CONTENTS

CONTENTS

Orige
befor   as a se
pline   gure with im
influe   the development of Christian spirituality.

This volume presents a comprehensive and accessible insight into
Origen's life and writings. An introduction analyzes the principal
influences that formed him as a Christian and as a thinker, his emer-
gence as a mature theologian at Alexandria, his work in Caesarea
and his controversial legacy. Fresh translations of a representative
selection of Origen's writings, including some never previously
available in print, show how Origen provided a lasting framework
for Christian theology by finding through study of the Bible a
coherent understanding of God's saving plan.

Joseph Trigg is Rector of Christ Church (Episcopal), Port Tobacco
Parish, La Plata, Maryland. His books include Origen: the Bible
and Philosophy in the Third-century Church (Atlanta 1983) and
Biblical Interpretation in the series Message of the Fathers of the
Church (Delaware 1988).

THE EARLY CHURCH FATHERS
Edited by Carol Harrison
University of Durham

The Greek and Latin Fathers of the Church are central to the creation of Christian doctrine, yet often unapproachable because of the sheer volume of their writings and the relative paucity of accessible translations. This series makes available translations of key selected texts by the major Fathers to all students of the early church.

MAXIMUS THE CONFESSOR
Andrew Louth

IRENAEUS OF LYONS
Robert M. Grant

Further books in this series will be on Ambrose and Gregory of Nyssa.

ORIGEN

Joseph W. Trigg

ONE WEEK LOAN

ROUTLEDGE

London and New York

First published 1998
by Routledge
11 New Fetter Lane, London EC4P 4EE

Simultaneously published in the US and Canada
by Routledge
29 West 35th Street, New York, NY 10001

Typeset in Garamond by Routledge
Printed and bound in Great Britain by
TJ International, Padstow, Cornwall

British Library Cataloguing in Publication Data
A catalogue record for this book is available from the British Library

Library of Congress Cataloging in Publication Data
Trigg, Joseph W., 1949–
Origen / Joseph W. Trigg.
(The early church fathers)
Includes bibliographical references and index.
1. Origen 2. Theology – History – Early church,
ca. 30–600 – Sources. I. Title. II. Series.
BR1720.O7T75   1998
270.1'092–dc21   97-23338
[B]   CIP

ISBN 0–415–11835–2 (hbk)
ISBN 0–415–11836–0 (pbk)

T

TO ROBERT M. GRANT

A NOTE ON
TRANSLATIONS

In the translations below I have tried to provide a readable English text as faithful as possible to Origen's intentions. In line with the first aim, I have often altered the sentence structure of the original. In line with the second, I have sought to avoid technical terms from later eras. On occasions where a reference to the original Greek wording has seemed helpful, I have included the original (transliterated) in the notes. (This is most often the case with *logos*, perhaps the most heavily freighted word in the Greek language.) Origen's work does not lend itself well to being excerpted. Although he often wrote at length, he wrote carefully and sparingly, characteristically accumulating arguments to lead his reader step by step to a logical conclusion. Except in the case of the *Commentary on Lamentations*, I have therefore presented integral works, or self-contained sections, with no omissions. Triple asterisks indicate gaps in the manuscript tradition. I have sought to make available works that reflect Origen's entire career, giving roughly equal weight to his Alexandrian and Caesarean periods. I have also sought to present works not previously translated into English or accessible only on expensive or out-of-print editions. These last two considerations militated against including texts from Origen's best-known works, *On First Principles*, *Contra Celsum*, and the occasional treatises, although I cite them generously in part I.

The chapter and section numbers (arabic and roman) in my translations and in references to Origen's works do not come from Origen himself. Like the chapter and verse numbers in the Bible, most of these were added for convenience in reference when these works were edited in the Renaissance. I use those commonly employed in modern editions. Pierre Nautin's *Origène: sa vie et son œuvre* provides a comprehensive list of these editions up to 1976.[1] The most important addition to Nautin's list appeared in 1990.

Edited by the late Caroline Hammond Bammel, it is the first of a projected four volumes of a new critical edition of the *Commentary on Romans*.[2] Other editions have appeared in the French series of texts and translations *Sources chrétiennes*, and in newer Italian and German series modeled on it, *Biblioteca Patristica* and *Fontes Christianae*.

In order to convey the sense of the text as Origen read and understood it, translations from Scripture are my own. No single modern translation could possibly convey the way Origen makes Scripture his own, often making brief allusions to passages or adapting their grammar to integrate them into a new context. In the commentaries on John and Lamentations, I have included a translation of the text in bold type before the passage that comments on it. In the case of the latter, my translations are from Rahlf's edition of the Septuagint. Unless he indicated otherwise, Origen's Old Testament citations are from this early translation by Greek-speaking Jews. His references may seem odd or unfamiliar because the Septuagint often translated the Hebrew differently from the way we would understand it or translated a different (and not necessarily inferior) Hebrew text from the traditional Masoretic text we have received. Sometimes, as in the case of the "angel of great counsel" (the Septuagint version of the phrase translated "wonderful counsellor" in the King James Version), it is hard to know whether we are dealing with an eccentric translation or a different text. Origen's New Testament text, to which he is an early and important witness, was essentially the same as ours. Even in this case, though, Origen often understood the text differently from the way modern translators do. An example is the familiar phrase in 1 Corinthians 13:12 translated "now we see through a glass, darkly." There, as we shall see, Origen understood in a precise technical sense the Greek phrase *en ainigmati* (in an enigma) – vaguely rendered as "darkly" in the King James Version. Likewise, in John 13:2, referring to the Devil's having given Judas the intention to betray Christ, Origen understood the Greek verb *ballô*, describing the Devil's action in a precise sense. Where modern versions usually translate this word as "put," Origen found in it an image of the Devil piercing Judas' heart with this intention as with an arrow. My translations also reflect Origen's own inconsistencies in his citations (from memory, it should be remembered) of biblical verses. Thus, for example, in Book 1 of the *Commentary on John*, Origen cites Revelation 22:13 – "I am the alpha and the omega, the first and the last, the beginning and the end" – in three different ways, none of which is quite the way we have received it.

I have indicated citations, references, and allusions to Scripture in parentheses. Where, in Origen's citations, the Septuagint text differs radically from the Hebrew text as we have received it, I indicate this by the abbreviation LXX. These references, of course, are not Origen's own. Most of these are identified by the editions I translate, although I have added a few of my own. Origen could only refer to a particular passage by giving the name of the book and citing a few words, as he does frequently, or by summarizing its contents, as he does below at the beginning of his Homily 12 on 1 Samuel. The names Origen uses for books of the Bible in our selections are the same as ours except in the case of the books we know from their Hebrew titles as 1–2 Samuel and 3–4 Kings, which he referred to by their Septuagint titles as 1–4 Kingdoms. In the case of the Psalms, where Origen could refer to something smaller than a whole book, he used the Septuagint numbering. References to Psalms maintain the Septuagint numbering Origen used and include in brackets the Masoretic (Hebrew) numbering we commonly use, when this differs. Abbreviations for biblical references are as used in the Revised Standard Version.

ABBREVIATIONS

Address	[Gregory Thaumaturgus], *Address to Origen*
CC	Origen, *Contra Celsum*
CGen	Origen, *Commentary on Genesis*
CJn	Origen, *Commentary on John*
CLam	Origen, *Commentary on Lamentations*
CLk	Origen, *Commentary on Luke*
CMt	Origen, *Commentary on Matthew*
CSong	Origen, *Commentary on the Song of Songs*
DH	Origen, *Dialogue with Heracleides*
EH	Eusebius, *Ecclesiastical History*
EM	Origen, *Exhortation to Martyrdom*
GCS	*Die Griechichen christlichen Schriftsteller, Origenes Werke*
H1Sam	Origen, *Homilies on 1 Samuel*
HEx	Origen, *Homilies on Exodus*
HEzek	Origen, *Homilies on Ezekiel*
HGen	Origen, *Homilies on Genesis*
HIsa	Origen, *Homilies on Isaiah*
HJer	Origen, *Homilies on Jeremiah*
HJos	Origen, *Homilies on Joshua*
HJudg	Origen, *Homilies on Judges*
HLev	Origen, *Homilies on Leviticus*
HLk	Origen, *Homilies on Luke*
HPs	Origen, *Homilies on Psalms*
Nautin	Pierre Nautin, *Origène: sa vie et son œuvre*, Paris, Beauchesne, 1977
OP	Origen, *On Prayer*
Origeniana	*Origeniana*, Bari, Istituto di literatura cristiana antica, Università di Bari, 1975

ABBREVIATIONS

Origeniana Tertia	*Origeniana Tertia: The Third International Colloquium for Origen Studies (University of Manchester September 7th–11th, 1981)*, ed. Richard Hanson and Henri Crouzel, Rome, Edizioni dell'Ateneo, 1985
Origeniana Quarta	*Origeniana Quarta: Die Referate des 4. Internationalen Origeneskongresses (Innsbruck, 2–6 September 1985)*, ed. Lothar Lies, Innsbruck, Tyrolia Verlag, 1987
Origeniana Quinta	*Origeniana Quinta*, ed. Robert J. Daly, Louvain, Peeters, 1992
Origeniana Sexta	*Origeniana Sexta: Origène et la Bible/Origen and the Bible, Actes du Colloquium Origenianum Sextum, Chantilly, 30 août –3 septembre 1993*, ed. Gilles Dorival and Alain le Boulluec, Louvain, Peeters, 1995
PA	Origen, *Peri Archon* (*On First Principles*)
Phil.	Origen, *Philocalia*
SC	*Sources chrétiennes*
SP	*Studia Patristica*
Str.	Clement of Alexandria, *Stromateis*
ZNW	*Zeitschrift für neutestamentliche Wissenschaft*

Part I

INTRODUCTION

1

THE MAKING OF A SCHOLAR AND THEOLOGIAN

Early life

We know Origen mainly through his thought. The loss of all but two of his letters deprives us of the rich human detail that enlivens and enriches accounts of comparable figures like Augustine or the Cappadocians. Eusebius, whose *Ecclesiastical History* provides most of our information about his life, had access to Origen's extensive correspondence in his library at Caesarea. He used it, along with further information that his mentor, Pamphilus, gathered for his *Apology for Origen*, to promote Origen as a scholar and saint.[1] We can supplement Eusebius with data gleaned from Origen's own works and from other sources, notably an *Address to Origen* composed by a student traditionally identified as Gregory Thaumaturgus. Pierre Nautin sifts through such information in his ground-breaking reconstruction of Origen's life.[2] Other scholars have challenged details of Nautin's work,[3] and he himself admits that many points are uncertain, but his basic outline is persuasive. Nautin subjects Eusebius to source criticism, establishing criteria for isolating information from reliable sources such as Origen's correspondence. He dismisses as hearsay stories about Origen's relationship to his father, whose very name – Leonides according to Eusebius – he considers doubtful. One such story is that Leonides was so amazed and impressed by his son's precocious inquiries about the deeper meaning of Scripture that he would often uncover his breast as he slept, kiss it with reverence as the shrine of a divine spirit, and thank God for deeming him worthy to be father of such a boy.[4] Even if not reliable, such stories indicate the impression Origen made on others. Nautin's outline, which I follow here, gives us a glimpse of an active and often embattled figure, recognized in his own time as a great man, who made intractable enemies as well as generous and loyal friends.

3

Origen was born around AD 185 and reared in Alexandria, one of the principal intellectual centers of the ancient world and long the home of a thriving and creative Greek-speaking Jewish community.[5] The origins of Christianity in Alexandria are notoriously hazy. We can be fairly certain that Christianity came to Alexandria early, that its matrix was Hellenistic Judaism, and that it was never homogeneous. Since Basilides and Valentinus, two of the earliest Alexandrian Christians we know of, were Gnostics, Walter Bauer postulated that Gnosticism preceded an orthodoxy imported later from Rome.[6] Papyrological evidence, however, demonstrates the early presence of a nascent orthodox community that employed particular manuscript abbreviations for divine names and that availed itself of Irenaeus's anti-Gnostic writings shortly after their publication.[7] Clement of Alexandria, writing during the decades around AD 200, is our first witness to this community. He advocated a "rule of truth" or "of the church," corresponding to the united testimony of the apostles.[8] He did not say what constitutes this rule, except that it affirms the unity of Scripture. This distinguished him and his believing community from heretical Gnostics who ascribed the Old and New Testaments to different gods. We may safely assume that he would affirm the enumeration of the church's principal doctrines in the Preface to Origen's *Peri Archon* (see below), one that mirrors those of other second- and third-century Christian writers.[9] At the same time, Clement remained open to the Gnostics' ideas and was relatively fair-minded toward them, an indication that the boundary between what we may call Ecclesiastical Christianity and Gnosticism was still porous during Origen's youth. As Origen matured, the church's self-definition became tighter under the leadership of Bishop Demetrius, whose oversight began while Origen was a youth.

The church in which Origen grew up defined itself not only by its commitment to the rule of faith, but by radical demands for Christian commitment. It thus formed Origen as, in the words of the Danish scholar Hal Koch, "an almost fanatical Christian of the most exclusive variety."[10] A *leitmotiv* of second-century Christian literature is the veneration of martyrdom as the ultimate expression of Christian commitment. This is especially true of the writings of Ignatius of Antioch, which Origen knew, and of the early martyr acts. Origen's own works provide vivid testimony that he was in full accord with this type of piety. His *Exhortation to Martyrdom* contains his most impassioned writing and, in a sermon given during a long period free from persecution, he expressed nostalgia for the days of the martyrs when "there were few believers, but they really did believe, and they traveled the strait and narrow way that leads to life."[11] Because the church forbade religious compromise with the Roman state, martyrdom was an ever-present possibility. Origen's church also self-consciously set itself apart from the larger Greco-Roman society by upholding a strict sexual morality and by valuing sexual renunciation. One of our earliest testimonies to Alexandrian Christianity is Justin Martyr's account of a young man who sought to disprove pagan calumnies by applying (unsuccessfully) to the Roman Prefect, Felix, for permission to be castrated.[12]

Eusebius reported that Origen's father taught his son the Christian Scriptures as he studied pagan Greek literature; certainly Origen's works – including, notably, his *Contra Celsum*, but other works as well, including the selection from the *Commentary on Genesis* included in this volume – evidence a splendid education, almost unrivaled among the Fathers. Origen clearly mastered the standard Hellenistic curriculum: the study of Greek literature along with mathematics and astronomy. His command of Scripture, likewise remarkable, also bespeaks a familiarity nourished from childhood. When Origen was 17 (around 203) his father died during a persecution under Septimius Severus, an Emperor who targeted converts and catechists in an apparent attempt to stem the spread of the church. This event confirmed his veneration of martyrdom and left him with a life-long sense of obligation. Thirty or more years later, in a homily delivered at Caesarea, he declared: "Having a martyr as a father is no advantage to me unless I live well and bring credit to the nobility of my birth, namely to his testimony and to the confession which made him illustrious in Christ."[13] Nautin argues that his father's martyrdom constituted a tie of blood that attached Origen to the church.[14] The accompanying confiscation of his father's estate left Origen impoverished and responsible as the eldest son for his large family.

Training as a *grammateus*

A wealthy Christian woman enabled Origen to complete his studies. He could then support his family in the respected occupation of *grammateus*, a teacher of Greek literature. These literary studies were one of the most significant factors shaping Origen's thought and his legacy.[15] As a *grammateus*, Origen made his own a four-stage method of approaching a literary text, a method Hellenistic grammarians developed at Alexandria four hundred years earlier for the study of Homer and other literary classics. These four stages are, respectively, textual criticism, reading, interpretation, and judgment.[16]

Textual criticism, an arcane specialty today, was practiced – in an age when all works were copied by hand and each manuscript was inevitably different – whenever a teacher and students sought to make sure they were all reading the same text. In earlier centuries Alexandrian scholars established criteria, including the detailed examination of variants, to arrive at the most plausible original reading. Origen's later text-critical work demonstrates his mastery of these techniques.

Reading, the second stage in the grammarian's approach to the text, simply meant reading the text aloud. This exercise, valuable as it is today, was indispensable in an age when manuscripts lacked lexical aids we take for granted: capital letters, spaces between words, and most punctuation marks. An important aspect of reading, especially in the absence of quotation marks, would be identifying the persona (*prosôpon*) speaking. Thus below, in his *Homily 5 on 1 Samuel*, Origen distinguishes words spoken in the persona of the narrator from words spoken, say, in the persona of the necromancer. Marie-Joseph Rondeau has shown the pervasiveness and subtlety of the technique of identifying *prosôpa* in Origen's works not just in his Scriptural interpretation, but in his response to Celsus.[17]

The third stage, interpretation (*exêgêsis*) involved bringing to bear information useful for understanding the text. At its most basic level, interpretation involved identifying the meaning of the words an author used (*glôssêmatikon*). Since the Homeric epics, the fundamental text in the Hellenistic curriculum, were written in an archaic dialect containing many words and constructions no longer current, such close attention to words themselves would be second nature for a *grammateus*. A second branch of interpretation was the study of the narrative itself (*historikon*). Such interpretation could include information we would regard as properly "historical" such as chronology, but could also involve applying information drawn from fields such as geography and the natural sciences. A third branch of interpretation, known as *technikon*,[18] dealt with the author's rhetorical procedures, beginning with his use of grammar and continuing with his use of figures of speech. An example of Origen's employment of such methods is his discussion in *Commentary on John* 32.112 of whether Jesus' statement in John 13:12 "[Do you] Know what I have done.[?]" should be read as question or a command. *Technikon* would also deal with the author's use of order (*taxis*) and plan (*oikonomia*) in light of a particular goal or intention (*skopos*). The concept of *oikonomia* would, as we shall see, assume great importance in Origen's thought. Early commentators on the *Iliad* gave as examples of skillful use of *oikonomia* Homer's providing Thetis a consistently helpful character so as to make her interventions seem appropriate, and his intensifying the pathos of Hector's death by leaving his wife Andromache unaware of the duel with Achilles so that she gains her first intimation of it by hearing the lamentation over his fall.[19] Origen would ordinarily deal with the book's *skopos* in an introduction to the book as a whole, as he does below in the opening chapters of Book 1 of his *Commentary on John*. A fourth branch of interpretation, *metrikon*, dealt with the meter and, more broadly, the style an author used. Included in the study of style would be the investigation of whether a particular narrative is intended as a factual account, one which would involve looking closely at its consistency and plausibility.

Fourth and finally, the *grammateus* would exercise judgment (*krisis*), evaluating the author's work and drawing helpful lessons from it for his students. As a general principle, applicable in all modes of interpretation, Origen would have learned that the best way to interpret a difficult passage in any particular author is to seek an explanation from another passage in the same author's work, the principle summed up by the phrase, "Clarify Homer from Homer."[20]

Origen's studies in this period may also have included further work in other branches of "general education" (*enkuklios paideia*) such as music, mathematics, and astronomy, the latter including what we call astrology. The student who composed the *Address* testified to the importance of the natural sciences in Origen's own teaching, crediting him with helping him move from an irrational to a rational awe in the face of the beauty and majesty of the "holy plan (*oikonomia*) of the universe."[21] The selection below from Origen's *Commentary on Genesis* displays an understanding of astrology (in spite of his rejection of it) and of astronomy unexcelled in any ancient Christian author. He also learned some principles of ancient medicine, which he would later apply in describing the therapeutic work of God in the soul.[22]

Encounter with Gnosticism

Origen's benefactor also provided accommodations for a teacher from Antioch, Paul, whom Origen characterized as a heretic. This person attracted great numbers, not only of heretics, but also of persons belonging to the orthodox party, to hear his teaching. Origen stated that he "loathed" Paul's doctrine, which was probably some form of Gnosticism, and that he never joined in the heretics' prayers, maintaining instead the "rule of the church."[23] Whatever Paul may have taught, Origen's works testify to an intimate familiarity with Gnostic doctrines, particularly those of Valentinus and Marcion, and to serious engagement with the challenges they presented to the church's faith, particularly as regards the goodness of the God of Israel and the extent of human free will. What defined Gnosticism for Origen, as for other Fathers, was not, as we might suppose today, its esotericism, but its denial that the God and Father of Jesus Christ was also the God of Israel, the creator of the world and giver of the Law. Such a position united Valentinus, Marcion, Basilides, and their followers, however they might differ on other matters. Marcion, reveling in the savage cruelty occasionally displayed by Israel's God in the Old Testament, used such incidents to prove that such a god could not be the loving and gracious Father whom Jesus came to reveal. Origen's initial impetus toward allegorical interpretation of Scripture may have come from the need to obviate Marcion's criticism. Marcion, along with Basilides and two of Valentinus's followers, Ptolemaeus and Heracleon, anticipated Origen in applying Hellenistic critical methods to the study of Scripture.[24] Origen's *Commentary on John* illustrates how such works could spur him to respond in kind. This is evident in the detailed response to Heracleon, who wrote his own commentary on the gospel, in the selection below from Book 13 of that work.

Of the Gnostics, Valentinus and his followers had the most profound influence on Origen. Like Marcion, they challenged the identity of Israel's God with the God and Father of Jesus Christ. Their doctrine of three natures of souls, the spiritual, the soulish and the material — corresponding to Gnostic adepts, ecclesiastical Christians, and non-Christians — seemed to deny free choice and moral responsibility, a prospect all the more disturbing because they could make a plausible Scriptural case for divine determinism. Even more important, Valentinian doctrines made sense in terms of an overall theological system for interpreting Scripture. Such a system, eliminating apparent Scriptural crudities and inconsistencies, appealed to thoughtful Christians. Reaction to Valentinianism so profoundly influenced Origen that Holger Strutwolf, in a recent monograph, can refer to Origen's work as "the reception of

Valentinian Gnosticism" into the mainstream of Christian thought.[25] By this he means not that Origen was a Valentinian, but that, by a process involving both acceptance and rejection, he, in effect, appropriated and transformed Valentinianism. An example is the way Origen treats Christological titles that take on an existence of their own as the Aeons in the Valentinian Pleroma; as we see in Book I of the *Commentary on John* below, he presents these as aspects of the divine and human natures of Christ.

Clement of Alexandria

Although, curiously, he does not mention him in his extant writings, we may presume that Origen came under the influence of Clement of Alexandria. Clement was an original theologian, not just an Origen *manqué*, but his theological writings adumbrated many themes that Origen would develop more fully and systematically. In particular, Clement pioneered using Greek philosophy and allegorical interpretation against the Gnostics.[26] He repeatedly juxtaposed insights from the Bible with ideas taken from Greek literature and philosophy, combining biblical and classical terminology or moving seamlessly from a citation of a pagan author to a similar idea in the Bible and vice versa.[27] Clement went so far as to suggest that, just as, in Paul's words, the Torah served as a pedagogue for the Jews until Christ came (Gal. 3:24), so philosophy served as a pedagogue for the Greeks.[28] This favorable attitude toward Greek philosophy did not extend to pagan religion, toward which Clement exhibited the same implacable opposition that characterizes all early Christian authors. Clement's writings demonstrate that Origen grew up within a distinct school of thought, a learned Christianity distinguished from Gnosticism by its loyalty to the church's rule of faith, which was already flourishing in Alexandria. Clement and Origen's shared concerns include a defense of the ecclesiastical tradition against the Gnostics on the basis of allegorical interpretation of the Bible and an eschatology in which God's punishments are purificatory rather than retributive. Both authors also distinguish between simple Christians motivated by fear and more advanced, spiritual Christians motivated no longer by fear but by love. The latter have a responsibility to guard certain advanced, secret doctrines from premature disclosure that would only harm the former.[29] A fundamental division of Christians between what he termed a "simpler" majority and a minority who are genuinely "spiritual" would constitute a prominent feature of Origen's thought, as we see, for example, when he discusses those who drink from Jacob's well in *Commentary on John* 13 below.[30] Clement sought to fulfill his responsibility for guarding advanced doctrines by composing the *Stromateis* in a deliberately obscure style, passing from one topic to another and hinting at one thing while demonstrating another in such a way as to kindle the interest of the mature while throwing the spiritually immature off the track.[31] Other important aspects of Clement's thought, particularly his stress on negative or apophatic theology, in which he is a precursor to the Cappadocians and Pseudo-Dionysius, evidently had less appeal for Origen.[32] Pierre Nautin considers Origen's decision to compose, as one of his first books, a work entitled *Stromateis* to be the strongest single piece of evidence that he came under Clement's influence. It is hard to imagine what would inspire Origen to choose such an unusual title (only otherwise attested in a work by Plutarch, a pagan author in whom he showed no interest) unless he intended it, at least in part, as a tribute to Clement, whose most important work bore that title. Unfortunately, Origen's work is no longer extant, except for fragments.[33] Even if he had written no such work, it is hardly conceivable that Origen, with his insatiable intellectual curiosity, would have neglected a figure as deeply learned as Clement, as long as the two were, as they seem to have been, in the same city at the same time.

One can, in fact, plausibly see Origen's treatise *Peri Archon* (also known as *On First Principles*) as the fulfillment of a theological agenda Clement set forth but never, so far as we know from his surviving works, fully achieved. This planned work would have been, in Brian Daley's words, "a systematic anti-Gnostic consideration of Scriptural doctrine, all as a prelude for a 'truly gnostic' account of the cosmos and God, based on the book of Genesis and consistent with the 'Rule of Truth.'"[34] Even if, as seems so likely, Clement exercised a formative influence on him, Origen characteristically went his own way, especially in his style. Although, as we can tell from the *Contra Celsum*, Origen knew Greek philosophy better than Clement and probably knew Greek literature at least as well, he gives an absolute privilege to biblical language and terminology. Furthermore, while he may be cagey in his expression of ideas that he deemed inappropriate and dangerous for immature Christians, his writing is always clear and cogent, logically building whatever case he chooses to make.

Jewish influences

Jewish learning also exercised a formative influence on Origen and remained a compelling interest to him throughout his life. Introducing him to Philo's works was one of Clement's most momentous legacies to Origen, and, through him, to subsequent Christian tradition. Philo, a first-century Jewish theologian from Alexandria, wrote treatises in impeccable Greek interpreting the Torah in terms of Plato and vice versa. Clement's massive, if usually unacknowledged, debt to Philo is evident throughout his work, especially in the *Stromateis*.[35] David Runia has recently shown that Clement is the earliest Christian author who, without question, knew Philo's works. He also shows that Origen's own library is the source of the manuscript tradition for all of Philo's surviving works. We may thus presume that Origen, who openly admired Philo, learned about him from Clement. Runia argues, persuasively, that Philo "furnished a new starting-point for more than two centuries of Alexandrian Christian theology," not by teaching Clement Platonism, which he already knew, but by teaching him how to relate Platonism to the Bible.[36] The allegorical method Philo used for relating Platonism to the Torah provided Clement with a method for refuting the Gnostics, who denied the identity of the God of the Old Testament with the God and Father of Jesus Christ. Philo also mediated the Platonic use of the metaphor of initiation into the mysteries (in Plato's case these were the Eleusinian and Bacchic rites that were the fundamental religious expression of his time) as an image of intellectual and moral transformation. In Philo allegorical interpretation of Scripture opens up a mystical understanding of the text inaccessible to those who were intellectually and morally unworthy of it.[37] Like the author of the Wisdom of Solomon, Philo thus, in effect, extends the Hebrew wisdom tradition, assimilating Greek philosophy just as that tradition had assimilated the wisdom of Egypt and Mesopotamia. Drawing on Philo, Clement and Origen extend that tradition still further.

Although the Jewish presence in Alexandria seems to have been weak in Origen's time, he not only encountered there the works of Philo but also found at least one Jewish teacher who helped him with Hebrew and introduced him to Jewish exegetical traditions. In his *Homilies on Jeremiah* Origen recalls a Jewish tradition explaining the presence of two call narratives in the Book of Isaiah. (The prophet rashly said "Here I am, send me" in chapter 6 and had to deliver a message no one wanted to hear. He was more careful when, in chapter 40, "a voice said, 'Cry'"; before accepting a second assignment, he asked, "What shall I cry?") Origen describes his informant as "a man who, because he had come to believe in Christ and had abandoned the law for something higher, fled his native land and arrived where we were living." [38] He thus seems to have been a Palestinian Jew who converted to Christianity and emigrated to Alexandria. Pierre Nautin identifies this man as "the Hebrew" whom Origen refers to in two other works from his Alexandrian period, his early *Commentary on Psalms 1–25*, included here, and *Peri Archon*. [39] This informant thus opened Origen's eyes to a rich living tradition of Scriptural interpretation on which he would draw throughout his life. It is easy to see why Origen would have found "very beautiful" this Hebrew's image (in the selection below from the former work) of the way one passage of Scripture unlocks the meaning of another. Not only would it have seemed exegetically sensible to a student of Greek literature, taught to "clarify Homer from Homer," but its esotericism would have appealed to a reader of Philo and student of Clement of Alexandria encouraged to seek through Scriptural interpretation an initiation to the knowledge of God. Recognizing his limitations in Hebrew, Origen also made it his practice throughout his life to check out linguistic information with Jewish informants. [40]

Ammonius Saccas

According to the pagan philosopher Porphyry, Origen also encountered the Platonist Ammonius Saccas during his formative years. [41] There is every reason to believe that Origen acquired his superb education in philosophy from him. Porphyry also tells us that, at what seems to have been a later time, Ammonius taught Plotinus, the pagan philosopher accounted the founder of Neoplatonism. Plotinus himself held in the highest esteem a fellow-student of Ammonius named Origen, the author of three (now lost) philosophical treatises. [42] The fellow-student whom Plotinus knew may, however, have been a pagan of the same name. [43] One evidence that they had a common teacher is that Origen and Plotinus are the first ancient authors to set forth the doctrine expressed below in our selection from Origen's *Commentary on Genesis*, that the stars are signs rather than causes. Presumably through Ammonius, Origen gained his familiarity with Plato, Aristotle, Stoic philosophers, and philosophers in the school we call Middle Platonism.

The importance of Origen's philosophical formation cannot be

overestimated, but it can easily be misconceived. We misconceive
Origen's debt to philosophy if we anachronistically see it as the
adoption of a rationalistic mentality foreign or antagonistic to piety.
Ancient philosophers were critical, as Origen was, of the
unthinking piety of the masses, but none of them – especially not
Platonists of Origen's time – questioned the reality of God. The
Platonists' goal was to follow their master's exhortation in the
Theaetetus to transform themselves with the help of wisdom so as to
become like the divine as much as possible.[44] We also misconceive
Origen's debt to his philosophical formation if we see it as the adoption of philosophic doctrines alongside or instead of the doctrines of
the Christian faith. Henri Crouzel has set forth the ways Plotinus
and Origen share similar doctrines, demonstrating that Origen did
not accept Platonism uncritically, but only when it was consistent
with the church's rule of faith.[45] But specific doctrines are not the
point; Origen became a philosopher. He made his own the precise
use of language and the inquiring, critical approach to reality incul-
cated by a rigorous philosophical training. As a teacher himself,
Origen would seek to replicate his formation by evoking from his
students the "the part of the soul that exercises judgment."[46] As
Pierre Hadot has pointed out, for Origen, as for all ancient lovers-
of-wisdom, philosophy was a way of life.[47] Eusebius testifies to such
a conception in praising Origen for "right actions of genuine philosophy," in marvelous conformity with the saying, itself an echo of
Plato, "as was his speech, so was his manner of life."[48]

This was a way of life which Origen, like most other early
Christians, found profoundly compatible with the Christian faith.
That faith, indeed, presented itself to the ancient world not just as
the *cultus* of a Jewish man-god, but as a philosophy. Thus Justin
Martyr referred to his conversion to Christianity, after finding all
the Greek philosophical schools inadequate to his quest, as his
reason for being a philosopher.[49] Similarly, Clement promoted the
biblical tradition as "the barbarian [that is, non-Greek]
philosophy."[50] As a teacher himself, Origen therefore employed the
study of philosophy, understood as an exercise involving moral
purification as well as intellectual training, as a necessary preparation for the study of Scripture.[51] Implicitly presenting his own
enterprise as a continuation of ancient Hebrew wisdom, Origen
described the books ascribed to Solomon – Proverbs, Ecclesiastes,
and the Song of Songs – as a progressive philosophical
curriculum.[52] This is the curriculum of mystical, physical, ethical,
and logical teachings that constitute the allegorical significance of

the "ways of Zion" in fragment XIV of the *Commentary on Lamentations* below. For Origen, as we see below in Book 28 of his *Commentary on John*, Jesus himself, who made his disciples like him, transforming them from servants into friends, is the ultimate teacher.

Becoming a Christian teacher and ascetic

When a new Roman Prefect renewed persecution during Septimius Severus's reign, he targeted catechetical instructors along with converts. Clement, who had no zeal for martyrdom, was probably among the Christian teachers who left town at this time. In their absence, some pagans interested in Christianity sought out Origen, the brilliant young Christian *grammateus*, to prepare them for baptism. Among these, a certain Plutarch actually was martyred. Fearless for his own life, Origen not only served as a catechist but visited the martyrs in prison and was present to encourage them at trials and executions.[53] During this heroic time, Origen acquired his identity as Christian teacher. Following Paul's words in 1 Corinthians 12:8, which he often cited, Origen considered his teaching vocation a divinely conferred gift of grace. He identified the teaching gift with the talents in Jesus' parable (Mt. 25:15–30), talents which the person receiving them had to use to best effect.[54] Origen assumed the role of Christian teacher on his own, without consulting his bishop; Demetrius, perhaps feeling that he had little choice, sanctioned him after the fact as a catechist.[55] This new-found identity probably induced Origen's conversion to a rigorously ascetic life in conformity with the gospel precepts to give away worldly goods. He abandoned his occupation as a *grammateus* along with his books of Greek literature so that he could devote himself entirely to teaching and the studying the Bible.[56] Nonetheless, in taking on a new identity, he did not forget what he had learned; in his earliest work, a *Commentary on the Song of Songs* composed during his youth (not the longer work of his maturity we have in Rufinus's Latin translation), he discussed the importance of ascribing biblical passages to the appropriate *prosôpa*.[57] It seems that Origen's youthful ascetic enthusiasm led him to follow what he then took to be a counsel of self-castration in Matthew 19:12. Eusebius tells us that Origen later regretted the act, and in his *Commentary on Matthew* he explicitly repudiated any such interpretation.[58]

2

THE MATURE YEARS AT ALEXANDRIA

Tension with Bishop Demetrius

Origen had the misfortune to mature as a Christian teacher at the very time when Bishop Demetrius, like bishops elsewhere, was exercising increasing authority over the church's teaching. Such authority left less and less room for a brilliant lay teacher operating with a divinely given charism. Origen, while sincerely submitting to the church's rule of faith and always open to informed criticism, never accepted a bishop's authority to tell him what to teach.[1] The tension between conflicting understandings of teaching authority inevitably intensified as Origen's reputation grew. It ultimately led to a rupture with Demetrius that made Origen's position in Alexandria untenable. This tension may explain why, around AD 215, Origen made a journey to Rome.[2] If he was seeking in Rome a more congenial place to function as a lay teacher, he went to the wrong city; but he probably did absorb there a more sophisticated perspective on issues of Trinitarian theology. A second wealthy lay patron, Ambrosius, whom Origen's teaching had won away from Gnosticism, enabled and encouraged him to take a fateful step in his career by furnishing him with copyists and calligraphers so that his lectures could become books.[3] With such support, Origen's reputation soon spread beyond the Christian community. First the governor of the Roman province of Arabia (roughly equivalent to modern Jordan) requested a visit with him.[4] Then, in AD 231, Julia Mammaea, mother of the young Emperor Alexander Severus, requested him to attend her in Antioch.[5] (The Severan imperial house no longer persecuted Christianity.) Such fame could not have helped relations with Demetrius, and Origen's journey to Greece via Caesarea in Palestine was, very likely this time, an attempt to scout out a new place to live. In the event, Theoctistus, the Bishop of

Caesarea, valuing his preaching, provided him a congenial place to settle. Theoctistus's ordination of Origen as a presbyter provoked a crisis in Origen's relationship with Demetrius, who was understandably incensed that another bishop should ordain a person under his jurisdiction. He also argued that Origen's self-mutilation made him unworthy of ordination and charged that in his *Dialogue with Candidus*, the transcript of a debate with a Gnostic, he had set forth the blasphemously heretical position that the Devil would be saved.[6] Even after Demetrius was succeeded, at his death in AD 233, by Heraclas, who had once been Origen's student, he was no longer welcome in the Alexandrian church. In AD 234 he settled permanently in Caesarea, a date which divides his career as a teacher into two roughly equal halves. Origen called these events his deliverance from Egypt.[7]

Early works

Although Origen remained, throughout his life, open to growth and change, his Alexandrian works set forth the approach to the Bible and to theology that would last him the rest of his career. His desire to gain the best possible access to the biblical text led to one of the great projects of his life, the *Hexapla*, an immense and complex word-for-word comparison of the Septuagint with the Hebrew Bible and other Greek translations. As best we can determine from accounts of the *Hexapla* and possible fragments, this consisted of a work in six columns: the original Hebrew; a Greek transliteration of the Hebrew; three more or less literal translations of Aquila, Symmachus, and Theodotion; and, finally, the church's Septuagint text, provided with critical markings to indicate where it diverged from the Hebrew.[8] For the book of Psalms, Origen added two Greek versions he himself discovered, one at the Greek city of Nicopolis and one near Jericho, where he discovered a number of Greek and Hebrew manuscripts cached, like the Dead Sea Scrolls, in a jar. Origen made use of the *Hexapla* throughout his life, beginning, as the fragments of his *Commentary on Lamentations* abundantly show, with his earliest works at Alexandria. Origen took it with him to Caesarea, but its massive size and highly specialized function meant that it was never copied, so that it eventually disappeared.

The first work which Ambrosius solicited from Origen was, most likely, the early *Commentary on Psalms 1–25*. This work is lost except for the fragment below and another small fragment, both preserved in the *Philocalia*, a fourth-century anthology of Origen's work on biblical interpretation and free will that also preserved the *Letter to Gregory* and our selection from the *Commentary on Genesis*. After this Origen wrote several now lost treatises: the *Dialogue with Candidus* already mentioned; *On the Resurrection*, which may also have been a transcript of a debate; his *Stromateis*; and *On Natures*, a refutation of what he understood to be the Valentinian doctrine that the soul's destiny depends on its nature. Another early work, his second commentary as a mature author, the *Commentary on Lamentations*, survives more fully. The selected fragments below illustrate, along with Origen's attention to the text itself, a way of interpreting biblical imagery that he would follow throughout his life. Thus below the interpretation of feet in fragment XXIII reappears decades later in Book 32 (sec. 71) of the *Commentary on John*.[9] Such interpretation stems from Origen's belief that an activity like walking or seeing, a part of the body, or an object like a jar of wine, each of which means one thing in the context of physical reality, means something different but similar in the context of spiritual reality. For a *grammateus*, a word with more than one meaning was a "homonym."[10] Homonymy applies to narratives as well as words. Thus the history of God's dealings with his people in the Old Testament takes on new meaning in the context of the church and of the individual soul. In this elevated interpretation, the Babylonian captivity stands for the soul's captivity by Satan because of its sins.[11] Similarly, the return from that captivity and the rebuilding of the Temple symbolize the restoration of God's dwelling-place in the human soul.[12]

In Alexandria Origen began commentaries on two major books, Genesis and John. He conceived both on a grand scale – Book 1 of the Commentary on John covers the gospel's first half verse! – and continued to work on them for much of his life. In the only extensive surviving fragment of his *Commentary on Genesis*, included below, Origen vindicates human freedom of choice against astral determinism. Book 1 of his *Commentary on John*, written in Alexandria, is included here in full. Origen begins it with an introduction to the gospel that constitutes one his fullest statements of exegetical principles. He goes on to analyze a homonym, the Greek word *archê*, the second word in Genesis and John, which can, among other things, mean "beginning" or "principle," and concludes with a discussion of the various Christological titles in Scripture, relating them as aspects (*epinoiai*) of the Logos in his divine and human natures.

Peri Archon

The scope and character of Peri Archon

The most fascinating of Origen's works, the one which has received the most attention from his time to ours, also comes from the Alexandrian period. This is the treatise now commonly referred to by its Greek title, *Peri Archon*, and also known as *On First Principles*, its title in G. W. Butterworth's graceful and accurate 1936 English translation.[13] The title can have – and Origen probably intended it to have – two meanings. As he himself explained in Book 1 of his *Commentary on John* below, *archai* can either be "fundamental principles of being," a meaning with a philosophical pedigree back to the Pre-Socratics, or they can be "elementary principles" of the Christian rule of faith. Origen wrote *Peri Archon* around AD 229, when he was in his early forties. It thus represents his mature theological position.[14] We possess it in its entirety only in a fourth-century Latin translation by Rufinus, a work intended for and reflecting the Latin-speaking Christian culture of the 390s rather than the Alexandrian Christian culture of the 220s. Nicola Pace's recent study of Rufinus's text shows how we have lost the subtlety and philosophical sophistication of Origen's language in the shift to Latin. Pace does not mention an example in the first sentence of Origen's treatise, which survives in a Greek fragment:

> All who believe and are persuaded (*pepeismenoi*) that grace and truth have come to be through Jesus Christ (see Jn 1:17) and know that Christ is truth, according to what he himself said, "I am the truth" (Jn 14:6), receive the knowledge that incites men to live well and blessedly from no other source than the very words and teachings of Christ.[15]

Here Origen, always careful about words, implicitly distinguished between simply "believing" that Christ is the truth and "being persuaded," presumably on the basis of rational argument, that this is so. We would be unaware of this from Rufinus's rendering of the first phrase, "All who believe and are sure (*certi*)." We have also lost some of Origen's theological formulations related to the Trinity, which, in the wake of the Arian controversies, sounded heterodox to Rufinus. Nonetheless, we still have, along with the basic shape and content of the book, a faithful picture of Origen's cosmology and eschatology, which Rufinus wished to promote.[16] Two extensive sections of *Peri Archon* survive in Greek in the *Philocalia*, and many fragments, often tendentious, survive in Greek and Latin. Butterworth, following the best edition of his time, incorporated these fragments into the text, giving them preference over Rufinus.

Origen's preface provides a key to his intentions. As we have seen, he begins by arguing that those who believe and are persuaded that Christ is God's word and truth must seek the truth through Christ's teachings. Since Christ is the Logos, these constitute the entire Bible, not just Christ's words recorded in the gospels. He then goes on to argue that

> because many who profess to believe in Christ disagree, not just in small and trivial matters, but also in ones of great and the greatest importance, that is about God, or about our Lord Jesus Christ himself, or about the Holy Spirit, and not just about these, but also about creatures, dominions and holy powers, for this reason it seems necessary before-hand to establish a firm line and distinct rule about each of these subjects, and then we can also investigate other subjects.

This "firm line and distinct rule" is the church's proclamation "truly preserved by an order of succession handed down from the apostles, remaining in the churches even to the present."[17] The doctrines the apostles proclaimed straightforwardly were:

1 "That God is one, who created and ordered all things, and who, when nothing existed, made the universe to be,"[18] and that "This just and good God, the Father of our Lord Jesus Christ (see Rom. 15:6), himself gave the law, the prophets, and the gospels, who is the God of the apostles and of the Old and New Testaments."[19]

2 "That Jesus Christ, the same one who came (see Jn 5:43), was generated[20] from the Father before every creature, who, when he had served the Father in the foundation of all things (see Pr. 8:22–31 and Wis. 9:9), for all things were made through him (Jn 1:3), in the latter days emptied himself and became a man (see Heb. 1:2 and Phil. 2:7), was incarnate, while he was God. and, having been made man, remained what he was, namely God. He assumed a body like our body, differing only in this, that he was born from a virgin and the Holy Spirit. And because then this Jesus Christ was born and suffered in truth

and not in appearance, that he truly died the common death,[21] and he was truly raised from the dead and, having conversed with his disciples after his death, was assumed into heaven."[22]

3 "That the Holy Spirit is associated in honor and dignity with the Father and the Son" and "that this Holy Spirit inspired each one of the saints, prophets, and apostles, and that there was not one Spirit in the Old Testament and another in those writings which were inspired at Christ's advent."[23]

4 "That the soul, having its own substance and life, when it departs this world, it will be compensated for its merits, either to inherit eternal life and blessedness, if its deeds are answerable to this, or to be delivered to eternal fire and tortures, if the guilt of its crimes deflects it in that direction, but that there will be a time of the resurrection of the dead, with this body, that what is now sown in corruption will rise in incorruption, and what is sown in dishonor will rise in glory (see 1 Cor. 15:42–3)." Furthermore, concerning the soul, the church proclaims "that every rational soul has free choice and will, but also that it is engaged in a struggle against the Devil, his angels, and the opposing powers, for these contend to weigh it down with sins, but, nonetheless, by living rightly and prudently, we strive to avoid such a calamity. From this the conclusion is that we are not subject to necessity, so that one way or another, whether we desire it or not, we are forced to do either bad or good things."[24]

5 That "devils or adverse powers" exist.[25]

6 "That this world was made and began to exist at a certain time and that because of its corruption it is to be destroyed."[26]

7 "That the Scriptures were written by the Spirit of God and have not just that sense that is evident, but another one hidden from most readers."[27]

8 "That there are certain angels of God and good powers, who serve to bring to its completion the salvation of men."[28]

Aside from ranking the existence of a hidden sense of Scripture among the fundamental articles of the faith (as we shall see, for Origen this is a corollary of its divine inspiration), this list faithfully represents the position of Christians like Irenaeus and Tertullian who differentiated themselves from Gnosticism. Nonetheless, such doctrines are only the elementary principles of theology:

But this ought to be understood. When the holy apostles were proclaiming faith in Christ concerning certain things which they considered necessary, they passed them on very straightforwardly to all believers, even to those who appeared somewhat listless in the investigation of divine knowledge, while leaving the reason for their assertions to be inquired by those who merited the more excellent gifts of the Spirit, and especially those who would acquire the grace of speech, wisdom, and knowledge from the same Spirit (see 1 Cor. 12:7–8). About other things they said, indeed, that they were so, but as to the how and the why, they kept silent, assuredly being so that each of those who were more studious among their posterity, those who would be lovers of wisdom (see Wis. 8:2), would have an exercise in which they could show the fruit of their intelligence, those, that is, who would prepare themselves to be worthy and capable of receiving wisdom.[29]

In the course of reciting the rule of faith, therefore, Origen signals areas where the apostles remained silent. These include: whether the Holy Spirit was begotten or not; whether the soul comes into existence at conception or has an earlier beginning; who the devils are and how they came to exist; "what existed before this world, or what will exist after this world"; "how God himself ought to be understood, whether he is corporeal and configured in some shape or is of another nature than corporeal"; and how and when the angels were created, and whether the heavenly bodies are or are not animated.[30] Origen concludes that:

It is therefore necessary for someone who desires to construct a coherent and organic whole[31] according to the commandment that says "Enlighten yourselves with the light of knowledge" (Hos. 10:12 LXX) to use points such as these [i.e. the doctrines handed down in the rule of faith] as elements and first principles, so that with clear and necessary arguments he may investigate what is true in individual matters, so that, as we have said, one organic whole may be constructed from examples and affirmations which he finds in the Holy Scriptures or which he discovers by careful investigation and direct pursuance of their consequences.[32]

21

Beginning with Basilius Steidle in an article published in 1942,[33] scholars have noticed that the four books of *Peri Archon* obscure a more fundamental four-part structure. The treatise incorporates two brief and two extended cycles dealing with a series of theological topics, beginning with the doctrine of God and descending down a chain of being to deal with the Son and the Holy Spirit, rational beings, and, finally, the material world. The preface and last chapter constitute the brief first and last of these cycles. The two extended cycles, constituting most of the work, are from the beginning of Book 1 through chapter 3 of Book 2 and from chapter 4 of that book through chapter 3 of Book 4. The first extended cycle deals with each of these topics in turn in a continuous narrative; the second deals in more detail with particular issues in roughly the same order. It ends with the topic of biblical interpretation, not covered in the first main cycle but enumerated in the preface. Gilles Dorival and Marguerite Harl have shown that such a structure conforms to a recognized philosophical genre dealing with "physics," the discipline dealing with the nature of reality, *archai* in the first sense above.[34] Nonetheless, as Brian Daley convincingly points out, on the basis of Origen's conclusion quoted above to his preface, the work is also clearly about *archai* in the second sense; it derives from the elementary principles of the faith, "the kind of integrated, demonstrative, logically coherent system of knowledge that in the Aristotelian tradition was called a 'science' (*epistêmê*)."[35]

Pierre Hadot cites Origen's *Peri Archon* of a procedure characteristic of ancient philosophical schools: building a philosophy on unquestioned basic principles. This, in his view, accounts for those schools' remarkable stability over centuries.[36] In establishing the church's rule of faith on a firm, rational basis, Origen effectively refuted the Gnostics, not by pointing out deficiencies in their systems, but by offering a coherent alternative. As he himself wrote, he also accomplished a still more important goal: "to outline the most conspicuous characteristics of the understanding of the Scriptures" by investigating precisely those doctrines most important for souls "who cannot otherwise attain perfection without the rich and wise truth about God." These are doctrines which the biblical authors, enlightened by the Logos, placed in Scripture so that those who devote themselves to the deep things of God (see 1 Cor. 2:10) might seek them out and which the Spirit of God deliberately concealed from those unable to bear the toil of such investigation.[37] Although *Peri Archon* sets out to examine these doctrines, his tentative expression of conclusions leaves in doubt the extent to which he thought that he had achieved a logically coherent system which he referred to as a "coherent and organic whole."[38]

The divine hypostases in Peri Archon

In his doctrine of God (the Father) Origen argued that incorporeality, utter unity, and simplicity distinguish God from the multiplicity of the material world. Against the Gnostics, he argued that God who is the Creator and Lawgiver of the Old Testament is also the God and Father of Jesus Christ. The Son is God's Logos ("Word" or "Reason") and Wisdom, a second divine hypostasis, subordinate to and eternally generated by the Father. Similarly, the Holy Spirit, the third divine hypostasis, shares in the Father's eternal existence. Origen cites his Hebrew teacher as saying that the two six-winged seraphim in Isaiah's Temple vision (Isa. 6:2–3) who cry "Holy, holy, holy is the Lord of hosts" are the Son and the Holy Spirit.[39] Origen valued this tradition because it provided an Old Testament attestation of two separate divine hypostases in addition to God the Father. These hypostases mediate the knowledge of God the Father to those worthy of it and hide that knowledge from the unworthy, just as, in Origen's reading of Isaiah, the wings of the seraphim partially reveal and partially hide God.[40] As a result of the Arian controversy, Origen's formulation of the Son's relationship to the Father occasioned a serious misunderstanding, not yet dissipated, which obscures his contribution to the history of Christian doctrine. From the fourth century on, Origen has been criticized for, in effect, importing into Christian doctrine a Platonic understanding of the relationship of the divine hypostases, in which the second is clearly inferior and subordinate to the first. This is the alleged foundation for Arius's heresy. In this spirit, opponents of Origen took the image of the Son and Holy Spirit as seraphim to mean that, like Arius, Origen thought they were created beings, differing from the angels only in dignity. Although the subordination of the Son and Holy Spirit to the Father was consistent with Middle Platonic understandings of the relationship between the divine hypostases, such "subordinationism," if we chose to call it that, was an unproblematic characteristic of Christian thought in Origen's time. Origen he did not need Platonism to suggest it to him; all he needed was the New Testament, in which the Son acknowledges the Father's superiority and acts in obedience to him.[41] Arius's notion that the Son and, by implication, the Spirit, are subordinate to the Father come not out of Origen's influence, but from theological conservatism.[42] Where Origen is original and distinctive is in his development of the concept of the eternal generation.[43] This doctrine, distinguishing the Son and Holy Spirit from all other beings, which were created in time and are subject to change,[44] provided the theoretical foundation of Nicene orthodoxy. It allows the Father to be the cause of the Son's begetting and the Spirit's procession, but in such a way that, in distinction from all other created beings, they share in the Father's eternal and incorporeal existence. Athanasius, the champion of Nicaea, gratefully cited *Peri Archon* 4.4.1 in this regard:

> If he is the "image of the invisible God" (Col. 1:15) the image is invisible. And I am so bold as to posit that, because he is also the "likeness" of the Father, there was no time when he did not exist. For when did God, who is called "light" by John when he says, "God is light" (1 Jn 1:5), not have the "radiance of his own glory" (see Heb. 1:3)? Would someone be so bold as to say that the Son began to exist after having not existed previously? When did the image of the unspeakable, unnameable and ineffable substance Father, the "imprint" (see Heb. 1:3) and the Word who knows the Father (see Mt. 11:27), not exist? For let the one who is so bold as to go ahead and say "There was a time when the Son was not" be aware that he is saying as well that Wisdom did not exist, that the Logos did not exist, and that Life did not exist. . . . But it is not possible nor is it safe, because of our weakness, to deprive God (in so far as we can do so) of having his only-begotten Son always united with him, who is the Wisdom "with whom he rejoices" (Prov. 8:30), since, in that case, he could not be understood always to rejoice.[45]

In a way characteristic of his use of philosophy, Origen found useful the Platonic concept of hypostasis as a way of speaking about the Son and the Holy Spirit as having a separate existence from the Father in the unity of the Trinity. Nonetheless he modified it in the direction of biblical faith by affirming the doctrine of creation out of nothing,[46] so that, in place of a Platonic continuity of being in an eternally existing cosmos, we have the biblical distinction between the Creator and the creation. Arius repudiated Origen when he affirmed that the Son came into being in time and out of non-existence.[47]

24

In the beginning of his discussion of Christ in *Peri Archon*, Origen sets forth the fundamental distinction between two natures: Christ's deity, by virtue of which he is the only Son of God, and his human nature, which he accepted in recent times to fulfill the divine plan (*dispensatio* in Latin = *oikonomia* in Greek).[48] This notion of divine plan, beginning with creation and including the election of Israel, in which Christ's incarnation and resurrection play the key role, has its roots in the New Testament and was fully developed by Irenaeus.[49] For Origen the *grammateus*, *oikonomia* would suggest the image of God as the author of the cosmos, planning all its intricacies and events much as Homer planned the *Iliad* or as God himself, as its ultimate author, planned the Bible. The divine nature, God's Logos, fully shares, as we have seen, in the Father's eternity and incorporeality. In a chapter suffused with awe, Origen discusses how the Logos also shares our full human nature. His taking flesh does not simply mean animating a body, but taking a human soul as well. Anticipating devotion to Mary as the Theotokos, Origen insists on the full union of these two natures, so that, in his words,

> it is to be believed that the Power of the divine majesty, that very Logos and Wisdom of God, in whom all things visible and invisible were created (see Col. 1:16), existed within the contours of that man who appeared in Judaea, and, in addition, the Wisdom of God entered a woman's womb, was born a baby, and uttered a cry just like other howling babies.[50]

This union is so intimate that Scripture habitually applies the properties of either nature to the other, so that the man Jesus Christ is called the Son of God and the Son of God is said to have died. The union of the Logos with his human soul actually precedes and makes possible his assumption of a human body, for, as he put it "it was not possible for God's nature to combine with a body without some medium."[51] The rational being which ultimately constituted Christ's human soul was the one such being that did not, to a greater or lesser extent, fall away from God after its creation (see below) but clung inseparably to him. It still remains a soul but it is no longer capable of separating from the Logos by choosing evil, by virtue of its "firmness of purpose, immensity of affection and unquenchable warmth of love, any notion of change or alteration was removed, and what was once a matter of choice was by a long condition of practice changed into nature."[52] Except for its presupposition that Christ's human soul was a rational being preexisting his human conception, this Christology – Christ in two distinct natures which retain their own integrity, the one fully God and the other fully and completely a man, natures so intimately and inseparably united that the properties of either one may be ascribed to the other – anticipates and foreshadows Chalcedonian orthodoxy. As the one Mediator between God and humanity, Christ not only unites the two natures but mediates between the absolute and simple oneness of God and the multiplicity of created beings. In *Peri Archon* Origen alludes to Christological titles, which he understood as aspects (*epinoiai*) of the Logos;[53] he develops their significance in the *Commentary on John*. Book 1 below (XX.119) shows how

> God is ... entirely one and simple, but the Savior, on account of the many – since God "designated" him "in advance as a propitiation" (Rom. 3:25) and first-fruits of all creation – has become many and is doubtless all things that every created being capable of liberation has need of from him.

As we shall see, Origen ascribes four of these (Wisdom, Word, Truth and Life) to the divine nature; the rest Christ (Resurrection, Way, Good Shepherd, etc.) he assumed with his human nature for the sake of the divine *oikonomia*.

The *divine* oikonomia *in* Peri Archon

Origen posited a two-stage Creation. In the first stage, God first creates rational beings, united to him by their free choice. All but one of these rational beings, the one which constitutes the human soul of the incarnate Christ, fell at least to some extent from this original unity with God. Some did not fall very far, so that their return is relatively easy. These are the angels and the spirits who animate the heavenly bodies, who serve those below them who have fallen farther. A second group of rational spirits fell so far from God as to be actively antagonistic, subverting the return of other rational beings to God. These constitute the demons or, as Origen calls them, the "adverse powers." A third class of rational beings occupy a middle ground. These are called "souls" (*psuchai*) because their once ardent love of God has "cooled" (*psuchesthai*).[54] By virtue of their creation in the image and likeness of God, as exhibited in their capacity to participate to some extent in God's virtues – by being merciful, for example, even as their heavenly Father is merciful (see Mt. 5:48) – these souls still retain a kinship to God.[55] The primeval fall of rational spirits brings into play a further step in God's *oikonomia*, a second stage of creation, that of our material cosmos. In unequivocal opposition to the Gnostics, Origen affirms this creation as an essential element in God's beneficent plan to bring fallen rational spirits back to himself.

The inequities of the world, of which Gnostics, especially Marcion, complained, stem from the diverse motions and declensions of rational spirits from their original harmony with God.[56] The creation we know is submitted to futility and awaiting its liberation (Rom. 8:19–22), serving as a place for these fallen rational spirits to recognize their alienation from God. Here God provides them an opportunity to begin a process of moral and intellectual purification that will ultimately restore them to their unity with him. God's *oikonomia* entails an exercise of providence that respects the free choice of rational creatures. Hal Koch, in a pioneering study of Origen, recognized that his entire system revolves around these two foci, divine providence and human free will.[57] In this plan God so arranges things that those beings farther along in their progress assist those who have made less progress. Thus, as Origen explains in a key passage, even the struggles of the adverse powers against them serve to make their ultimate victory more secure:

> I suppose that God the parent of all things arranges each individual event for the salvation of his whole creation through the unspeakable calculation of his Word and Wisdom, in such a way that each spirit or soul (or whatever else rational beings ought to be called) should not be compelled by force against its freedom of choice into any action except that to which the motion of its own mind leads – for in that case their freedom of choice would be taken away from them, which would certainly change the quality of their nature itself – and at the same time the diverse motions of their wills should fit together in a suitable and useful way for the harmony of one world, so that, when some need help, others can offer help, while others bring about conflicts and struggles for those who are making progress, so that their zeal may be proven and they may hold their restored position more securely after their

victory, because they have confirmed it by the difficulties of those who exert themselves.[58]

For Origen the cosmos may be a difficult place with conflicts and struggles, but it is fundamentally beneficent. Furthermore, its marvelous order bespeaks the unimaginable skill of its Creator. Origen suggests that the ultimate purpose of the cosmos lies in the opportunity it provides for rational spirits to become like God voluntarily and through their own efforts. Although Plato sets forth this ideal, it comes ultimately from Moses. In a characteristic exegetical argument, Origen points to a discrepancy between Genesis 1:26, where God says "Let us make man in our own image and likeness," and the following verse, where God makes man simply "in the image of God." God makes rational creatures in his image by endowing them with reason and freedom of choice. Nonetheless, "the perfection of God's likeness was indeed reserved for the consummation" so that they might obtain it by their own earnest efforts to imitate God.[59] Implicit in this understanding of the cosmos is the idea, which Origen inherited from Clement, that God's *oikonomia* extends not simply to the cosmos as a whole, but to each individual rational spirit.

Origen always maintains that "it lies with us and with our own actions whether we are to be blessed and holy, or whether through sloth and negligence we are to turn away from blessedness into wickedness and perdition."[60] Hendrik Benjamins has recently shown how Origen's understanding of God's *oikonomia* underlies his discussions of freedom of choice from a philosophical perspective. The most important of these is Book 3, chapter 1 of *Peri Archon*, a chapter preserved in Greek. There Origen draws masterfully on the resources of Greek philosophy to develop a concept of *oikonomia* inconceivable apart from the biblical notion of a benevolent, personal God. From the Stoics he takes the concept of a chain of events in which nothing happens accidentally. From them he also took arguments vindicating a sphere of human freedom. However, this freedom is no longer, as with the Stoics, in the face of an inexorable and impersonal fate, but in the face of the loving, personal God. From the Platonists he takes arguments vindicating a beneficent divine providence that arranges the world for the best. However, this providence is no longer just for the cosmos as a whole but for each individual soul. From the Platonists also Origen takes the concept of the preexistence of souls as a way to explain apparent injustice in the way providence operates.[61] Thus Origen explained the distinction between souls who are vessels of honor and those who are vessels of dishonor in Roman 9, not on the basis of unmerited election, but on the basis of those souls' behavior before they were conceived in the womb.[62] Origen presents grace and free will not as mutually exclusive, but as complementary. We see this in his interpretation of another problematic text, "So it depends not on man's will or exertion, but on God's mercy" (Rom. 9:16). He argues that Paul is not denying human agency but appropriately indicating that God's share in our salvation far exceeds ours. Paul is like a sailor who, at the conclusion of a safe voyage, ascribes all the credit to God. The sailor does not for a moment suppose that he could have arrived safe at harbor without his own skill at navigation. Even so, he is far more impressed by God's role in giving favorable winds, hospitable weather, and the stars as a guide.[63]

Eschatology in Peri Archon

Peri Archon made Origen, as Brian Daley describes him, "without a doubt the most controversial figure in the development of early Christian eschatology."[64] While conceding "a touch of anachronism," he goes on to describe Origen's eschatological thought as "an attempt to de-mythologize the accepted apocalyptic tradition of the Scriptures and popular Christian belief in a constructive, reverent and pastorally fruitful way."[65] Daley points out that, more than other early Christian thinkers, Origen stresses the relevance of eschatology to the ongoing spiritual life of Christians. In Origen eschatology is in continuity with the rest of the divine oikonomia. This process begins now in those cooperating with God's grace and continues "bit by bit and by stages as boundless and immense ages pass by, seeing that the amendment will occur and the correction is followed through painstakingly in each individual."[66] Origen writes that "as the eye naturally seeks light and vision and our body by its nature desires food and drink, so our mind harbors a natural and proper desire to know God's truth and to learn the causes of things."[67] He goes on to say that God would not have given us this longing to no purpose, but so that it might be satisfied. Origen thus understood the Christian hope as a continuing education. Souls who have departed this life will pass through "a lecture hall or school"[68] where they learn to understand the mysteries of Scripture and the underlying reason for the diversity and variety of the natural world, including animals and trees. Then, ascending through the heavenly spheres, they will come to understand the nature of the stars.[69] This process of education is also a process of moral purification, since its goal is to "see God," which is "to understand him through purity of heart."[70] The personal spirituality and pastoral concern that animate this eschatological vision shine through in a passage where Origen explains why the Holy Spirit is known as "Comforter" (*Paraklêtos*):

> Anyone who deserves to participate in the Holy Spirit, when he has learned his unspeakable mysteries, undoubtedly obtains consolation and gladness of heart. Because, by the Spirit's revelation, he has come to know the reasons for all things that happen, and why and how they happen, his soul can never be disturbed in any way or experience any feeling of sadness.[71]

Two aspects of Origen's eschatology have been problematical from his day to ours, both of them related to one of its key principles, eschatology, namely that "the end is always like the beginning."[72] First, if the end is always like the beginning, and all rational creatures were originally at one with God, will not all eventually be restored to that unity? Borrowing a term from Acts 3:21, Origen refers to this eventual restoration of unity as *apokatastasis*, the return of all things. (Although, as far as we can tell, he did not use *apokatastasis* in this sense in *Peri Archon*, he did do so elsewhere, including *Commentary on John* 1.XVI.91 below.)[73] Second, if the ultimate source of all things is the incorporeal godhead, will not corporeal existence, entailing, as it does, the possibility of a differentiation from God, ultimately cease to exist when God is all in all? These implications of Origen's eschatology ran counter to two fundamental early Christian beliefs: the belief that God will condemn the wicked to eternal punishment and the belief that the final Christian hope is for the faithful to be restored to their bodies in the resurrection of the dead. For those souls which have not fully achieved the return to God for which the cosmos exists, Origen suggests that there may be

> some future healing and correction, certainly quite harsh and full of pain for those who have refused to obey the Word of God, yet a process of instruction and rational training through which those who already in the present life have devoted themselves to such activity and, by having had their minds purified, have attained here and

now to a capacity for divine wisdom, may advance to a fuller understanding of truth.[74]

Origen alludes to such a process of purification after death in *Homilies on Jeremiah* 12.3 below, explaining to sinners that they "must taste something very bitter, being under God's careful management, so that, having been corrected, [they] may be saved." In this purification we make our own fire as we burn with remorse for our evil deeds.[75] Such ideas, which he shared with Clement, provide a possible basis for the doctrine of Purgatory.[76] Elsewhere Origen hints that the notion of eternal punishment, while not actually true, serves a useful function, since it encourages simpler Christians, still motivated by fear, not to be complacent.[77] He also raises the possibility that God has created worlds both before and after this one.[78] He carefully distinguishes this possibility of multiple worlds from the Stoic doctrine that, because the same inexorable sequence of causes will remain, each subsequent world will be identical.[79] The logic of his system suggests that all rational beings will return to their original unity with God, and he leaves open the possibility that even devils will be saved.[80]

Second, if the end is like the beginning, and God, simple and changeless by virtue of his incorporeality, is the beginning from which all things come into being, does not the ultimate Christian hope entail the abandonment of corporeality? Such a conclusion ran counter to contemporary Christian understandings of the resurrection of the body. Origen strongly criticized the views simple Christians held, castigating "disciples of the letter alone" for indulging their own desires and lusts and supposing that "that the promises for the future are to be expected in terms of bodily pleasure and luxury," imagining that they will eat and drink and even order servants around. While accepting and using the Revelation to John, he implicitly rejects any literal understanding of the Millennium promised in chapter 20 of that book. Appealing to 1 Corinthians 15, he argues that such persons do not follow the Apostle Paul's thinking about the resurrection of a "spiritual body" (1 Cor. 15:44).[81] Later, Origen would make the same argument in his *Contra Celsum*. Origen ostensibly leaves the ultimate status of corporeality open, but he apparently cannot conceive of a continuing role for corporeality once all things have returned to their union with God. Again, he derives this position from 1 Corinthians 15, in which the Apostle wrote that "this corruptible must put on incorruption and this mortal body must put on immortality"

(1 Cor. 15:53). In a manner characteristic of a *grammateus*, he focuses on the verb and argues that "putting on" incorruption and immortality should be interpreted in terms of Paul's exhortation in Romans 13:14, "Put on the Lord Jesus Christ." Plausibly interpreting Paul, Origen envisages two stages in our souls' return to God. In the first stage we will be clothed in more pure and subtle bodies, different from the ones we have now, which cannot be conquered by death. In the second stage, "when at last material nature little by little passed away," death is swallowed up in victory (see 1 Cor. 15:54) so that God will be "all in all" (1 Cor. 15:28).[82] Origen argues elsewhere in *Peri Archon* that the soul's attainment of likeness to God also entails incorporeality.[83] There is no reason to believe that Origen substantially altered his eschatological vision. As we shall see, the *Contra Celsum*, one of his last works, is consistent in this regard with *Peri Archon* and the same is true of another late work, the *Commentary on Matthew*.[84] In this teaching Origen distinguished his views from those of simpler Christians whose views on the bodily resurrection and on the eternal punishment of the wicked have, in fact, dominated the Christian tradition. Nonetheless, we can overestimate Origen's departures from traditional eschatology. Henri Crouzel has pointed out how nuanced Origen's position was, and Charles E. Hill has shown that his rejection of millennialist eschatology had just as good a pedigree as his adversaries' position.[85]

Biblical interpretation in Peri Archon

The first three chapters of *Peri Archon*, Book 4 deal with biblical interpretation.[86] They begin with two arguments for the Bible's divine inspiration. The first is that Scripture must partake of divine power in order to influence for the better the great mass of humanity, not just a few intellectuals. Besides Moses and Jesus no lawgiver has ever had any influence outside his own people, yet people of all nations flock to conform to the standards of the Old and New Testaments, even though doing so exposes them to the hatred of idolaters.[87] The second is that Scriptural prophecies have been fulfilled long after they were made.[88] Because these prophecies pointed to him, it is only with the advent of Jesus that the divine presence in the prophetic discourses and spiritual character of the Mosaic law, previously hidden, came to light, so that anyone who brings care and attention to the Bible will feel a "trace of enthusiasm" from that divine presence. Origen the *grammateus* readily

32

admits that the style of Holy Scripture is mediocre (compared, presumably, to Homer or Plato) because, as Paul wrote, "We have this treasure in earthen vessels" (2 Cor. 4:7), but, even so, this is the pattern of the divine *oikonomia*: just as we must seek a profound cause when people from all over the world commit their lives to an obscure Galilaean, so the Bible's divine power clothed in a humble style impels us to seek a profound hidden meaning. [89]

Origen asserts that literal interpretation makes Christian orthodoxy untenable. Unless we seek a non-literal meaning in prophecies – for example Isaiah 11 prophesying that when the Messiah comes the wolf will lie down with the lamb – the Jews can make a good argument that Jesus falsely called himself the Christ. (Origen criticizes the Jews for excessive literalism, as we see also in *Homilies on Jeremiah* 12.13 below, even though, as we have seen, his own esoteric interpretation has roots in Judaism.) Similarly, Gnostics point to the literal meaning of some passages – for example, "A fire has been kindled in my fury" (Deut. 32:22; Jer. 15:14) and "I am a jealous God, visiting the Sins of the Fathers upon the children to the third and fourth generation" (Ex. 20:5) – to prove that the Creator-God whom the Jews worship is imperfect and not even good. Unfortunately, "the simpler of those who boast of belonging to the church, even as they take for granted that there is no God greater than the Creator, which is sound on their part, nonetheless they take for granted things about God that they would not believe about the most savage and the most unjust of men."[90] If the church accepts such naïve biblical interpretation, it leaves itself defenseless before its adversaries.

Origen is famous for propounding in *Peri Archon* a threefold interpretation, in which Scripture has bodily, soulish, and spiritual meanings. His intent was not to say that each passage has precisely three meanings, but that Scripture meets the needs of rational creatures at different levels of progress.[91] Some passages, indeed, have no bodily sense, even though all have a spiritual sense.[92] This is because God's Logos has, in fact, so "planned" the Scriptures as to include "snares, obstacles, and" even "impossibilities" to force the intelligent interpreter to get beyond the obvious sense of the text.[93] God's *oikonomia* thus accounts for difficult Scriptural texts as part of a divine strategy of revelation and concealment that enables the spiritual to attain "that which is hidden" of 1 Cor. 2:7.[94] Our selections below from Origen's homilies exhibit him speaking movingly of the anguish involved in failing to understand a passage as he describes Mary and Joseph's search for Jesus and also undertaking with zest the "struggle" of explaining difficulties in the passage about the Witch of Endor. Scripture's goal is to conceal God's truth from those "unable to bear the burden of examining such momentous things" even as it reveals that truth to the spiritually minded.[95]

Origen points out a number of passages where the literal sense presents "obstacles" and "impossibilities" that impel the intelligent reader toward a deeper, spiritual sense. The first mentioned are inconsistent and absurd statements in the early chapters of Genesis, on which Origen was preparing a commentary at the time, but he finds examples from the entire Bible, the New Testament included. He makes it clear that, although most of the Bible's narrative is factual and most of its laws were meant to be observed, there are nonetheless some passages, albeit few, that have only a spiritual meaning.[96] Origen's standards for what is literal may strike the modern reader as obtuse, as when he argues that Jesus' injunction "if someone strikes you on the right cheek" (Mt. 5:39) is incredible because most assailants, leading with their right hand, would actually strike the left cheek first.[97] We should not, however, expect Origen's categories for what is literal to correspond to ours, especially when, as Northrop Frye has pointed out, what we ourselves mean by "literal" is far from clear.[98] The spiritual interpretation that penetrates to the profounder sense requires two things: (1) obedience to Jesus' command to "search the scriptures" (Jn 5:39) by devoting prolonged, careful, and exact examination to them; and (2) God's assistance, which "breaks in pieces the gates of brass" (Isa. 45:2) that hide the "treasures of wisdom and knowledge" (Col. 2:3).[99] God's assistance is particularly vital for understanding the gospels, which demand "the mind of Christ" (1 Cor. 2:16) for their interpretation.[100] Origen elaborates on these spiritual qualifications in *Commentary on John*, Book 1 below.

Origen's discussion of Scriptural interpretation in *Peri Archon* stands beside Augustine's *On Christian Teaching* as a classic of biblical hermeneutics. Nonetheless, it makes sense only in connection with Origen's actual practice. It is to be hoped that the selections from Origen's works here will be helpful in that regard. One of today's foremost Patristic scholars, Manlio Simonetti, identifies three fundamental principles that, in practice, govern Origen's interpretation of Scripture. These are:

1   a practical principle, "utility" (*ôpheleia*, see 2 Tim. 3:16), how the text addresses the spiritual concerns of those who are to hear it interpreted;

2 an ideological principle, how the text relates to Christ; and
3 a structural principle, how, given Origen's Platonic view of
   reality, we can move from the sensible to the intelligible levels
   of being.[101]

The Epistle to the Hebrews, which speaks of the law as a shadow of
good things to come (Heb. 8:5), provides Origen Scriptural prece-
dent for the third principle. Our selections below include numerous
examples of each of these principles in action. Thus, for example, we
see Origen concerned with usefulness at the beginning of *Homilies
on 1 Samuel* 5, when he asks how the biblical narrative "touches" his
hearers, relating liberation from exile to Christ in *Commentary on
Lamentations*, fragment II, moving from the sensible to the intelligible levels of being in his discussion of the spiritual meaning of
footwashing in *Commentary on John*, Book 32. In practice also, as
Theresia Heither has recently pointed out, Origen's discursive style
effectively brings the reader into a dialogue with the biblical text by
raising hypothetical objections and answering them.[102] Finally, as
important as the Bible was to Origen – and practically all of his
work is pervaded by biblical language and concerned in one way or
another with biblical interpretation – our selection from the
Commentary on John, Book 13 makes clear that he saw it not as an
end in itself, but as a gateway to deeper knowledge.

3

MAN OF THE CHURCH AT CAESAREA

Caesarea

In 234 Origen left Alexandria permanently for Caesarea in Palestine, where Bishop Theoctistus had ordained him as a presbyter. This was to be his only real home for the rest of his life. There, with Ambrosius's assistance, he continued to publish, producing most of the works that have come down to us and becoming one of the most prolific authors of Antiquity. There too, as a presbyter, he had the opportunity to preach at the eucharistic gathering as well as to teach, and was also involved at least twice in examining bishops for heresy. Although smaller than Alexandria, Caesarea was, like Origen's former home, a prosperous seaport and seat of Roman administration. It was also a splendid location for a student of the Bible.[1] As we see below in his *Commentary on Lamentations*, fragment XCIII, Origen already knew Palestine as the "holy land" (he is one of the first authors to use the term in its present sense).[2] He made use of the opportunity to gain a better understanding of biblical geography and to pursue his quest for manuscripts. Even more importantly, Caesarea had a flourishing Greek-speaking or bilingual Jewish community with which Origen had extensive, if touchy, intellectual relations. He not only consulted rabbis for technical information but made himself familiar with Jewish traditions, so much so that his works provide a valuable window on Palestinian Jewish thought of the time.[3] There also is tantalizing evidence that Jewish scholars, perhaps Rabbi Hosha'ia, may have borrowed Origen's copies of Philo's works.[4]

A student's testimonial

It is in Caesarea, at some time no earlier than 238 and no later than 245, that a student composed the *Address to Origen*, which provides a picture and a reflection of the man and of his teaching methods.[5] The author is traditionally identified as Gregory Thaumaturgus (i.e. "Wonderworker"), also identified as the recipient of Origen's *Letter to Gregory* below.[6] Gregory ascribes his encounter with Origen to a "marvelous *oikonomia*."[7] Divine providence, working through his guardian angel, accomplished this by taking him from a home in which he was brought up in error, worshipping false gods, to Caesarea, where Origen had arrived after being driven out of Egypt.[8] Arrived there, his angel gave him over to Origen's *oikonomia*, "and then perhaps somehow he rested, not out of any weariness, for the race of divine ministers cannot be wearied, but because he had conferred me to a man who would exercise all possible providence and care."[9] In his account, Origen first trains him in philosophy, beginning with ethics, understood in an entirely practical way as, in Robert L. Wilken's words, "training in virtue."[10] He also uses Greek philosophy to teach him physics and logic. With this necessary preparation, Gregory can go on to the study of the Christian Scriptures. Regarding them, Gregory presents Origen as a uniquely inspired exegete, partaking of the same Spirit who originally inspired the oracles (i.e. the Christian Scriptures).[11] His unmediated access to the Logos is guaranteed by his having, as his personal guardian angel, the Logos himself, the Angel of Great Counsel.[12] Gregory explains that such insight is necessary because Scripture is obscure, either because God deliberately veils the meaning from the unworthy, or because it is actually plain but seems difficult to us.[13]

Gregory's account of Origen's teaching practice demonstrates how he exercised God's providence along with human care for his pupil. Its fundamental concern was integrating the student's personality, or, more precisely, reintegrating it, into the image and likeness of God. Thus Gregory states that Origen "taught that part of our soul which it falls to the lot of dialectic alone to correct," namely its rational part, "but also its lowly part," the part moved by affections and appetites.[14] In his teaching about the natural world, Origen enabled his pupil to move from an irrational to a rational awe in the face of its beauty and majesty of the "sacred *oikonomia* of the universe and its irreproachable nature," the higher and lower parts of the soul entertaining the same emotion.[15] Such integration involved the union of theory and practice. Gregory stresses that Origen's students did not simply learn about the principles of morality but, in so far as possible, and he demurs in his own case, they exercised the virtues themselves.[16] The hallmark of such education is personal appropriation of ideas as opposed to simply knowing information. Gregory contrasts Origen favorably to an earlier teacher in Roman law, whom he simply sought to please out of obedience rather than out of love for his subject.[17] Evidently the genuine teacher's goal is not to have the student reproduce his ideas but to become like himself. In the Socratic tradition, such a teacher's role is not to inculcate ideas but to serve as a midwife, enabling the student to develop his own. Origen must have self-consciously placed himself in this tradition, since his student described him as attaching himself "very Socratically" to his students, his words being like the bit to a wild horse.[18] Unlike pagan teachers of rhetoric, who were concerned only with purity of style, Origen was concerned that his students learn how not to be deceived.[19] Guarding against deception therefore played a special role in Origen's teaching of Greek philosophy, which, Gregory says, he taught capably by virtue of prolonged study.[20] Origen disapproved the tendency of the Greeks to be convinced by the doctrines of the first philosophers they ran across and sought to inculcate his students against such an uncritical attitude.[21] To assure that his student would develop his own critical sense, Origen would exercise *oikonomia* in the ethical sense, accommodating himself to his pupils by deliberately concealing his own opinions. He would often present doctrines he considered sound in an offhand way and those he considered specious with seriousness, only revealing his actual opinion after his students had grappled with them.[22] The *Address* thus presents an Origen whose actual pedagogy reflects the ideal of Christ himself, the teacher whose aim is to transform his disciple into his own likeness. Origen sets forth this pedagogical ideal in his discussion of footwashing in our selection from Book 32 of the *Commentary on John*.

Preaching

As a presbyter at Caesarea Origen seems to have preached regularly, at least for some years, at the eucharistic gathering. His homilies provide our fullest access by far to Christian preaching in the ante-Nicene period. On the basis of them, Nautin has argued that the Caesarean church heard the entire Bible in its eucharistic services over the course of a three-year period.[23] (See the opening of Origen's fifth homily on 1 Samuel below, which indicates that four lengthy chapters of 1 Samuel had just been read.) Origen's procedure was to go through a passage that had just been read and explain it, roughly verse by verse, while drawing out its moral implications. Two-hundred and five homilies survive in Latin translations by Rufinus or Jerome and twenty on Jeremiah and one on 1 Samuel survive in Greek.[24] Four homilies, two that survive in Greek and two on Luke preserved in Jerome's translation, are included here.

Although Origen's homilies constitute, in effect, commentaries on the books on which he preached, he treated the homily as a distinct genre from the commentary. His homilies are more hortatory, much more concise, less technical, and less speculative than his commentaries. As a teacher, Origen recognized that he was not speaking to the learned audience at the eucharistic gathering, but, as a teacher, he also sought to make his hearers a bit more like himself by initiating them into the transformative study of Scripture. He therefore sought to provide them an example of a reverent and, above all, prayerful approach to the Bible that they could apply themselves.[25] His preaching style was therefore "homiletic" in the root sense of the word, that is, conversational.[26] He frequently asks hypothetical questions, as in the fifth homily on 1 Samuel, where hypothetical debating partners are aghast that the great prophet Samuel could actually be in hell. He frequently employs the second-person singular as if he were addressing each member of the congregation individually – "You, a sinner, must taste something very bitter . . . so that . . . you may be saved." or "Just as you, when you read the Scriptures . . . " (*Homilies on Jeremiah* 12.3 and *Homilies on Luke* 19.5, below). In the thriving port of Caesarea he singled out avarice and lust for particular attention. Origen also warned his congregation against heresy and false ideas. Following his principle of utility, he consistently provides an allegorical interpretation to a historical narrative or a legal edict. Thus Gideon's fleece (Judg. 6:36–40) symbolizes the transition from Judaism to Christianity; the dew of Moses that originally alighted only on the Jewish people now leaves them dry and alights on the surrounding gentiles.[27] The commandment to keep alight the fire on the altar of holocaust (Lev. 6:12–13), applies to "the fire of faith and the lamp of knowledge" in Christians.[28] He frequently preaches about Scriptural interpretation. Thus the grass in Psalm 36:2a [37:2], "they are dried up swiftly like grass," reminds him of Jezebel's attempt to seize Naboth's vineyard and replace it with a field of grass (1 Kings 20). This suggests an allegory about the continuing danger that carnal wisdom (Jezebel) will replace spiritual interpretation of the Bible (Naboth's vineyard) with carnal interpretation (a field of grass).[29] He also maintains a high doctrine of the preached word. Thus he criticizes his congregation for their inconsistency in being (rightly) scrupulous not to lose one crumb of the eucharistic bread while being negligent about applying their understanding so as to not to lose one detail of God's word.[30] This criticism is one indication that Origen's homilies were sometimes ill received; in one homily he scolded members of his congregation for not listening and in another he complained that they did not want to hear what he had to say.[31] Although his thoughtful homilies pointedly address moral and spiritual concerns, Origen evidently was not a preacher who could (or necessarily wanted to) control a congregation like John Chrysostom or Augustine.

On the Passover and Dialogue with Heraclides

In his early years at Caesarea Origen continued to work on his *Commentary on John* and *Commentary on Genesis*. During these years he may have composed his treatise *On the Passover*, recovered in 1941 in a cache of books hidden in an ancient quarry at Tura near Cairo.[32] In it philology contributes to spiritual insight. Origen begins by making short work of Christians who ignorantly identify the Hebrew word *pascha* (Passover) with the Greek *paschein* (to suffer) so as to interpret the Passover as a prefiguration of Christ's passion. The Jewish Passover, described in Exodus 12, for which he gives a spiritual interpretation, is not Christ's passion, but our passage into a transformed life in Christ.

The cache at Tura contained another previously unknown work, Origen's *Dialogue with Heraclides*. This was not a literary dialogue like those of Plato but an actual transcript of a hearing investigating a bishop on charges of heresy. Origen was evidently called in to share his theological expertise. The circumstances are similar to another occasion we know about from Eusebius. There Origen played a prominent role in the investigation of Beryllus, bishop of Bostra in what is now Jordan, whose writings implied that Jesus Christ did not subsist on his own before his Incarnation, nor even then did he have his own proper divinity distinct from the Father. According to Eusebius, Origen, after a close investigation, successfully straightened out what was unorthodox and persuaded Beryllus by his reasoning.[33] From Origen's questions at the beginning of the *Dialogue with Heraclides*, he suspected that Heraclides held views similar to those of Beryllus.

Besides showing Origen as a respected proponent of orthodoxy, the *Dialogue with Heraclides* provides a significant glimpse of impor-

tant elements in his theology. He brings Heraclides to the point of
agreeing that "we need not dread to say that in some way there are
two Gods, but in some way there is one God."[34] Besides affirming
that the Savior is God yet distinct from the Father, Origen argues
that the Son assumed full human nature: body, soul, and spirit. In a
statement that prefigures Gregory of Nazianzus's famous formula,
"What is not assumed is not healed,"[35] he affirms the soteriological
necessity of Christ's assuming full humanity:

> So then our Savior and Lord, wishing to save man as he did,
> for this reason wished to save the body, just as he wished to
> save the soul as well; he also wished to save the remaining
> part of man, the spirit. The whole man would not have
> been saved unless he had assumed the whole man.[36]

The *Dialogue* ends with Origen explaining his theological anthro-
pology in response to a question "Is the soul the blood?" In this
discussion Origen identifies the inner and outer human beings
spoken of by Paul in 2 Corinthians 4:16 and Romans 7:22 with the
two creation narratives in Genesis. Genesis 1:26, where human
beings are created in the image and likeness of God, narrates the
creation of the inner human being, and Genesis 2:7, where God
formed the first man from the dust of the earth, the creation of the
outer human being. Of these the first, by virtue of being in God's
image, is "immaterial, superior to all bodily existence." Therefore,
in answer to the original question, Origen sets forth the principle of
homonymy:

> Just as the outer human being has the same name as the
> inner, so also do the parts of his body, with the result that
> each part of the outer human being has a name corre-
> sponding to a part of the inner human being.[37]

This inner human being also has spiritual senses corresponding to
the senses of the outer human being and may undergo a spiritual
death corresponding to but more serious than the death of the outer
human being.

On prayer

In those same years Origen received a request from Ambrosius
and from a lady, Tatiana, to write a treatise on how and, more

importantly, why we should pray. They specifically asked him to set forth and refute the arguments of those who consider prayer superfluous. Origen's response, his treatise *On Prayer*, accessible in several excellent translations,[38] elicited his powers as a spiritual guide, a philosopher, an interpreter of Scripture and an upholder of orthodox Christian doctrine. He opens the treatise with a statement that "a clear, exact and appropriate account of the whole matter of prayer" is humanly impossible but "becomes possible by the exceeding grace of God (see 2 Cor. 9:14) to those who are no longer servants, but friends of the Logos (see Jn 15:14–15)." He therefore prays that the Spirit enable him to perform so weighty a task.[39] Origen deals with objections to the need or efficacy of prayer in a self-contained philosophical discussion of providence and free will.[40] His primary endeavor, however, was not so much to defend the efficacy of prayer as to redefine it. He argues that we should look on prayer not as a way to obtain benefits, especially earthly benefits, from God, but as a means of becoming more like God. The very act of prayer, bringing with it the benefit of a settled condition, prevents sins and promotes good deeds.[41] Indeed, by separating itself in prayer from the concerns of the body, the soul lays aside its condition as a soul, that is a rational being whose ardor for God has cooled, and becomes more spiritual.[42] Origen reinterprets the material benefits received by the saints of the Old Testament in spiritual terms. Thus, just as God answered Hannah's prayer for a child, so he answers the prayers of those today who find their reason barren and their minds sterile, enabling them through the Holy Spirit to conceive discourses filled with true insights.[43] Origen interprets Paul's exhortation to "pray without ceasing" (1 Thess. 5:17) to mean that the whole life of a saint should be one unbroken prayer, including virtuous deeds as a form of prayer. Nonetheless, "what is commonly called prayer" is also a necessary part of such a life.[44] He therefore discusses when and how one should engage in private prayer, recommending, for example, an orientation toward the East.[45] In doing so he provides a precious insight into early Christian practice. The centerpiece of Origen's treatise is a detailed interpretation of the Lord's Prayer. Ever the *grammateus*, he carefully discusses differences between the Matthaean and Lucan versions before engaging in a verse-by-verse analysis that includes, among other things, an insightful discussion of the uses of temptation.

An Exhortation to Martyrdom

In 235 the Emperor Alexander Severus and his mother, Julia Mammaea, lost their lives at the hands of troops who installed Maximinus Thrax, an Emperor who did not share his predecessor's favorable attitude to Christianity. Because of his wealth and associations with the previous regime, Ambrosius, along with Protoctetus, a presbyter associated with him, had reason to fear arrest and execution. Their situation called forth another short treatise, Origen's *Exhortation to Martyrdom*. In it Origen encourages his friend to meet steadfastly his prospective fate: "I pray you," he writes,

> throughout the present struggle to remember the great reward laid up (see 2 Tim. 4:7–8) in the heavens for those who are persecuted and reviled on account of the Son of Man (Mt. 5:11–12), and to rejoice and to exult and to leap for joy just as the apostles rejoiced when on one occasion they were esteemed worthy to suffer insults for his name (Acts 5:41).

He echoes his older contemporary, Tertullian, saying:

> If we wish to save our soul, so that we may receive it back as better than a soul, let us lose it by martyrdom. For if we lose it for Christ's sake, throwing it to him in dying for him, we purchase for it true salvation.[46]

Ambrosius will find tranquillity if he allows the mind of Christ to speak in him as he meditates on the Psalms:

> And if sometimes you feel distress in your soul, may the mind of Christ within us speak to the soul – even as your own state of mind does what it can to confuse even this mind of Christ – saying "Why, my soul, are you sad? And why do you disturb me? Hope in God, for I will make my confession to him" (Ps. 41:6 [42:5]).[47]

He makes short work of rationalizations that might tempt his patron to temporize. Believing in Christ in his heart will avail him nothing unless, when the test comes, he also confesses Christ with his mouth (see Rom. 10:10).[48] Neither should he think that names are indifferent, so that he could dissemble by worshipping the true

God under the name of Zeus.[49] Origen the "almost fanatical Christian" still remains a *grammateus*, listing variants when he cites from the gospels exhortations to be steadfast in the face of persecution.

We might speculate that Ambrosius received with mixed feelings a treatise so urgent about his putting his neck on the line, but there can be no question of Origen's sincerity; the *Exhortation to Martyrdom* reveals the living piety behind the theology of *Peri Archon*. Origen thus sets forth the cash-value of a belief in the divine *oikonomia*:

> Since God evidently watches over the movement of the heaven and the stars in it and over that which takes place by his divine skill in earth and sea, in the birth and nurture of all kinds of animals and in the origin and growth of all plants, it would be absurd for us to close our eyes and not to look to God, but in fear to turn our eyes upon men who will soon die and be handed over to the punishment they deserve.[50]

As in *Peri Archon*, eschatological hope entails understanding Scripture:

> With profound meaning Isaiah says: "I gave Egypt for your ransom and Ethiopia and Syene for you, for you were precious in my sight" (Isa. 43:3–4)." The right meaning of this and other such sayings you will understand if you have a love of learning in Christ and already wish to surpass that which is seen through a glass, in an enigma (see 1 Cor. 13:12), and hasten towards him who has called you.

Such understanding of Scripture is, however, but a step toward the ultimate Christian hope, the immediate knowledge of God:

> Then, as never before you will comprehend face to face, as friends of the heavenly Father. Friends learn not by obscure hints, or by mere knowledge of sounds and words, symbols and types, but by a vision through which they attain to the nature of intelligible things and the beauty of the truth.[51]

Even more clearly than in *Peri Archon*, this hope entails sharing God's immateriality:

I consider that they love God with all their soul who with a great desire to be in fellowship with God withdraw and separate their soul not only from the earthly body but also from any sort of body. Such persons accept the putting away of the body of humiliation (see Phil. 3:21) without distress or emotion when the time comes for them to put off the body of death (see Rom. 7:24) by what is considered to be death.[52]

In 238 Ambrosius's anxieties ended when Maximinus fell by the same violent means that brought him briefly to power. With his assistance, the remaining fifteen years of Origen's life were astonishingly productive, even by Origen's standards. He composed more volumes of his mammoth *Commentary on John* along with multi-volume commentaries on Matthew, Luke, most of the Pauline letters, the Psalms, and most of the Old Testament wisdom and prophetic books. Of this output, we possess certain volumes of the *Commentary on John*, two of which are represented here, and about half of the *Commentary on Matthew*, surviving either in Greek or in an anonymous Latin translation. Apart from fragments, the only other commentaries that survive are those on the Song of Songs and on Romans, both in translations by Rufinus.

Commentary on the Song of Songs

Origen seems to have composed the *Commentary on the Song of Songs* during a prolonged sojourn in Athens. Nautin speculates that he may have gone there because of tension with hitherto supportive bishops in Palestine.[53] Jerome, gave it his highest praise: "Origen, who in other books excelled everyone else, on the Song of Songs excelled himself . . . so that it seems to me that in him is fulfilled the Scripture, 'The king has brought me into his storehouse' (Song 1:4)." We have three books translated into Latin by Jerome's erstwhile friend, Rufinus. Origen opens his preface with a brief characterization of the book:

This little book is an epithalamium, that is, a wedding song, written by Solomon in what appears to me to be the form of a drama. He sang it from the perspective of a bride being married who burns with an ardent love for her groom, who is the Word of God. Thus the one who loves him is either the soul made in his image or the church.[54]

45

As a *grammateus*, Origen establishes its genre: a wedding song in which characters or *prosôpa* (a bride and groom, and, as he goes on to say, their friends) have dramatic parts. Throughout his commentary he pays attention to the dramatic context in which these characters speak. As a spiritual interpreter, he identified the groom as the Word of God and the bride as either the individual soul or the church. In identifying the bride as the church Origen follows in a Christian tradition already attested by Hippolytus, one that probably derived from Jewish identification of the bride with Israel.[55] We find such nuptial imagery for the relationship between God and his people in some Hebrew prophets and, far more abundantly, in the New Testament (most notably in Ephesians 5, which speaks of marriage as a "mystery" signifying the relationship of Christ to the church). The identification of the bride as the individual soul may have been Origen's innovation. If so, such identification follows naturally from his view that God's *oikonomia* applies to the individual as well as to the collective. Henri Crouzel has pointed out that for Origen the church functions in many ways like the third divine hypostasis of Plotinus, the Soul in which individual souls participate.[56]

As we have seen, Origen considered the Song of Songs to be the third book in Solomon's progressive series providing instruction in philosophy. As such, it deals with the culmination of philosophy, intimate and unmediated communion with God. To profit from its teaching the person reading it must, therefore, have reached spiritual maturity:

> But first we must know that, just as childhood is not moved to passionate love, so the babyhood and childhood of the inner man is not allowed to receive these words – those, that is, who are nourished in Christ with milk, not solid food (see Heb. 5:12 and 1 Cor. 3:1–3) and, at this initial stage, desire the rational and guileless milk (see 1 Pet. 2:2). For in the words of the Song of Songs is that food concerning which the Apostle said: "Moreover, solid food is for the perfect" and requires hearers, "who, in order to accept it, have their senses exercised in the discernment of good and evil" (Heb. 5:14).[57]

Although almost all of Scripture has a meaning that is appropriate for the spiritually immature, this is not true of the Song of Songs: its erotic imagery can easily lead them astray:

If someone has access to it who is a man according to the flesh
only, for such a person there issues no small risk and danger.
Because he does not know how to listen to the language of
love purely and with chaste ears, he diverts everything he
hears away from the inner man to the outer, carnal man, he
turns from the spirit to the flesh, and nourishes in himself
carnal desires, and on the occasion of divine Scripture seems
to be moved and incited to the lust of the flesh.[58]

Because it has no positive message for the immature and can so
easily lead them astray, Origen approves a Jewish custom of keeping
the Song of Songs, along with the beginning of Genesis and the
beginning and end of Ezekiel, out of the hands of the spiritually
immature.[59] The Song of Songs is for those who have the immediate
and intimate access to the Logos about which Origen speaks in
detail in *Commentary on John*, Book 1 below.

Although Origen believes that the Song of Songs has an entirely
spiritual meaning and considers it dangerous for the immature, he
resolutely affirms its eroticism. Its lush imagery is no embarrassment to be papered over by a sterile, spiritualizing interpretation,
but an opportunity to draw on a profound human experience to illu-
minate the human relationship with God. The power of erotic love
is evident in a wife who wants to do whatever pleases her husband;
in the same way mature souls in an intimate relationship with God
act out of love rather than mere fear.[60] To sever the connection
between a fundamental human emotional drive, sexual love, and the
love of the bride for her divine bridegroom would destroy the
homonymy between the inner and the outer man, between human
beings as created in the image of God and human beings as created
from the dust of the earth. In the Prologue to his *Commentary on the
Song of Songs* Origen sets forth this principle in much the same
terms as in his *Dialogue with Heraclides*.[61] He was well aware that
the Scriptures he read in Greek, including the Song of Songs,
almost always used the relatively uncommon word *agapê* for love
and avoided the usual word, *erôs*, but he argued that these concepts
are the same.[62] Although the Swedish theologian Anders Nygren,
in his influential work *Agape and Eros*, attacked Origen for identifying concepts that should have been kept separate, more recent
scholars have effectively upheld Origen's interpretation. They have
shown that, as a theoretician of love in the Christian tradition,
Origen has no peer but Augustine, many of whose positions he
anticipates.[63]

INTRODUCTION

For Origen, nonetheless, the Song of Songs is as much about biblical interpretation as it is about love. When the groom tells the bride, in verse 1:15, "Your eyes are doves," this is because "she understands the divine Scriptures, no longer after the letter, but after the Spirit and sees in it spiritual mysteries, for a dove is the symbol of the Holy Spirit."[64] Mature Christians for whom the Song of Songs was intended could be said to have entered the king's storehouse (Song 1:4), as Jerome once believed Origen had. They had access, that is, to "Christ's secret and hidden mind," so that, with Paul, they could say, "we have the mind of Christ . . . so that we may understand the gifts bestowed on us by God," (1 Cor. 2:16 and 2:12, which Origen often cites together in this way).[65] The word "mind" (Greek *nous*) also means "sense" or "meaning";[66] the soul that has Christ's mind thus, by God's gracious gift, perceives things as Christ does, thereby having access to the "treasures of wisdom and knowledge" (Col. 2:3) hidden in him.[67] Origen may have considered his interpretation of verse 1:5 "I am dusky [or, in other versions, black] and beautiful" as such a treasure. We have just seen an understanding of an oracle concerning Egypt, Ethiopia and Syene promised as a reward of martyrdom and in *Peri Archon* the meaning of "the diversity of races" mentioned in Scripture is a hidden truth, a mystery one might hope to learn in the afterlife.[68] In his commentary Origen identifies the "black and beautiful" bride with Ethiopians in Scripture: among others, Zipporah, Moses' Ethiopian wife, with the Queen of Sheba. As such, he argues that she is an image of the gentile church.[69] Such divinely given insights do not exhaust God's truth, but belong to an ever-continuing process in which all rational beings participate. This is especially clear in Origen's interpretation of 2:4, "bring me into the house of wine":

> That wine, which issues from the true vine (Jn 15:1), is always new. In the case of those who advance in learning, their understanding of divine knowledge and wisdom is always renewed. This is why Jesus said to his disciples: "I shall drink that new wine with you in the kingdom of my Father" (see Mt. 26:29). For the understanding of hidden things and the revelation of secrets is always renewed by the wisdom of God, not simply for men, but for angels and heavenly powers.[70]

The *Commentary on the Songs of Songs* is thus another book, like the *Exhortation to Martyrdom*, that leads us into the heart of Origen's

48

piety. Nowhere is this more evident than in his interpretation of verse 1:2, "Let him kiss me with the kisses of his mouth," where the bridegroom's kisses are insights into the meaning of Scripture.[71] Such language indicates that, for Origen, mystical experience, if we choose to call it that, is as much cognitive as it is affective. The Song of Songs thus teaches us that biblical interpretation is itself erotic.[72]

Commentaries on Paul's epistles

Charles Bigg, in his 1886 Bampton Lectures, characterized Clement and Origen as participants in "the first of those Pauline reactions, which mark critical epochs of theology."[73] Specifically, they, along with Irenaeus, effectively recovered the Pauline writings from Gnostics and brought them back into the mainstream of the Christian tradition. Nonetheless, Origen has, at least until recently, received little credit as a major interpreter of Paul and even less as a Paulinist thinker. His *Commentary on Romans*, the only one of his Pauline commentaries to survive more or less intact, is only now appearing in modern critical edition after having been the orphan among his major works.[74] The neglect or disparagement of Origen's Paulinism is initially puzzling since, besides being trained in the analysis of literary texts, he was culturally and linguistically closer to Paul than any other major interpreter. Nevertheless, his interpretation lies outside the mainstream of Pauline interpretation in the Western tradition, from Augustine through Luther to Bultmann, a tradition concerned almost exclusively with the individual's salvation by grace. For Origen, rather, Paul was the apostle of spiritual transformation – the transformation of human apprehension of God from the oldness of the letter to the newness of the Spirit and the transformation of believers into the image of Christ. Paul was also the preeminent theoretician of the spiritual interpretation of Scripture, which, for us, is necessary for such transformation.

Only recently, particularly in the wake of studies that take seriously Paul's Jewish identity, have scholars begun to recognize the value of Origen's Pauline interpretation. Thus Peter Gorday demonstrated how Origen's interpretation of Romans 9–11 integrated three otherwise troublesome chapters into the epistle as a whole, and a colloquium of Italian scholars have examined sympathetically his interpretation of the hardening of Pharaoh's heart in Romans 9:14–18.[75] Theresia Heither, in a recent study of Origen's *Commentary on Romans*, takes Origen seriously as someone who can help us understand Paul. She shows how Origen views Romans as a whole within the context of Paul's life and thought, relating each individual passage to that coherent whole as he explains its peculiarities of style and expression. She does not accept a priori that salvation by grace alone is the "essential and exclusively essential" element in Pauline theology and judge Origen wanting for not finding it so. [76] In Origen's interpretation of Romans, Paul dealt specifically with two aspects of a transfer of religion: on the one hand, from the Jews to the gentiles and from the Old to the New covenants, and, on the other, from the letter to the Spirit or from the outer to the inner man. Thus Paul gave a new, spiritual meaning to key Jewish concepts such as law, Israel, and circumcision. Heither also shows how Origen dealt sensitively with individual passages. Thus, for example, in his interpretation of Romans 5:12–14, he clarifies the fundamental lines of Paul's soteriology without oversimplifying a difficult passage.

Although we have lost the rest of Origen's commentaries on Paul, Origen cites and comments on key passages from the other Pauline epistles throughout his works. Origen made no distinction between Pauline and Deuteropauline literature, but epistles now considered genuine, particularly 1 Corinthians, are central to his thought. Apparently he never attempted a commentary on 1 Corinthians, although he did preach on it; perhaps he saw no need to pay special attention to a book he dealt with lavishly throughout his works.[77] The selections presented here, except for the brief *Letter to Gregory*, show how Origen uses that epistle to buttress key concepts. Thus the discussion of the gifts of the Spirit in 1 Corinthians 12 authenticates his own role as teacher (*Commentary on Lamentations* fr. CXVI; see also *Peri Archon*, Preface 3, quoted above). Likewise, verse 1:24, where Paul refers to Christ as the "wisdom of God and the power of God," links the Logos of John 1 with the Wisdom of Proverbs 8:22 (*Commentary on John* 1.55). He generalizes verse 9:22, where Paul speaks of becoming all things to all people, to apply to Christ and to the angels (*Commentary on John* 1.217 and 13.99). 1 Corinthians is particularly important for Origen's eschatology. It provides a key text for purification after death, verses 3:10–15, where fire proves each person's work, destroying what is built with wood, hay, and stubble even as the person is saved. It also provides, in chapter 15, an account of resurrection suggesting that, in the end, God will be "all in all" (v. 28).

Our selections illustrate how 1 Corinthians also provided key texts for holding up Paul as a model spiritual person. Thus in

Commentary on John 1.42 we see how Paul's discussion of how he accommodated himself to the Jews in verse 9:22 also provides a pattern for the spiritual man who accommodates himself to simple believers. As a spiritual person, Paul was, for Origen, foremost, in one recent scholar's phrase, the "master of Scriptural interpretation."[78] Origen uses both Corinthian letters to show how Paul set forth and put into practice a spiritual hermeneutic. The single most important passage in this regard is 1 Corinthians 2, a passage that is as vital for Origen's hermeneutics as chapter 15 is for his eschatology. He begins his twelfth Homily on Jeremiah with a reference to 1 Corinthians 2:14, "The soulish man does not receive the things of the Spirit of God. They are foolishness to him." That homily ends with a discussion of Jeremiah (13:17 LXX), "if you do not listen in a hidden manner," that recalls verse 2:7, "we speak the wisdom of God in a mystery, that which is hidden, which God fore-ordained before the ages for our glory." ' According to verse 2:10 God does, through the Spirit, reveal this hidden wisdom. Origen echoes this verse in *Homilies on 1 Samuel* 5.10 below concluding that his exposition has demonstrated that "everything is marvelously written and is understood by those to whom God reveals the interpretation." In *Commentary on John* 1.35 and in *Homilies on Jeremiah* 12.3 below Origen cites another vital verse, 10:11, "these things [i.e. the Old Testament narratives] were written down for our instruction," to demonstrate that Scripture's hidden meaning meets the spiritual needs of Christians. Origen uses 1 Corinthians 13 to argue that Scriptural interpretation is an open-ended process, never complete in this life. As in *Commentary on John* 13.58 below, he appeals especially to verses 9 ("we know in part") and 12 ("now we see through a mirror in an enigma," Greek *en ainigmati*). In the latter verse Origen, like other Fathers, takes entirely seriously the Greek phrase "in an enigma" ("dimly" in the Revised Standard Version) as a technical term pointing to an allegorical interpretation.[79] Key texts for Origen's spiritual hermeneutic from 2 Corinthians are, notably: 3:6 ("the letter kills, the spirit gives life"), indicating the danger of literalism; 6:12 ("words no one could speak"), indicating the need for discretion in dealing with divine mysteries; and 4:7 ("we have this treasure in earthen vessels"), justifying the Bible's humble style in comparison with Greek literature. Although controversial in his own time and later, Origen's use of 1 Corinthians deserves to be taken seriously for bringing to the fore aspects of Paul's thought which later interpreters, including most in our own time, have neglected or suppressed. Robert Grant argues concerning 1 Corinthians 15 that "In dealing with the problem of the resurrection his interpretation is both grammatical and 'spiritual' and certainly comes closer to the meaning of Paul than that of his opponents."[80] The same might be said of the esotericism in 1 Corinthians 2.

Such principles, drawn heavily from 1 Corinthians, determine Origen's own approach to Paul's writings and to Scripture as a whole. They are intimately associated with his concept of a divine *oiko mia*. Origen explains in his *Commentary on John* that Paul acted as a "steward [*oikonomos*, i.e. one who practices *oikonomia*] of the mysteries of God" (1 Cor. 4:1). Such a steward seeks out, as, "the appropriate time for introducing [certain] doctrines, so as not to harm the person listening and to calibrate carefully what is to be left out or added, even when he observes the appropriate time."[81] Thus Origen argues that, in Romans 5:12–14, a notoriously difficult passage, Paul deliberately leaves out important information. He compares Paul to the servant of a great king, who may indeed display the wealth of his master to impress others with the king's power, but who is careful not to divulge information that would enable the king's enemies to steal into his storerooms on their own. Thus when Origen speaks in the Preface to *Peri Archon* of the apostles' having set forth certain doctrines straightforwardly while being silent about others, leaving them for those who would be lovers of wisdom, he generalizes from Paul to the New Testament as a whole.

Contra Celsum

Late in his life, most likely in 248 or 249,[82] Ambrosius sent Origen a copy of a work entitled *True Logos* by Celsus, a long-departed author. Although we cannot be certain who Celsus was, Origen took him to be the Celsus who was a friend of the second-century satirist (and enemy of Christianity) Lucian. James Francis has recently made a case that such an identification is plausible.[83] Evidently written in the late second century, it might be called an anti-apology, a pagan response to pleas for toleration by Christian authors. Its title, implying that Christians proclaimed a "False Logos," is evidence that Celsus knew of a Logos theology such as that taught by Justin at Rome before his death in 156, and he seems to be responding to arguments like those of Justin or Aristides.[84] Beginning with the accusation that Christians constitute an illegal, secret society and ending with an indictment of their refusal to worship the Emperor, his work constituted, in effect, a brief in defense of persecution. The parlous state of the Empire, threatened as never before by inflation, internal dissension, and external invasion, induced in some pagan intellectuals an apocalyptic mood as Rome celebrated the millennium of its founding in 247. Some blamed Christians, favored by the reigning Emperor, Philip the Arab, who tolerated Christians and with whom Origen himself had been in correspondence,[85] for Rome's disarray. Ambrosius, sensitive after his last brush with persecution, must have found the circulation of Celsus's treatise disturbing; he looked to Origen for a response. The need to provide arguments against renewed persecution was probably more pressing than any need to reassure weak Christians who might be disturbed by Celsus's arguments. (Origen pointed out that the Apostle Paul, when he enumerated things that might even conceivably separate us from the love of God in Christ [Rom. 8], did not include "arguments" in the list.[86]) Although hesitating to rescue from oblivion a work he had never heard of before, Origen undertook a detailed refutation in eight books, his *Against Celsus* (commonly known by its Latin title, *Contra Celsum*). As it happens, this is his longest work preserved in Greek and in its entirety, a testimony to the value subsequently placed on it.

Celsus's criticisms are satirical and hard-edged, but demonstrate a real acquaintance with the New Testament. Celsus also had a clear-sighted perception of Christianity's departures from and threat to Greco-Roman social and cultural values. The way he deals with Christian claims that Jesus performed miracles shows that he was no rationalist in the post-Enlightenment sense. He does not argue that these never occurred, but accuses Jesus of having performed them by the means of magic arts.[87] Although Origen assumed that a friend of Lucian would be an Epicurean – conveniently enough for polemical purposes, since Epicureanism was the least popular philosophical sect in his day – he came to admit that this was not the case.[88] Celsus was, rather, a conservative Platonist, fully supportive of traditional pagan cults even though understanding them as expressions of worship for one God. Celsus actually considered himself a more consistent monotheist than the Christians, who worshipped Jesus Christ as a second God.[89] His God is entirely transcendent, dealing with the world through inferior beings, demons, that is, gods worshipped in the pagan cultus. All the more rich for being varied, worship offered to these demons redounds to the one God.[90] Evil comes about as a result of matter, which God did not create. Although Plato was, in Celsus's opinion, the clearest and most authoritative exponent of this doctrine, it represented an "ancient *logos*" shared by all peoples. [91] All peoples, therefore, had a responsibility to maintain their ancestral worship. Christians, however, would lure them away from such worship. Thus, as Robert Wilken points out, Celsus pursues "not simply a debate between paganism and Christianity, but a debate about a new concept of religion. Celsus sensed that Christians had severed the traditional bond between religion and a 'nation' or people."[92]

Celsus's affirmation of a *philosophia perennis* has resonance in our time, as do his objections to Christianity's presumption that God's only concern in all the cosmos is the human race. Humans, he argues, are not even the only rational animals for God to be concerned about; birds must be rational, since they foretell the future, and elephants, since they keep their oaths.[93] Although he accepted God, demons, and magic along with traditional pagan cults, Celsus also represented a philosophical tradition that subjected religion to rational scrutiny. Christians, he argued, broke with that tradition by urging on their followers an irrational fideism, saying such things as "Do not ask questions, just believe," "Your faith will save you," and "The wisdom of the world is an evil, and foolishness is a good thing."[94] While allowing that Jesus might have impressed people by magic arts, he refuses to accept the apparition of the Spirit at Jesus' baptism or the accounts of his resurrection, impeaching the veracity of testimony.[95] Although the most consistent impression Celsus leaves is that Christianity is unspeakably tacky by the standards of elite Greco-Roman culture, he also raises objections that go to the heart of Christian theology. The Christian doctrines of Creation and Incarnation, in his view, fatally compromised the transcendence of God. Creation made God responsible for matter and the evil inevitably associated with it.[96] The Incarnation, besides hopelessly confusing sensible and intelligible realities, would involve an irrational change on God's part from a better mode of existence to a worse.[97] Regarding the Incarnation, Celsus took advantage of the rejection of Jesus on the part of Jews. In a section in which he attacks Christianity from the perspective of Jew, Celsus asks: "What God is not believed when he appears among men, especially when he manifests himself to those who are expecting him? Why indeed should he not be recognized by those who had been waiting for him for a long time?"[98] Nonetheless, although Jews, unlike Christians, had persisted in ancestral traditions long enough to be tolerable, they had little beyond that and their rejection of Christ to recommend them.[99] He regarded them as Egyptians who, like Christians, had abandoned their traditional religion under the influence of another charlatan, Moses, who performed magic tricks.[100]

Universally respected for his learning, Origen was, simply by being who he was, a refutation of Celsus's charge that Christians discouraged thought. (Celsus might still have taken heart from the reaction to Origen on the part of Christians who did not care to be dismissed as "simpler.") Origen's attitude toward miracles, for example, was much like Celsus's, not denying their possibility but subjecting them to rational criticism.[101] While uncompromising about Christian partici-pation in the pagan worship of the Emperor, Origen was also willing to agree with Celsus so far as to grant that the Empire played a positive role in God's *oikonomia*. He considered Jesus' birth in the principate of Augustus to be a sign that the *Pax Romana* was God's way of preparing the world for the gospel.[102] Furthermore, many things Celsus found objectionable – not to say ludicrous – in Christianity, Origen objected to just as strenuously: irrational fideism, belief in a vindictive and otherwise anthropomorphic God, an expectation that Christians would someday reanimate their corpses. The opportunity to score points off simpler Christians by refuting Celsus was probably an inducement to comply with Ambrosius's request.

Origen's use of the *Contra Celsum* to defend himself against those ("simple" in his opinion) who objected to his ideas is most evident in his response to Celsus's charges that Christians conceive of God as a celestial cook planning to set fire to the world and that they irra-tionally hope to reanimate their corpses. Like ancient Greek philosophers, who may themselves have learned it from "the more ancient race of the Hebrews," Christians teach

> that a cleansing fire is applied to the world, and possibly to each of those who need the chastisement and healing brought by fire. It burns but does not consume those who do not have matter that needs to be cleansed by that fire, but it burns and consumes those who have built the building, figuratively speaking, of their deeds, words, and thoughts out of "wood, hay, and stubble" (1 Cor. 3:12). For the divine oracles say that the Lord will visit each of those who require such treatment "like the fire of a smelting-furnace and like a cleanser's herb" (Mal. 3:2) because of the evil matter derived from vice that has amalgamated with the soul.

But, although Scripture, rightly understood, represents this fire as entirely beneficial in its effects,

The prophet Isaiah will also testify that we do not say that God applies fire like a cook, but as a God who is a bene-factor to those needing punishment and fire in what was written in the oracle to a sinful nation, "Because you have coals of fire, sit on them, so that they will be a help to you" (Isa. 47:14–15, LXX).

Nonetheless, most Christians admittedly do not understand this because "the Logos, having accommodated himself to what is appro-priate for the crowd who happen upon the Scripture, mysteriously speaks harsh words with wisdom to induce fear in those who could not otherwise turn away from the dissolution of sins." Immature Christians are thus like infants who must be scared into good behavior:

> And perhaps just as one adapts what one says to infants in proportion to their infancy, in order to exhort them to turn to the better even though they are children, even so to those whom the Logos calls "the foolish of the world," "ignoble," and "despised" the superficial interpretation of punishments is appropriate, since they have no inducement to avoid many evils without a motivation through fear and the portrayal of punishments.

"Even so," Origen writes, "the attentive reader will find an indica-tion of the purpose of the harsh and severe language brought to bear on those who endure them." He justifies speaking so openly because "I have been constrained to hint at things not suited to those who believe simply and who need simple statements in words accommo-dated to them", so as not to leave the charge unrefuted if Celsus should say: "when God will apply fire just like a cook."[103] Origen responds to the charge that Christians hope to reanimate their corpses with the claim that:

> Neither we ourselves nor the divine Scriptures say that those who have once died will live again in the flesh without its having undergone any change for the better when they rise again from the earth. Celsus slanders us in saying so. Let us listen to the many Scriptures speaking of the resurrection in a manner worthy of God. It will suffice for the present to cite the text from Paul in First Corinthians, where he says: "But someone will ask, 'How are the dead raised? And with what will they come?' Fool,

in your own case what you sow does not activate, unless it dies, and when you sow, you do not sow the body that will come to be, but a bare seed, perhaps of wheat or of some other plant, and God gives it a body as he wills, and to each of the seeds its won body" (1 Cor. 15:35–8). . . . We hear the Logos teaching at length about the difference between the one which is, in a manner of speaking, sown and the one which is, as it were, awakened by him: "It is sown in corruption, it is awakened in imperishability. It is sown in dishonor, it is awakened in glory. It is sown a soulish body, it is awakened a spiritual body." Let him who is able, comprehend what he had in mind when he said: "As is what is earthy, so are they who are earthy, and as is what is heavenly, so are they who are heavenly. And just as we have borne the image of the earthy, so we shall bear the image of the heavenly" (see 1 Cor. 15:42–9).

Origen admits that the passage in question is obscure, but ascribes that obscurity to deliberate reticence on Paul's part:

Nonetheless, the Apostle, wishing to hide things not to be said in this passage and unsuitable for the simple and to the hearing of the ordinary crowd who are influenced toward improvement by believing, was compelled nonetheless, so that we should not misunderstand him, to say, after the words "we shall bear the image of the heavenly": "This I say, brothers, that flesh and blood cannot inherit the kingdom of God, nor can the corruptible inherit incorruptibility." And being well aware that there was something ineffable and mystical about this passage, as is fitting for someone leaving behind in writings the sense of his thought, he added: "See, I tell you a mystery" (see 1 Cor. 15:49–51). This is precisely the way to allude to doctrines that are very profound and very mystical and appropriate concealed from the many. Thus it is written in Tobit, "It is a good thing to conceal the king's mystery," then, with regard to what is famous and appropriate for the many, properly managing the truth, "It is a good thing to reveal gloriously the works of the Lord" (Tob. 12:7).[104]

After a learned comparison with pagan philosophical ideas, he concludes that "we say that, just as the seed of grain is awakened as an ear, so a certain rational principle (*logos*) exists in the body, by means of which the body 'is awakened in incorruptibility' (1 Cor. 15:42)."[105]

Origen applies to the *True Logos* the same close attention and techniques learned as a *grammateus* that he applies to biblical passages. These enable him to point out where Celsus misquotes biblical passages or takes them out of context. He is particularly effective at showing the implausibility of Celsus's hypothetical Jew. Like a schoolboy fumbling through his first exercise, Celsus breaks the most basic rule in the creation of a *prosôpon*: having one's character speak in an appropriate way.[106] Origen's philosophical learning also enabled him to give Celsus's quotations from Plato the same critical attention. Thus, for example, he correctly pointed out that the well-known passage in Plato's *Timaeus* (28C): "to find the Maker and Father of this universe is difficult, and after finding him, it is impossible to declare him to all men" does not, as Celsus assumed, imply that God is "indescribable" and "nameless," but rather that God can be known by only a few. [107]

Origen turns the tables on Celsus's arguments about Christianity's obscurity with an elegant illustration from Plato; considering Jesus' vast impact on the world, his poverty and obscure upbringing is all the more reason to believe that he was no ordinary man:

> Plato's Seriphian[108] reproached Themistocles, who had attained renown for his generalship, with not having derived his fame from his own character but from his having happened to be from the most remarkable country in all of Greece. Themistocles, a reasonable man, recognizing when he heard this that his country had contributed to his fame, replied "If I had been a Seriphian, I would not have been so famous, but neither would you have become a Themistocles if you had been born in Athens." Our Jesus also, reproached for having been born in a village and that not even a Greek one, nor from any nation held in honor by the many, defamed as one who was the son of a woman who made her living by weaving and as one who left his homeland to work as a hired laborer in Egypt, and thus, in accordance with the example just cited, not just born a Seriphian, that is, from the smallest and most obscure island, but even among Seriphians, so to speak, the least

noble, was nonetheless able to make a sensation before the whole world of men, not just more than Themistocles the Athenian, but more than Pythagoras, Plato or any other of the world's sages, or kings, or generals. Who, therefore, unless he is investigating the nature of things superficially, would not be struck with admiration for this man who has overcome all circumstances that would make for obscurity and has been able to surpass in glory and all famous people whatsoever?[109]

When Celsus states that Jesus, in teaching about turning the other cheek, is borrowing and cheapening the celebrated passage from Plato's *Crito* (49B–E) where Socrates, about to take the hemlock, argues that we must not return injustice with injustice, Origen responds that even if Jesus came after Plato, Moses and the prophets, who taught the same doctrine, came before him. Besides, it is their words that have actually had widespread beneficial effects:

> Is it not then an established fact that when, according to Celsus, Jesus says in a coarse style "To someone striking you on one cheek, offer also the other" and "To someone taking you to law for your cloak, let him have your tunic as well" (Lk. 6:29; Mt. 5:40), he promoted and illustrated his doctrine with more real-life usefulness by speaking this way than Plato did in the *Crito*, who is not only incomprehensible to the ignorant but scarcely understood by those who have received a good education until they have specifically studied the venerable philosophy of the Greeks.

Origen also points to the sexual continence practiced, along with all the other virtues, by ordinary Christians. These people live in a way philosophers advocate but cannot achieve even for themselves, much less inculcate in others.[110] (On the other hand, in the *Commentary on Matthew*, written about the same time, he sought to shame greedy Christians by holding up the example of Crates, a pagan Cynic philosopher who liberated himself by giving away all his possessions.[111]) Just as philosophy, despite its good doctrines, has little effect on lives, so, even though it effectively criticizes pagan polytheism, it still connives with it.[112] Although Celsus has little good to say about him, Origen argues (following Philo and Clement) that Moses taught Platonic philosophy long before Plato. Thus Moses and the prophets, in practicing homonymy, implicitly taught the inferiority of the sensible reality to a higher, non-sensible reality:

> The most ancient doctrine [*logos*] of Moses and the prophets knows that genuine things have the same names as things that are more generally known by those names here, for example, a "genuine light" (1 Jn 2:8) and a "heaven" (Gen 1:6–8) that is not the same as the vault of the sky and a "Sun of justice" (Mal. 4:2) that is different from the sensible one. Also in one concise expression it says that, in contrast with sensible things, none of which are genuine, "God, his works are genuine" (Dan. 4:34), classifying the works of God as genuine and classifying as inferior his so-called "handiwork" (Ps. 101:26 [102:25]).[113]

Origen's open but critical response to the Greek philosophical heritage in the *Contra Celsum* implicitly belies assertions that he somehow betrayed biblical faith by reinterpreting it in Greek philosophical terms. Such an attitude colored Adolf Harnack's deeply learned and often admiring presentation of Origen in his *History of Dogmas*.[114] Harnack believed that early Christians like Origen fundamentally misunderstood their own tradition, failing to perceive a discontinuity between Greek metaphysics and the simple message of Jesus or, as later theologians would put it, between Greek thought and Hebrew thought. Neo-Orthodox theologians of the next generation, otherwise critical of Harnack's theological liberalism, tended, like Nygren, to accept uncritically his belief that Origen "secularized" the gospel by interpreting it in Greek philosophical terms. As we see below in his *Letter to Gregory*, Origen held that Greek philosophy leads to error when it contradicts the church's rule of faith, even as he also considered philosophy a useful adjunct to Christianity. In the *Contra Celsum* Origen was clear about the need to accept philosophy critically. He gives no ground on his belief that God created the material world.[115] More importantly, he gives no ground on the issue of God's Incarnation in Jesus Christ. God's becoming a human being is at the heart of the divine *oikonomia*, since only thus could God eradicate the evil in human nature while respecting our free will.[116] Using Platonic concepts against Celsus, Origen argues that, because of God's immateriality, God's presence in Christ does not mean that God left one place to go to another.[117] The Incarnation belongs to a pattern of divine condescension that applies to Scripture as well.[118] Such divine condescension is indispensable, Origen argues; we cannot return to God unless God first comes to us. Thus after correcting Celsus's interpretation of Plato on the knowability of God, Origen takes the occasion to add that "We affirm that human nature is not sufficient in any way to seek for God and to find Him in His pure nature, unless it is helped by the God who is the object of the search."[119] The Incarnation is God's way of making himself accessible to our limited human understanding. Once we have known Christ after the flesh, we can then, but only then, advance with his assistance to know him as the Logos of God and through him to know the Father.[120] At its heart, therefore, Origen's last major work is a vindication not simply of the Incarnation, but of God's grace.

Persecution and death

Revived interest in Celsus's *True Doctrine* did, in fact, presage a new hostility toward Christianity in Roman ruling circles. In 249 Decius overthrew Philip the Arab and launched the most deadly and effective persecution the church had yet seen. He sought to force all inhabitants of the Empire – except Jews – to worship the pagan gods, requiring them to obtain papers certifying they had done so. As it turned out, because Decius's reign was short, the church suffered most from internal dissension over how to deal with those who had obtained certificates. Decius also went specifically after Christian leaders, executing Fabian, bishop of Rome, and imprisoning Origen's supporter, Alexander, bishop of Jerusalem, who, like Bishop Babylas of Antioch, died in prison. Origen was also imprisoned and tortured, but not executed, evidently in the hope that a recantation on his part would be more valuable to his persecutors than his death. As a result, he survived the persecution, but, apparently, with his health broken, so that he died within a year or so of regaining his freedom.[121] An unequivocal death by martyrdom would have been better for Origen's posthumous reputation.

4

A CONTROVERSIAL
LEGACY

Origen became the archetypal Christian scholar, fully engaged in prayer and in the life of the church, filled with a love for Jesus Christ and, by his learning and intelligence, earning awed respect even from those not sharing his faith. He drew deeply on every possible source – among them Jewish tradition, philology, philosophy, and the natural sciences – to aid him in his principal enterprise, interpreting Scripture. He was convinced that, by means of such study, he was drawing closer to God and helping others do so. His impact on subsequent Christian tradition was immense and is still, to a large extent, unappreciated.

Origen's importance as the chief theoretician of allegorical interpretation has long been recognized. In four magisterial volumes on medieval exegesis, Henri de Lubac has amply documented the truth of the statement he quotes from the pioneer of modern biblical criticism, Richard Simon: "Most of the Fathers who lived after Origen scarcely did anything but copy his commentaries and other treatises on Scripture" and "even those who were most opposed to his sentiments could not keep from reading them and profiting from them."[1] His allegorical interpretation was popular because it enabled Christians to use the whole Bible as the church's book; Manlio Simonetti argues that, before Origen, the Old Testament functioned for Christians as scarcely more than a quarry for proof texts.[2] Origen's exegesis had such a profound and lasting appeal, not just because it satisfied a need, but because it was persuasive. His spiritual interpretation was not founded on some arbitrary set of correspondences, but rather on a conviction that God's *oikonomia* operates in the same way in Scripture and the natural world, in the salvation of the cosmos and in each individual soul, and in the inner and in the outer man. One can therefore make analogies from one to another of these spheres. He thus provided a way to interpret the entire Bible that was self-consistent and relevant immediately to spiritual needs. Postmodernism, by breaking with the assumptions that the interpretation of a text means the determination of a univocal authorial intention, promises the possibility of a new hearing for Origen's spiritual interpretation.

Nonetheless, Origen's fame as an allegorist has often distracted scholars from other aspects of his approach to the Bible. His greatness as an interpreter and his influence on subsequent Christian tradition lie even more in his precise attention to detail – *akribeia*, "accuracy," is one of his favorite words – and reverence for the text itself. It is this attitude that he recommends in his *Letter to Gregory* (section 4), saying, "We need great application when we are reading divine things, so that we may not be precipitous in saying or understanding anything concerning them." Such application means being attentive to what a text has to say even if that is disconcerting, as in his fifth homily on 1 Samuel below. This attitude made him, as the author of the *Hexapla*, the foremost textual critic in the Early Church. Manlio Simonetti and Bernhardt Neuschäfer have demonstrated this is Origen's great, if unacknowledged, legacy to Antiochene exegesis. Thus such interpreters as Theodore and Theodoret, even though critical of Origen's allegory, were often truer to his spirit than his successors in Alexandria.[3]

In the sphere of doctrine, we have already noted the way Origen lays crucial foundations for the definition of doctrine of the Trinity and of the person of Christ. He also provided a way to relate divine grace to human free will that proved congenial to the Greek theological tradition, a congeniality that accounts for the preservation of many of his writings on the subject. As we have seen, Origen distinguished himself from the Platonic tradition by insisting on the necessity for God's grace if human beings are to become like God. Origen just as firmly defended human moral responsibility, refuting philosophers and astrologers who would urge that human actions are predetermined. He made a convincing case that God's foreknowledge does not predetermine human actions and that God's providence fully respects human free will. This way of relating human and divine activity in a continual process of human transformation provided the chief theoretical model for the Christian ascetic tradition.[4] It is thus the source of Gregory of Nyssa's notion of *epektasis*, a continual straining toward God.[5] Recent studies have shown how pervasive Origen's influence was on emerging Egyptian monasticism, including Antony of Egypt.[6] Through John Cassian, who imbibed this Origenist approach from Evagrius Ponticus, Origen's approach to grace and free will became, even in the West, a standing alternative to Augustine's approach, which tended to present them as mutually exclusive.[7] We see an echo of this in the controversy over free will between Erasmus and Luther, since the former depended heavily on Origen's *Peri Archon*.[8]

In spite of his lasting and pervasive influence, Henri Crouzel has aptly applied to Origen Simeon's phrase, "a sign which shall be spoken against" (Lk. 2:34).[9] He has aroused both fascination and repulsion, sometimes, as in the case of Jerome, both reactions in the same person. Christian tradition has not found him easily assimilable because he put forward views, particularly on eschatology, that were unacceptable in his own time or, in the case of his doctrine of the Trinity, found so later. This unacceptability was due in part, but only in part, to misunderstanding and misattribution. That tradition has, nonetheless, found him hard to dismiss because he defended the orthodoxy of his own time and, perhaps more than any other single person, laid the foundations for the orthodoxy of subsequent generations. Acknowledged saints respected him as an authority, he was the glory of the church in his day, and he died as a confessor in the communion of the church. Manlio Simonetti has argued that Origen's thought was the product of a unique period, early in the church's organizational evolution, in which relatively great intellectual freedom was possible.[10]

Origen has remained a controversial figure. As recently as 1981 Ulrich Berner could depict modern Origen scholarship as still to a large extent polarized between advocates of positions that have been argued more or less continuously since Jerome and Rufinus gave them classic expression.[11] Some scholars upheld what Berner identified as a "systematic" interpretation. They follow Origen's earliest detractors by arguing that he used allegorical interpretation of the Bible to read Platonism into Christianity. According to them, he treated the church's doctrine as an episode within a larger system in which the corporeal world comes into being as a result of the fall of rational creatures from the contemplation of God and it will end when they are reunited with him. Others upheld a "non-systematic or mystical" interpretation of Origen. According to them, he was a loyal son of the church who (perhaps unadvisedly) speculated about certain doctrines later to be rejected by the consensus of the faithful. Nonetheless, by their account, his fundamental concern was mystical communion with God, a process furthered by his insights into the deeper meaning of Scripture.

Even before Jerome and Rufinus, the basic arguments pro and

con begin to emerge. Our first clear literary records of controversy
about Origen come from the end of the third century and the
beginning of the fourth. In this period, Methodius attacked his
views on the resurrection and his allegorical interpretation of
Scripture.[12] We see Methodius's views reflected in the work of his
contemporary, Eustathius of Antioch, whose favorite epithet for
Origen was "dogmatist," meaning, apparently, someone who made
up his own doctrines.[13] At the same time, Pamphilus and Eusebius
of Caesarea, who had access to Origen's library, were his defenders.
Pamphilus began an *Apology for Origen*, part of which survives in a
translation by Rufinus.[14] Pamphilus, like Methodius, died in the
so-called "Great Persecution" of 303–12, the wholesale assault on
the church launched by the Emperor Diocletian. Afterwards,
Eusebius completed that work and, in making Origen the hero of
his *Ecclesiastical History*, preserved most of what we know about his
life. For most of the fourth century Origen was respected despite
lingering uneasiness over the issues Methodius raised. The editors of
the *Philocalia* presented him as a Scriptural interpreter and defender
of free will while leaving his views on creation and eschatology out
of their anthology. Basil of Caesarea implicitly rejected Origen's
interpretation of the opening chapters of Genesis, while Diodore of
Tarsus and Theodore of Mopsuestia, leaders in the emerging
Antiochene school of interpretation, more openly attacked Origen's
principles of interpretation. Perhaps as a result, the word "allegory"
(*allêgoria*) fell out of favor, being replaced by "contemplation"
(*theôria*) even on the part of authors like Gregory of Nyssa whose
"contemplation" is indistinguishable from Origen's "allegory."[15]

   In the last decade of the fourth century Epiphanius of Salamis
launched what has come to be known as the First Origenist
Controversy, attacking Origen as the source of the hated Arian
heresy as well as a holder of heretical views on creation and eschatology. This was the controversy where Jerome and Rufinus became,
for Latin Christianity, the spokesmen of opposing sides. In their
quarrel over the translation of *Peri Archon*, Jerome accused Rufinus,
with justification, of deliberately softening expressions offensive to
contemporary standards of orthodoxy (even though he, Jerome, just
as deliberately sharpened them). Exacerbated by latent tensions,
particularly within Egyptian Christianity, and by personal rivalries
and animosities, this controversy permanently damaged Origen's
reputation.[16] We see its reflection in the attitude of the one early
Christian writer whose achievement and influence exceeded his;
Augustine never knew Origen's works well and, in spite of initial

interest and genuine affinities, grew increasingly hostile toward his ideas.[17]

The so-called Second Origenist Controversy of the sixth century did still more damage. The Emperor Justinian revived and sharpened Epiphanius's accusations in his *Letter to Menas* in 543, a condemnation seemingly upheld by the Second Council of Constantinople in 553 (ironically the tercentenary of Origen's death as a result of torture under Decius). Justinian ordered the destruction of Origen's books along with those of two other theologians in his tradition, Didymus the Blind and Evagrius Ponticus.[18] Like many earlier critics, Justinian lacked not only sympathy but even genuine understanding of Origen, whose thought he knew only from snippets taken out of context from *Peri Archon*.[19] It is also an open question to what extent, in both of these controversies, the views of others were actually ascribed to Origen. At the very least, views which Origen presented as results of rational investigation always open to modification were treated as absolute and unequivocal doctrinal pronouncements. Such a presentation was more characteristic of Evagrius Ponticus, who held many of Origen's views, but put them forward without rational justification as a higher knowledge for the spiritually mature.[20] Such a style of presentation is also more characteristic of Clement, on whom Evagrius depended as well.[21]

Justinian's condemnation did not carry the same weight in the Latin West as in the Greek East, so that Origen remained a respected authority in Western Christianity through the Middle Ages. The Renaissance saw a revival of interest in Origen, including critical editions of his works, along with a revival of controversies about him. His ideas had profound influence on Erasmus and other humanist reformers, but proved unattractive either to the Catholic or to the Protestant orthodoxy that emerged from the era of Reform.[22] Generally speaking, Origen has appealed again and again to those who would prefer not to choose between infidelity and obscurantism and has just as consistently threatened those who believe that they already have answers to all important questions.

Part II

TEXTS

COMMENTARY ON
PSALMS 1–25, FRAGMENT
FROM PREFACE

Introduction

Written in the early 220s, this is one of our earliest examples of Origen's writing. It is an excerpt from the preface to Origen's first, Alexandrian, Psalm commentary which the editors of the *Philocalia* chose to illustrate Origen's hermeneutic principles. It recounts the "very beautiful tradition" concerning biblical interpretation provided by a Jewish informant and, in section 4, posits an analogy between God's self-revelation in Scripture and in the natural world. This analogy establishes what Charles Bigg called a "sacramental mystery of nature"[1] that is the foundation of Origen's approach to biblical symbolism.

The translation is from Origène, *Philocalie, 1–20 et Lettre à Africanus*, ed. Marguerite Harl and Nicholas de Lange = *SC* 302, Paris, Cerf, 1983, pp. 240–4.

Text

1   The divine discourses say that the divine Scriptures are locked and sealed by the key of David and also, indeed, by that seal of which it is said: "The imprint of a seal, a holy thing to the Lord" (Ex. 28:36), that is, locked and sealed by the power of the Lord who gave them. John teaches that they are locked and sealed in Revelation, saying:

> And to the angel of the church at Philadelphia, write: "Thus says the one who is holy, who is true, who has the key of David, who opens and no one shuts, who shuts and no one opens, 'I know your works, see, I have furnished before you an open door, which no one can close'"
>
> (Rev. 3:7–8)

and a little later:

> And I saw to the right of him who sat upon the throne a book written inside and out, sealed by seven seals. And I saw another mighty angel proclaiming in a loud voice: "Who is worthy to open the book and to break its seals?" And no one in heaven, on earth or under the earth could open the book and see it, and one of the elders said to me, "Do not grieve, see, the Lion of the tribe of Judah, the Root of David, has triumphed so as to open the book and its seven seals."
>
> (Rev. 5:1–5)

2   Isaiah writes, concerning sealing only:

> And all these words will be to you like the discourses of this sealed book. If one should give it to a man who knows letters saying "Read this" he will say "I cannot read it, for it is sealed," and should you give it into the hands of a man who does not know letters and say to him "Read this" he will say "I do not know letters."
>
> (Isa. 29:11–12).

These things must be considered to be said, not just of the Revelation to John and of Isaiah, but of all divine Scripture. For it is unanimously agreed by all who even moderately understand the divine discourses that they are filled with riddles, parables, dark sayings, and various other forms of obscurity hard for human nature to comprehend. This is just what the Savior intended to teach when he said – on the assumption that the key was in the possession of scribes and Pharisees who were making no effort to find a way to open the Scriptures – "Woe to you, lawyers, because you have taken away the key of knowledge. You yourselves do not enter, and you do not allow those coming to enter" (Lk. 11:52).

3   As we are about to begin the interpretation of the Psalms, we shall disclose a very beautiful tradition handed on to us by the Hebrew[2] which applies generally to the entire divine Scripture. For the Hebrew said that the whole divinely inspired Scripture may be likened, because of its obscurity, to many locked rooms in one house. By each room is placed a key, but not the one that corresponds to it, so that the keys are scattered about beside the rooms, none of them matching the room by which it is placed. It is a diffi-

cult task to find the keys and match them to the rooms that they can open. We therefore know the Scriptures that are obscure only by taking the points of departure for understanding them from another place because they have their interpretative principle scattered among them. In any event, I think that the Apostle suggests a similar approach to understanding the divine discourses when he says: "And those things we speak are not in discourses instructed by human wisdom, but in ones instructed by the Spirit, interpreting spiritual things by means of spiritual things" (1 Cor. 2:13).

* * *

4   But if "the oracles of the Lord are undefiled, refined silver, unadulterated with earth, purified seven times" (Ps. 11:7 [12:6]) and if the Holy Spirit has prompted them with deliberate precision through the servants of the Word (see Lk. 1:2), we must not miss the analogy,[3] since the wisdom of God has permeated the whole of Scripture even to the individual letter. This is indeed why the Savior said: "Not one iota or one stroke will pass away from the law, until everything comes to be" (Mt. 5:18). For just as the divine skill in the fabrication of the world appears not only in sky, sun, moon, and stars – all of these being bodies through which it courses – but it has acted on earth in the same way even in the meanest material object, since even the bodies of the tiniest creatures are not despised by the Artisan,[4] and even less the souls present in them, each of which receives in itself a particular property, a saving principle in an irrational being. Nor does the Artisan despise the earth's plants, since he is present in each of them with respect to their roots, leaves, possible fruits, and different qualities. So with regard to everything recorded by the inspiration of the Holy Spirit we accept that, since divine providence has endowed the human race with a superhuman wisdom by means of the Scriptures, he has, so to speak, sowed traces of wisdom as saving oracles, in so far as possible, in each letter.

5   One must by all means be persuaded, once one has accepted that these Scriptures are the work of the world's Creator, that those who investigate the Scriptures will confront issues as serious as do those who investigate the rational principle[5] of creation. Indeed, even in Creation there exist some problems which human nature finds it hard or impossible to resolve, but the Creator of the Universe is not to be blamed on this account; for example, we do not ascertain the cause of the creation of basilisks or other venomous beasts. In the

71

case of someone who perceives the weakness of our race and that it is impossible for us to comprehend the rational principles of God's skill even when they have been contemplated with very precise attention, the reverent procedure is to refer the knowledge of these matters to God, so that later, if we are deemed worthy, the things to which we piously pay attention may be revealed to us. Similarly, in the divine Scriptures one must see that there are many problems hard for us to resolve. As for those who, having abandoned the Creator, presume to take refuge in a God whom they have invented, let them resolve the difficulties that we have just presented. After such audacious impiety, let them persuade their conscience to be at peace with their proposals concerning the matters just investigated and the difficulties we have just raised. But if the difficulties remain no less intractable, once they have separated themselves from the godhead, would it not be more pious for them to stay with the common understanding of God, namely that the author of existence is contemplated by means of the creation, and to declare nothing godless and impious concerning such a great God?

COMMENTARY ON LAMENTATIONS, SELECTED FRAGMENTS

Introduction

The fragments from Origen's *Commentary on Lamentations* survived, as other fragments of Origen's works did, in *catenae* (chains), Byzantine biblical commentaries formed by stringing together brief passages excerpted from older commentaries. In spite of the obscurity that comes from the loss of context, we find in this, one of the earliest of Origen's commentaries (between 222 and 225, according to Nautin),[1] the same approach to the Bible that he continued to employ throughout his life. Origen initially approaches the text as a *grammateus*, establishing the work's form in Hebrew, setting it in a historical context, comparing translations, and, where necessary, identifying *prosôpa*.[2] Note, in fragment XXV, Origen's concern, without using the term, to identify the *prosôpon* of the speaker when Lamentations 1:9 switches from a third-person voice, presumably to be identified as the *prosôpon* of the prophet Jeremiah, to a direct address to God in the second person ("See, Lord, my humility . . . "). In his attempt to understand the text in its historical context, Origen draws on Josephus's account of a similar circumstance, the siege of Jerusalem in AD 70 (fr. CIX). As we see in the fragments on Lamentations 1:4, 1:9, and 1:10, Origen first uses such grammatical techniques to establish the literal sense of the text, which then provides the basis for an elevated sense.

Jerusalem in captivity to the Babylonians symbolizes, at the higher level of interpretation, the soul in captivity to the demons. The gentile nations that loot the temple and even enter its holy of holies are a mob of vices that overcome the soul's governing faculty (*hêgemonikon*) and invade the sanctuary of reason (*logos*) where God can reside (fr. XXVII). Such a captive soul has entered a state of confusion (frs X and LII). This is why the "ways of Zion," the four philosophical disciplines that lead to the truth, "mourn" because they are no longer traveled (fr. XIV). Origen always maintains that, even in the punishments Jerusalem undergoes, God is acting mercifully, with no wrath or vindictiveness, to bring her back to himself. In spite of the severity of his chastisement, God is not the soul's enemy, but, rather, "like an enemy" (fr. XLVI), since he actually acts for the soul's own benefit. Fragment CXVI, the longest of the fragments and the last in our selection, deals with Lam. 4:20, traditionally regarded as an important Old Testament testimony to Christ. It anticipates what Origen says about the relation between the two testaments in our selection below from Book 1 of the *Commentary on John* and testifies to Origen's belief in a continuing prophetic charism.

The text is from *Commentary on Lamentations* from *GCS* 6, ed. Erich Klostermann and revised by Pierre Nautin, Berlin, 1983, pp. 235–79.

Text

And it came to pass after Israel was taken captive and Jerusalem was laid waste, Jeremiah was mourning and made this lamentation over Jerusalem and said:

I   Jeremiah, while the people are captive in Babylon, makes his lamentations over the city, the country, and the people because of what had happened. He makes these laments in individual stanzas beginning with each letter of the Hebrew alphabet. After composing a lament beginning with each letter up to tau, the last letter of the Hebrew alphabet, he repeats the process beginning with aleph, going through the twenty-four letters four times.

II   If we see that the soul – which is contemplative by nature, able to survey and attend to things that exist[3] – has become subject to the Devil or even his angels, and altogether subject to the hostile powers, we shall somehow understand both the captivity and the one taking captive. But taking refuge in Christ, who proclaimed, according to the prophet Isaiah, "release to the captives" (see Lk. 4:18; Isa. 61:1), we shall be liberated from captivity, even if he who takes captive has succeeded in putting us in bondage. For Jesus came to "lead those in bondage out of their bonds and those sitting in darkness from the house of custody" (Isa. 42:7).

III   The Hebrews say that the books of the Old Testament have the same number as the letters of the alphabet because they are an introduction to all knowledge of God, just as the letters of the alphabet are an introduction to all wisdom for those who learn. For this reason they are fourfold[4], perhaps because bodies have been composed of four elements[5]. * * * Lamentations is not found in the versions of Aquila and Theodotion, but only in Symmachus and the Septuagint. * * * Someone might investigate why, since the title of the book, Lamentations, is in the plural, it says "this lamentation" in the singular in the prologue. But although there are many parts, assigned to the letters, all have a single reference, referring to one subject, Israel.

How does the city sit solitary, that was filled with people; she who was filled with gentiles has become like a widow, she who ruled over the land has become subject to paying tribute (Lam. 1:1).

VII   It is appropriate to refer "filled with people," understood according to the letter, to the Israelites dwelling there, and "filled with gentiles," as mentioned earlier, to proselytes. In the elevated sense, since it is more natural and assured for theoretical matters rather than practical ones to refer to the soul, the multitude of people would symbolize the blessed Jerusalem's wealth of theoretical insights, and the multitude of gentiles her large number of good works. * * * She that was filled with people sits solitary because the bride has been abandoned by her bridegroom the Word, so that she who once was filled with the gentiles just mentioned has become like a widow.

VIII   As far as the letter is concerned, the tone of amazement in the reference to Jerusalem is fitting because of the sad change that had left her that was filled with people sitting solitary, so that her solitude is desertion. For she once had as her husband the presiding living Word, and when he was present to assist her, she attended on him, but she had since been widowed and abandoned by him because of her sin. * * * This will sufficiently explain what is said, but, as to the meaning, Jerusalem flourishing and filled with people and with gentiles, and ruling over the land, is the divine soul. And it is not remarkable, if the perfect soul is not addressed as a house, a farmstead, or – better than this – as a village, nor even as a city, but is called Jerusalem, distinguished above all cities and honored by God, because she has been invested by wisdom and virtue with far greater renown than even the greatest city, with all its multitude of buildings. * * * Just as it is possible to see Jerusalem prospering, filled with people and with gentiles and ruling in the land, so, if virtue is liable to change, it is sometimes possible to see her made solitary, acting as a widow and a slave, so that she pays tribute to the enemy who exercises dominion over her, in the manner of a soul fallen away from the truth.

IX What must one say also concerning the city that, after having ruled the land, has been so enslaved by her enemies that she continually pays tribute, paying to evil rulers whatever tribute they exact; even though they never exact anything beneficial? Indeed, whenever any of us stumbles, he pays some tribute to Nebuchadnezzar, whose name means, "seated and recognition of straitened circumstances," and not just to Nebuchadnezzar, but also to his satraps.

Mourning she mourns in the night, and her tears are upon her cheeks, and there is no one to console her from all those who love her. All those who befriended her have rejected her, and they have become enemies to her (Lam. 1:2).

X In the case of the first lament, beginning with aleph, we can maintain the literal sense. In the case of this one, what would someone say, when a city is said to have mourned in the night, so that her tears are upon her cheeks? Evidently one says "city" to indicate those whom we would refer to as its inhabitants, who are also paying tribute, and in their mourning calling to mind how they have gone from such peace and freedom into such a great slavery and wretchedness in order to mourn. How also shall we interpret "in the night," except that, in the time of a common rest for all men, the city has remembered its disasters, that is those who dwell in the city do not cease to mourn, and they mourn with their tears falling streaming down their cheeks? Mourning is most intense for them and tears flow down, because there is no one to console them from so many lovers, since each of those who had befriended her has rejected friendship toward her and has exchanged it for hatred. Who are those, therefore, who, according to the letter, loved her earlier, of whom there is not one to console her? Perhaps they are the rest of the cities of Judah, because, in the same way, they had loved the mother city, but did not console her in time of distress.

* * *

Let this suffice concerning the literal meaning. But if the discourse, as we have shown in earlier discussions, should refer to the perfect soul as "Jerusalem," that soul is said to mourn, coming into confusion[6] after having fallen from her native land. Thus she is in the opposite situation from those who laugh the laughter that comes from joy and gladness, which our Lord promises to those who mourn a blessed mourning, saying, "Blessed are those who mourn now, because they shall laugh" (see Lk. 6:21). In Job also it says that "the mouth of the true shall be filled with laughter" (Job 8:21); this, indeed, is why one of the Patriarchs was named "Laughter" (see Gen. 21:6). Thus he who is groaning because of being in the tent – as the Apostle set forth, saying "for we who are in the tent are groaning as a result of being weighed down" (2 Cor. 5:4) – and longing for the laughter and the divine gladness in the promise, mourns the mourning that is most nourishing and beneficial for the soul.

XI We think that love is more divine and, so to speak, spiritual, but friendship is bodily and more human.[7] Doubtless we should ascribe nothing base to one who loves, because "there is no one to console her from among all those who love her" refers only to those who are better, but "All those who befriended her have rejected her, and they have become enemies to her" refers to those who are worse. Indeed the worse have rejected her and become her enemies; but the better have simply not consoled her.

The ways of Zion mourn because no one arrives at a feast, all her gates have been removed, her priests lament, her virgins are led away, and she has been embittered in herself (Lam 1:4).
XIII The literal sense is this. The law says, "Three times a year each of your males shall appear before the Lord your God" (Dt. 16:16). The people were conscientious, after the building of the Temple in Zion at the time of Solomon, to fulfill this commandment. And around Jerusalem, where the cities of Judah are, roads lead from every direction toward Zion. These the prophet speaks of as lamenting sadly because of being in captivity and complete desolation. There was also great prosperity and gladness in them in the days when the inhabitants of Judah hastened from all directions to the festival on Mount Zion. Since there were many gates built on all sides of Zion, the discourse says "they have all been removed, and the priests groan," evidently because they are no longer able to accomplish priestly activities on the feasts and other days – either because they have been taken into captivity or because no one comes to them requesting priestly acts of worship. But also "the virgins," it says, of Zion are "led away," evidently by enemies who have taken control.
XIV The meaning is this: since the ability to look toward a goal and to contemplate is called "Zion," the many ways are the various

disciplines – mystical, physical, ethical, and logical – that lead to the apprehension and observation of what is set before us. All these ways, therefore, lament whenever someone has lost these disciplines and is confused, since they are no longer traveled, as they were when these "ways" were crowded, because they were by being examined, and, so to speak, traversed. They lament being deserted, not being inquired of or passed through, because those who travel on them have disappeared and, taken into captivity by the passions, have been diverted to inferior pursuits.

Her uncleanness is before her feet, she has not remembered her last things; she has degraded her important things, there is no one to comfort her. See, Lord, my humility, because the enemy has been magnified (Lam. 1:9).
XXIII   According to the bodily interpretation, what is now said concerning Jerusalem means this: the uncleanness of Jerusalem is an impediment, but the prophet has left it to us to understand what sort of impediment it is. He indicates, indeed, that her uncleanness is what impedes her walking, but, while such is the case, he also indicates that she has not remembered her last things.[8] But whoever has these last things before his eyes and sees why he is assailed by sins will not sin. For this reason, therefore, her uncleanness is an impediment to her; and because she has not remembered her last things – her wonderful and great things, things which she had because they were worth being concerned about – she has degraded and brought to wretchedness things that originally were important and great beyond all praise. But also after all this there was no one to comfort her who had repeatedly degraded her great things. Therefore, recognize, Lord, my wretchedness when I speak, since the wicked one is magnified because of what has happened to my fatherland.

* * *

One must, to be sure, investigate, according to the laws of elevated interpretation, if it is possible to be involved in some uncleanness without being responsible for it. Let us look at the first thoughts of the Lamentation. Such a soul has fallen away entirely and is in uncleanness, an uncleanness that hinders her from proceeding on the holy way. Just as the holy Moses was ordered by God to remove his sandals when he entered a holy place (see Ex. 3:5) and the same occurred to his successor Joshua (see Jos. 5:15) – for it was inappropriate for the feet to be wearing dead hide in a holy place – so if anyone is going to proceed without impediment, he must not just remove sandals, but needs also to wash off the uncleanness that has occurred because the feet are dusty. And we think that the Savior's pouring water into a basin to wash his disciples' feet is a symbol of this, when he said to Peter, who because he did not understand the mystery tried to prevent him, "If I do not wash you, you have no part with me" (Jn 13:8) and "What I am doing you are not aware of now, but later on you will know" (Jn 13:7).[9] Will it not be necessary for the uncleanness gathering about the feet of the soul, so to speak, to require Jesus, so that he may wash it away and we may have part in him? But if it remains present, it will be an impediment to our walking along the way according to sound reason,[10] namely the Savior who says, "I am the way" (see Jn 14:6).

XXIV   It is evident that the healthy soul, or the one desiring to be so, performs actions so as not simply to look to the present, but to look ahead also toward the future results to be expected from what it has accomplished. And if, in the case of something regarded as beneficial in the present, it foresees its turning sour in the future, it acts to reject what seems pleasant at the time, so not to fall into some difficulty later on. On the other hand, if something is arduous in the present, but this apparent unpleasantness offers good prospects, it willingly dedicates itself to austerity, even though it is initially repugnant, instead of devoting itself to activities that are initially enjoyable but have an unpleasant outcome.

XXV   It says that, suffering all these things, the one figuratively called Jerusalem did not abound in comforters. Moreover, having abandoned the reason[11] within her so as to be wholly dominated by the passions, she has lost her helper, the one always arming her against distress, along with the attitude that puts her on guard against things to be considered repugnant. After this it says "See my" – the citizen's – "humiliation," as if a relative of the soul should say: "This suffering belongs to me, a citizen; because I have been taught humane feeling,[12] it is my misfortune. Therefore, Lord, attend, and do not finally abandon the one who has undergone the aforementioned sufferings. Do not overlook her enemy, wickedness, I say, which has been magnified and poured down on her." It is possible that "See, Lord, my humility" is spoken figuratively by the reason[13] that subsists in the soul, dishonored and humiliated, having lost, so to speak, its proper dominion.

The oppressor has extended his hand over all her desirable things; for she has seen the gentiles entering into her holiness, those whom I ordered not to enter your congregation (Lam. 1:10).

XXVI   Of course the "desirable things" of Jerusalem must be understood as the things in the Temple, both those suitably arranged for divine worship in the holy of holies and those otherwise believed divine because they were stored in the Temple, the golden lampstand and so on. Indeed the people were convinced that these were stored in the Temple for the glory of God, and esteemed them above all else, preferring to suffer hardship themselves from their enemies than to allow any of them to fall into the hands of enemies. It was customary for those in the circumcision to refer to the Temple as "holiness".

XXVII   Jerusalem had suffered something most incredible during the time of captivity: for the gentiles, whom God commanded not to enter the congregation, were seen walking in the "holiness," where it was not even permitted for Israelites to enter. Only priests (with purifications not available to ordinary people) were considered worthy there. But enemies had penetrated into forbidden places, even entering the place where only the high priest entered, after many purifications, once a year (see Heb. 9:7).

* * *

But if Jerusalem, as we have already proposed, is such a captive soul, it must be understood that the good properties which she has by nature as an ornament – the means by which she worshipped the divine, hidden in places forbidden to anyone except reason, the high priest[14] – are called her "desirable things." But the enemy has taken control of all these things in the fray, oppressing the one not fighting well for herself, but rightly abandoned by divine assistance. Extending himself by his active power toward depravity, he has looted the governing faculty[15] and left the soul that has fallen away from God bereft of good properties. Also, "nations" in our passage must be understood allegorically as the mob of vices "entering" into the governing faculty that was crafted to be capable of containing God and to be the true "holiness" of the person wishing to rely on a pure mind. These very "nations" God everywhere prohibits from entering the congregation. For what else should we more properly consider to have been prohibited by God from entering the soul numbered in God's church than the works and the intention of the flesh, since these are truly nations at enmity with God? For the flesh does battle against the Spirit (see Gal. 5:17), because the intention of the flesh is at enmity with God, since it is not subject to the law of God, nor can it be (see Rom. 8:7).

He has bent his bow like an enemy, he has made strong his right hand like a foe, and he has killed all the precious things of my eyes in the tabernacle of the daughter of Zion. He has poured out his wrath like fire (Lam. 2:4).

XLVI   Indeed the enemies also dared to perpetrate massacres in the Temple with God's permission. "Like an enemy" is well put, for God does not chastise out of enmity, but out of a desire to benefit either those who suffer or those who observe his chastisement.[16] The Temple is called "tabernacle" after the former sanctuary, and "bow" is the retributive power, according to Habbakuk, "Stretching you stretch your bow, says the Lord, against the scepters" (Hab. 3:9), which are clearly adverse rulers and authorities. But the Son, as the "right hand" of God the Father, has swiftly prevailed, destroying the very idols they had set up in the Temple of God (for these are the "precious things of the eyes"), killing, instead of the idols, the demons dwelling in them.

The Lord has handed over[17] his altar of incense, he has shaken off his holiness, he has crushed in the hand of the enemy the wall of its heavy things; they had given voice in the house of the Lord as in the day of festival (Lam. 2:7).

XLIX   He handed over the vessels for worship, since he was no longer well pleased with the sacrifices offered by the impious, as in "whole offerings of rams and fat of bulls and of goats I do not desire" (Isa. 1:11). He also handed over the restraining wall of the city's dwellings, even the palace, as Symmachus translated. But the adversaries, when they had also taken the Temple, boasted, as in a total victory, for the rest of the festival. The soul's altar of incense is the rational faculty, through which the passions, put to death, are offered as a sacrifice.

Her gates have sunk into the ground, they have destroyed and crushed her bars, her king and her rulers are among the gentiles, there is no law, and her prophets do not receive visions from the Lord (Lam. 2:9).

LII   Indeed they [the gates] are as invisible as if they were put away beneath the earth or the sea. But king, rulers, false prophets –

as well as her law, which they had broken by choice before
succumbing – have been destroyed by the pressure of servitude. The
gates of the soul are the senses, which, when it sins, are overwhelmed by the passions and become earthy. And those powers of
the soul that guard it are undone when the reigning mind is
destroyed and when the ruling rational faculties are among the
passions, so that the law and order of the soul are destroyed and it
becomes full of "Babylon" or "confusion," having no faculty of fore-
sight coming to the rescue from God.

**How has the gold become dim, and how has the good silver
altered? The holy stones have been poured out at the beginning of every alley (Lam. 4:1).**
XCIII   They are holy since they are elect because of the fathers (see
Rom. 11:28) or because of those saints left with Jehoiachin, whom
he compares to fruitful fig trees (see Jer. 24:2–5).

* * *

The ways out from the holy land[18] "lead away to destruction" (see
Mt. 7:13) and to what Babylon means,[19] "so that they may be
instructed not to blaspheme" (1 Tim. 1:20). But you could say that
the lamentation refers to those who have turned aside from piety,
especially notorious persons who led others into error, "abandoning
the spring of living water, becoming shattered cisterns that can no
longer hold water" (see Jer. 2:23).[20] So they are as if they were
poured out, bewailing their error too late.

**Her Nazirites had become purer than snow, they shone more
than milk, what was torn from them was redder than gems of
sapphire. Their appearance has become darker than soot, they
are not recognized in the passages, their skin sticks to their
bones, they have dried out, they have become like wood (Lam.
4:7–8).**
CII   Symmachus has "Her undefiled ones were distinguished
beyond snow, brighter than milk, their condition was redder than
admirable things, their limbs were sapphire, their appearance
darker than soot." The text speaks of those sanctifying themselves to
God, for "Nazirites" means "sanctified". This is why Symmachus
and Theodotion rendered "those sanctified" in Amos as "Nazirites"
(see Amos 2:12). Moses has also mentioned them (see Num. 6) and
Samson was one (see Judg. 13:5). And they were present among the

Jews. Because of their purity they were compared to snow, because of their brilliance to milk, but they were reddened by discipline, having been tested in those things which they promised to God. Their elect, evidently the piece torn out, have a heavenly manner of life, appropriate to the color of sapphire. They also had golden veins, to which Symmachus likens their state of mind, by piety possessing what is incorruptible and fiery.

Her watchers have been tossed about in the alleys, they have been stained with blood, so that no one can touch their clothing (Lam. 4:14).
CIX Symmachus says: "They have become unstable, blind in the alleys, they are defiled with blood, so that no one can touch their clothing". Scripture calls the angels "watchers" in Daniel (see Dan. 4:10). Perhaps these were the ones by whom the law was given through Moses, according to "if indeed the law spoken through angels" (Heb. 2:2). Such beings, therefore, who were in attendance even in the divine temple itself, were tossed about and abandoned it. For Josephus in the account of the siege narrates how "by night the priests entering the temple, as was their custom for the services, said that they had apprehended a movement and after that the voice of a crowd saying 'we are departing from here'."[21] According to Symmachus it says that they had become unstable, straying, and blind in the alleys. For there was "no distinct vision" (see 1 Sam. 3:2). No king, no prophet, no leader was left, since, indeed, "it belonged to him for whom it was reserved, who was the expectation of the gentiles" (see Gen. 49:10).

They have hunted our little ones, so that they cannot walk upon our streets, our time has come, our days are fulfilled, our time is upon us (Lam. 4:18).
CXIV Having been accepted by the Savior as "fishers of men" (see Mt. 4:19), the disciples hunted Jews who were infants in understanding, those who were not strolling the wide and broad (see Mt. 7:13) way of their fathers; whom the Savior hinted at saying "let the little children come to me" (Mt. 19:14).

The spirit of our face, Christ the Lord, was taken away in their depraved activities, concerning whom we said "In his shadow we shall live among the nations" (Lam. 4:20).[22]
CXVI Some have said that among those who are prominent, [the prophet] specifically laments Josiah, for [the pious] were hoping

through his piety to reestablish Jerusalem in glory in the midst of
the nations, for Jerusalem is in the midst of the nations. [Josiah] is a
type, [these interpreters] say, of Christ, because he was put to death
because of the people's lawlessness. And indeed [Josiah] was not
involved in the people's depraved activities, but he was taken away
because, even though cautioned by a prophet, he met Pharaoh Neco
in battle, even though Neco did not want to fight against him (see
2 Chr. 35:20–5).[23] Moreover, according to the divine Apostle, "a
veil is placed on the face of the Jews when they read Moses, but if
they were to return to the Lord, the veil would be removed, the
Lord is spirit" (2 Cor. 3:15–17). But by prophetic utterance he calls
the Lord "spirit." Even though those who encounter the veil could
not say "The spirit of our face, Christ the Lord," those who are
"beholding with unveiled face the glory of the Lord as in a mirror"
(see 2 Cor. 3:18) could say so. These latter are those for whom the
Lord is always present to the eyes of the mind. This makes it clear
that the spirit working in the prophets was Christ, the same one
who, when incarnate, said "I am present, the very one who is
speaking" (Isa. 52:6; see also Jn 4:26), himself being spirit, Lord,
and Christ.[24] This is the one they took away when they were first
destroying among themselves the seeds of piety.[25] But after we have
been taken away, we the prophets can conclude that the spirit of our
face no longer has a place among them, so that we live under the
shadow of Christ, no longer with the Jews, but among all the
nations, seeing that "the kingdom of God – taken from them"
because of the outrage against Christ –"has been given to the
nations" (see Mt. 21:43). Behold, indeed the prophets live in us,
speaking about him and proclaiming, but no longer among them,
those then and now implicating him in their own depraved activities and daily blaspheming him.[26] But Aquila says "spirit of our
nostrils" and Symmachus "breath of our nostrils". For those who are
beloved of God are breathing Christ in everything, because they
have him before their eyes. It should be known that just as Christ,
being a spirit, spoke in the prophets, so also did the Father, for Paul
says in Hebrews: "In various ways and in many manners God who
spoke in ancient times in the prophets, has in the last days spoken
to us in a Son" (Heb. 1:1); so also the Holy Spirit, for the Savior
says: "well did the Holy Spirit say in Isaiah, 'they hear with hearing
and do not understand'" (Mt. 13:14, Isa. 6:9).[27] In the letter to the
Corinthians Paul, speaking of the charisms, including prophecy,
says: "In all these works one and the same Spirit, directing each one
as he wills" (1 Cor. 12:11), that is, authentically, not slavishly. You

could say that the spirit of the face,[28] namely Christ, is the spirit of prophecy that will be given to us, for this is the face[29] of the prophets. But the spirit is a charism, the shadow is law, according to "for the law, having a shadow of the good things to come" (Heb. 10:1). Therefore the prophets lived in us and in the shadow of the law. The prophetic charism, which is the outcome of all prophecy, is Christ, that is, from Christ, "for Christ is the end of the law and the prophets" (Rom. 10:4). It could be said of the persons[30] of apostles and believers that "in him we live and move and have our being" (Acts 17:28), thus we say that we live in his shadow, that is, in imitation of him. For the divine Apostle says "be imitators of me as I am of Christ" (1 Cor. 11:1).

COMMENTARY ON GENESIS, FRAGMENT FROM BOOK 3

Introduction

This is the longest fragment we possess from Origen's *Commentary on Genesis*, composed in Alexandria around 229, shortly before *Peri Archon*.[1] It comes from the third of thirteen books, commenting on the first four chapters of Genesis. Here Origen deals with verse 1:14, in which the Septuagint refers to the stars as being established "for signs" (*eis sêmeia*). In keeping with what we may presume to have been the intention of its original Priestly author, Origen sees the text as an implicit criticism of astrology. The compilers of the *Philocalia* preserved this passage among others that vindicate human free will, which Origen refers to as "what is within our power" (*to eph' hêmin*).[2] If the stars determine our character, Origen argues, moral responsibility is no longer within our power, and we can neither be praised for doing well nor blamed for doing ill.

Origen's argument provides the best example in this volume of his use of the rhetorical genre "problems and solutions."[3] In section 6 he lays out four problems and, in the remainder of our section, deals with each of them in turn. He endeavors to show that knowledge of future events does not imply causation. This applies, in particular, to God's total knowledge from the perspective of eternity. Origen found the Scriptural description of the stars as "signs" to be congruent with the use of the same terminology by Platonic philosophers. His argument is sufficiently close to that of Plotinus in *Enneads* 3.1, 5–6 and 2.3 that we must assume a common source, most likely their common teacher, Ammonius Saccas. Plotinus also argued that the stars are signs (*sêmeia*) and criticizes astrology for implying that the stars are evil or capricious, but, while denying that they determine our character, he allows that the stars may exercise some influence. The stars are like letters in which those who know how to read this sort of writing can ascertain future events, "discovering what is indicated (*sêmainomenon*) by analogy," but the stars do not cause these events.[4] Using the terminology of the apocryphal *Prayer of Joseph*, Origen readily admits, by virtue of the analogy between Scripture and the cosmos, that the stars are "the tablet of heaven" which the angelic powers can read. In fact, they receive instruction from God by reading stars much as we do by reading the Bible. Nonetheless, Origen argues, for logical and scientific reasons, that we, as human beings, cannot predict the future by means of horoscopes.

The translation is from Origène, *Philocalie, 21–27*, ed. Éric Junod = *SC* 226, Paris, Cerf, 1976, pp. 130–66, 174–204.

Text

1   It is of the utmost necessity to discuss how the luminous bodies – the sun, the moon, and the stars – become signs. The many nations who are strangers to the faith of Christ are not the only ones who lose their footing concerning the topic of destiny. They reckon that everything that occurs on the earth, as well as to each individual person, and indeed even to irrational animals, is due to the combination of the stars called planets with those of the zodiac. Many presumed believers also fret themselves about the possibility that human affairs are subject to necessity and must ineluctably turn out as the stars, in their various configurations, direct. It follows from those who assert these things that what lies within our power is eliminated and with it any possibility of praise and blame or any distinction between acceptable and blameworthy behavior. If things are as they hold, there is no longer any point to the announcement of God's judgment, his warnings to sinners that they risk chastisement, and the honors and blessings addressed to those who have dedicated themselves to better things. None of these have any reasonable purpose. And if one considers the consequences for personal piety of what they assert, faith is vain as well, Christ's coming is pointless, as are the entire divine plan of the law and the prophets and the efforts of the apostles to establish the church of Christ. Even Christ himself, according to some who dare to say so, has been subjected to the constraint of the movement of the stars on account of his birth, and accomplished and suffered what he did, not because the God and father of the universe had endowed him with extraordinary powers, but because the stars did so! From such

godless and impious doctrines it also follows that believers must believe in God because they have been induced to do so by the stars.

Let us inquire of them, what was God's intention when he made such a world? Was it that men should be impassioned with feelings appropriate to women without being the least bit answerable for their licentiousness while others act like wild beasts on the pretext that God has so ordered the universe that its movement makes them do so, abandoning themselves to the most cruel and utterly inhuman practices, even murders and piracies? Why also should we speak of what happens among men and of their sinful actions, multitudinous as they may be, when whoever holds such noble opinions has cleared them of all charges by ascribing to God responsibility for everything that is done maliciously and reprehensibly?

2   If some of them, in order to defend God, say that there is another, good God who is the source of none of these things, but that all such things depend on an Artisan, I respond that, first, they cannot demonstrate what they wish, that this Artisan is just. [5] For how can they reasonably assert that he is just who is, according to them, the father of such evils? Second, one must examine what they say about themselves. Are they subject to the movement of the stars, or are they free and, while they are living, no power is exercised over them from that source? If they say that they are subject to the stars, there clearly follows a result which they do not want, namely that stars have granted them this awareness and that the Artisan is the one who has suggested, on account of the movement of the world, the doctrine of a God imagined to be superior. If they reply that they are outside of the laws of the Artisan administered by the stars, it follows, unless what they say is an unproved assertion, that they must attempt to lead us in a more compelling way, establishing the difference between a mind subjected to birth stars and destiny, and another free from the power of such things. It is clear to those who know such persons that, upon being requested to, they can by no means provide such an explanation.

In addition, prayers are superfluous, because they are pronounced in vain, for if events must necessarily occur, and the stars make them happen, nothing can happen contrary to the relations of the stars to each other, so that it is irrational to ask of God that he give us such things. But why must we draw out this discourse any longer, establishing the impiety of this doctrine of necessity, one which ordinary people reject out of hand? What has been said is sufficient for a general illustration.

3   Let us call to mind how, in examining "Let the luminous bodies be for signs," we have arrived at these considerations. Those who know the truth about particular incidents are either personal witnesses who describe such incidents accurately, since they have personally observed what was either undergone or performed, or they know about these incidents by hearing about them from persons who report them without having themselves made them happen. Let us, for now, set aside the possibility that the actual passive or active participants, in describing what they had done or undergone, have brought to a non-participant knowledge of what happened.

Let us posit that a first party learns from a second party – in no way responsible for these incidents – that certain incidents had happened or were going to happen to a third party. Nonetheless, the first party does not recognize that his informant, the second party, was not actually responsible for these past or future events. That first party would assume that the second party reporting these past or future events had caused, or was going to cause, the incidents concerning which he provided information. Nonetheless, obviously, he would be mistaken in making such an assumption.

Thus someone chancing upon the prophetic book that foretells Judas's betrayal, and learning what was to happen, might think, on seeing that very thing fulfilled, that the book was the cause of what had happened later, since he had learned from the book what Judas was to do, or – realizing that the book was not the cause – he might blame it on the author, or the one who inspired it, namely God.

Now in the prophecies concerning Judas, the texts themselves, on examination, show that God was not the author of Judas's betrayal, but had only shown that God knew in advance the things Judas was to do out of his own wickedness, without being the cause of them. In the same way, if one delves deeply into the reason why God knows all things in advance and the texts in which he has, so to speak, imprinted his foreknowledge, one would comprehend that one who foreknows is not necessarily the cause of the things fore-known, any more than are the texts that receive the imprints of the words of foreknowledge from him who foreknows.

4   To anyone who knows about the power of God's intelligence, it is obvious from the notion of God itself, even apart from Scripture, that God knows every future event long before its occurrence. But should one need to establish this from Scripture, the prophets are full of such examples. According to Susanna, God knows everything before it comes to be, as it says: "Eternal God who knows secrets,

who knows everything before it comes to be, you know that these men have borne false testimony against me" (Sus. 42–3). In the Third Kingdoms [1 Kings] the name and deeds of one who was to reign as king were recorded most clearly many years before his birth in this prophecy: "And Jeroboam made a feast on the eighth month, like the feast celebrated in the land of Judah, and went up to the altar which he made at Bethel with the calves which he made" (1 Kings 12:42). A little farther on its says:

> And behold a man of God from Judah has come in the word of the Lord to Bethel, and Jeroboam has stood at his altar to sacrifice, and the man of God called upon the altar in the name of the Lord and said "Altar, altar, thus says the Lord, 'Behold, a son has been born of the house of David, Josiah is his name, and he shall sacrifice upon you the priests of the high places who sacrificed upon you, and the bones of men he shall burn upon you. And he has given you a marvelous sign in that day, saying, "This is the marvelous sign of which the Lord spoke, saying, 'Behold, the altar breaks asunder, and the fat upon it is poured off.'"'"
>
> (1 Kings 13:1–3)

A little farther on it says: "And the altar broke asunder, and the fat upon the altar was poured out according to the marvelous sign which the man of God had given in the word of the Lord" (1 Kings 13:5).

5   And in the Book of Isaiah, a long time before the Babylonian captivity – and it was a long time after the captivity when Cyrus arose, the King of the Persians who assisted in the construction of the temple that occurred in the time of Ezra – Cyrus is specifically named in:

> Thus says the Lord God to Cyrus, my anointed, whose right hand I have grasped to reduce nations to obedience before him, and I shall break the power of kings, and I shall open gates before him, and cities shall not be shut. I shall march before you and level mountains, and I shall shatter gates of bronze, and I shall crush bars of iron, and I shall give you the treasures of darkness, the hidden ones, things unseen I shall open to you, so that you may know that I, the Lord God who calls you by name, am the God of Israel.

For the sake of my servant Jacob and Israel my chosen, I
shall call you by name and receive you.

(Isa. 45:1–4)

It is clearly shown by these words, that because of his people, whom
Cyrus benefited, God gave him authority over many nations in spite
of his unfamiliarity with the Hebrew religion. It is also possible to
learn these things from the Greeks, who have recorded things
concerning the Cyrus who is the object of this prophecy.

In addition, in the Book of Daniel, during the time when the
Babylonians were ruling, the empires that were to follow him were
shown to Nebuchadnezzar. But they were shown in an image: the
Babylonian Empire was named golden, the Persian silver, the
Macedonian bronze, and the Roman iron (Dan. 2:37–40). Later, in
the same prophet, we find prophesied the affairs of Darius and
Alexander, and of the four successors of Alexander the Emperor of
the Macedonians, and of Ptolemy, the ruler of Egypt, surnamed
Lagus:

Behold a he-goat from the goats shall rule from the West
over the face of the whole earth, and the he-goat will have a
horn between his eyes. And he went to the ram that had
horns, which I saw seated before Ubal, and he ran against
him in the face of his strength. And I saw him coming up
to the ram, and he became furious with him, and he struck
the ram and broke both his horns, and the ram did not have
strength to stand before him, and he threw him to the
ground and trampled on him, and there was no one to
deliver the ram from his hand. And the he-goat from the
goats magnified himself exceedingly. And as he prevailed
his great horn broke, and four other horns arose from its
base in the directions of the four winds of heaven. And
from one of them arose one strong horn, and it magnified
itself exceedingly in the direction of the South and West.

(Dan. 8:5–9)

Why is it necessary to speak about the prophecies concerning
Christ, such as Bethlehem the place of his birth, Nazareth the place
of his nurture, his withdrawal to Egypt, the miracles he performed,
and how he was betrayed by Judas whom he had called to be an
apostle? These are all signs of God's foreknowledge. But the Savior
himself said, "When you see Jerusalem besieged by armies, then

91

know that the time of its devastation is near" (Lk. 21:20). For he predicted the thing that later occurred, the final destruction of Jerusalem.

6 Now that we have demonstrated, not inappropriately, that God is prescient, it must be understood, in order to discuss how the stars have become signs, that the stars are so ordered as to move – those we call planets turn in courses opposite to the fixed – so that those who apprehend signs from the configurations of the stars may know all things in particular and in general. These are not men, for the capacity to apprehend truly from the movement of the stars whatever each individual man has done or undergone is far beyond human ability. But they are the powers which, for many reasons, necessarily know these things, as, in so far as possible, we shall demonstrate below.

But being troubled by certain observations, or by the teaching of angels who had overstepped their proper order and, to the detriment of our race, had taught certain things concerning these matters, men have supposed that those beings [the stars] from whom they think that they apprehend signs are themselves the causes of those things, of which the Word says that they are signs. It is these very matters that we shall immediately treat concisely and, in so far as possible, with the greatest care.

These, then, are the issues posed for us:

1 How what is within our power is preserved, granted that God foreknows from eternity about those things reckoned to be accomplished by each person.
2 How the stars are not the agents of everything that happens among men, but only the signs.
3 That men cannot have a precise knowledge concerning these things, but they are set forth to powers[6] greater than men.
4 For what cause God made the signs in order to provide knowledge to the powers.

7 And now let us look at the first point, the very one concerning which some Greeks[7] are wary. Supposing that events are subjected to necessity and that no domain within our power is preserved if God knows all things that are going to happen, they have recklessly accepted an impious doctrine in place of one that is, by their account, worthy of God, but, as far as they can see, takes away what is within our power and thus makes otiose praise and blame, the approval of virtues, and the censure of vices.

These Greeks also say that if God has known from eternity that a certain man would be unjust and would do such unjust things, and if God's knowledge is infallible, the man foreseen to be such will be unjust in any case and could not possibly be other than unjust, his being unjust will happen of necessity and it is impossible for him to do anything else except the very thing that God knows. If he could not possibly do anything else, and no one can be blamed for failing to do what is impossible, it is in vain to hold the unjust person responsible for his actions. From the unjust man and unjust acts he passes to other sins and then, in contrast, to acts considered virtuous. And they say that from God's foreknowledge of the future it follows that what is within our power cannot be preserved.

8   Against [these Greeks] it must be said that God, when he undertook the beginning of the creation of the world – since nothing has come to be without a cause – surveyed with his mind everything that was going to happen, because, when one thing happened, something else was the result, a result that brought on another consequence, which, in turn, caused something else to happen. Thus, having surveyed events all the way to the end, he knows the things that will come to be without being responsible for each individual occurrence about which he has knowledge.

If one person should see another person who is acting in a fool-hardy way – say, walking with reckless abandon on a slippery path – the first party's realization that the second party is going to slip and fall does not make him responsible for that person's having slipped. Similarly, we must understand that God has seen with foreknowledge what sort of person each man would be, the causes for his being such a person, and the particular things he will either do wrong or do right.

And, if we must say that foreknowledge is not the cause of what happens, it follows that when someone does sin, God is not implicated in the action of the person whose future sinning he has foreknown. But, paradoxical as it may seem, the truth is that the future event is itself the cause of such foreknowledge. It does not happen because it was known, but it was known because it is going to happen.

A distinction is required. If someone should interpret "It will happen in any event" to mean that what is foreknown will necessarily happen, we shall not grant this. We do not say that, since God foreknew that Judas would be a traitor, it was entirely necessary that Judas should become a traitor. Indeed, prophecies concerning Judas register reproaches and accusations of Judas, confirming to everyone that his blame was merited. Blame would not be applied to him if he had to be a traitor of necessity and it was not possible for him to be like the rest of the apostles. See if this is not evident when we adduce this citation:

> Let there be no one to have pity on his orphans, because he did not remember to exercise mercy, and he persecuted the poor man, the destitute, and the broken-hearted to bring about his death. He has loved cursing, and it has returned to him; he did not want blessing, and it has departed far from him.
>
> (Ps. 108:12, 16–17 [109:12, 16–17])

If someone interprets "It will happen in any event" to mean that these things will happen but it would be possible for them to happen otherwise, we would agree with him that this is correct. For God to be mistaken is not possible; it is possible, concerning things that could happen or not happen, for him to think that they happen and that they do not happen.[8]

9 To be as clear as possible, we say we explain the matter as follows. If it was possible for Judas to be an apostle like Peter, it was possible for God to know concerning Judas that he would stay as an apostle like Peter. If it was possible for Judas to become a traitor, it was possible for God to know, concerning him, that he would be a traitor. If Judas is a traitor, God, who foreknows the truth, by his foreknowledge of the two aforementioned possibilities – given that only one of these possibilities will occur – foreknew that Judas would be a traitor. But the event about which he had this knowledge could have happened otherwise, and God's knowledge could say, "It is possible for him to do this, but the opposite is also possible; both being possible, I know that he will do this." God would not say, "It is not possible that this man should stumble" nor would he say, for example, in delivering an oracle about someone, "It is not possible for him to be temperate." To avoid stumbling is absolutely beyond human ability, but we do have an ability to live either temperately or licentiously.

Since both abilities exist, he who does not heed discourses intended for conversion and education gives himself over to the worse, and he who seeks the truth and wants to live according to it gives himself to the better. The former does not seek truth, because he is inclined to pleasure. The latter investigates carefully concerning the two abilities, being convinced by common notions[9] and by a hortatory discourse. To repeat, the former chooses pleasure, not that he is incapable of spurning it, but because he makes no effort; the latter despises it, because he sees the disgrace that often accompanies it.

10 The following is an additional argument that the foreknowledge of God does not confer necessity on the things that it comprehends: often the God of the Scriptures calls the prophets to preach repentance, not affecting to know in advance whether those who hear will turn from their sins or remain in them. As it says in Jeremiah: "Perhaps they will hear and repent" (Jer. 33:3 [26:3]). God is not ignorant of whether they will or will not hear, when he says: "Perhaps they will hear and repent." Nonetheless, he says this to indicate that either possibility mentioned could equally well happen. In this way his foreknowledge, announced in advance, will not prematurely discourage those who hear it, making it appear a matter of necessity that they lack the power to turn from their sins and that this foreknowledge is itself the cause of their sins. By the same token, those who are unaware that God foreknows their good behavior are enabled to live virtuously, maintaining a vigorous struggle against evil, since foreknowledge does not occasion complacency, inducing them to relax their firm resistance to sin on the pretext that what has been announced in advance will be sure to happen in any event. In this way foreknowledge could be an impediment to good behavior.

In every way, therefore, God, who plans[10] the world's affairs so that they may turn out beneficially is reasonable in blinding us to the future. Knowledge of his plan would release us from the struggle against evil, and it would so inure us to abandoning the struggle against sin, supposing we could take the result for granted, that we would quickly be subject to it. So there is an inherent conflict between becoming entirely good and gaining foreknowledge that this will happen in any event. For to become a truly good person, beyond the measure of virtue we already have, requires a vigorous and sustained effort. But, if it were acquired in advance, the knowledge that one was to become virtuous in any event would relax discipline. Therefore it is expedient for us not to know whether we shall be good or bad.

11 Since we have said that God blinds us to the future, let us see if we can clarify a passage needing investigation in Exodus: "Who is it who has made deaf and mute, clear-sighted and blind? Is it not I, the Lord?" (Ex. 4:11).[11] Following our line of reasoning, God has made the same man clear-sighted and blind, seeing what is present,

and blind as to the future. Being deaf and mute does not require our explanation in the present context.

We also agree that numerous things that are not within our power are causes of things that are within our power. If these things had not happened – I speak of things not within our power – certain things within our power would not have been accomplished. But these things within our power were accomplished as a consequence of things that had happened previously which were not within our power, even though it is possible that other actions on our part could have followed these things that had happened previously.

If someone should speculate that what is within our power depends on nothing else, so that our choice would not depend on things that happen to us, he forgets that he is a part of the world, surrounded by human society and by the environment.

I think that I have sufficiently demonstrated, in this summary of the arguments, that the foreknowledge of God does not entirely subject things foreknown to necessity.

[Sections 12–13 in the *Philocalia* are a passage from the *Contra Celsum* dealing with the same subject.]

14   Well, we must maintain that the stars are not at all the agents of human affairs, but only signs. It is clear that in the former case, namely that a certain configuration of stars is considered to cause events that happen to man – for let our discourse investigate this now – we cannot, to begin with, understand today's configuration concerning one particular person to have produced past occurrences to one or more other persons; anything that produces an effect must be earlier than the effect produced. But according to the discipline of those who vouch for such arts, events touching human affairs that happened prior to the configuration are supposed to be predicted.

They vouch that, after having somehow established the birth hour of a particular person, they can establish how each of the planets relates perpendicularly to a certain degree of a sign of the zodiac, or, in a certain minute in it, which star of the zodiac chanced to be on the horizon in the east, which was in the west, which was at the meridian and which was at the opposite meridian.

And once they posit that the stars (which according to them constitute a configuration) have a particular configuration at the time of the birth of a particular person, then, by means of the time of birth of the person they are dealing with, they examine not just the future but the past, including things that took place before the birth and conception of the person in question: what sort of person the father was, rich or poor, sound of body or deformed, of good or bad character, indigent or affluent, following this or that occupation, and the same things concerning the mother and any older brothers and sisters there may chance to be.

15 Let us assume for a moment that they determine the exact position of the stars – we shall later demonstrate that this is not the case. Let us then ask those who claim that human activities are submitted to necessity by the stars how a particular configuration today can have produced events in the past. For if it is impossible to discover in this way the truth concerning past events, it is evident that the stars, by being moved to certain positions in the sky, have not produced events that had happened long before they ever assumed those positions. In this case, indeed, someone, admitting that they do provide true information, after having examined what they say concerning future events, will say that the stars provide this information not as agents, but only as signs. If someone should claim that the stars do not produce past events – but that other configurations cause those events and the present configuration only signifies them, but that future events are displayed by the configuration formed at a person's birth – let that person indicate the difference between being able to demonstrate that some things are perceived to be true on the basis of their having been produced by the stars, but that others are true only on the basis of their being signified by them. If they cannot supply this difference, they ought reasonably to assent that nothing takes place in human affairs because of the stars, but, as we have already said, they are, perhaps, signified.

It is as if someone should comprehend the past and future, not from the stars, but from the mind of God through a particular prophetic word. For as we have already demonstrated, God's knowing what each person will do does not impair what is within our own power. In the same way the signs which God has ordered simply as indications do not restrain what is within our power.

But just like a book containing the future prophetically, the entire heaven can, by being God's book, contain the future. We can, therefore, understand in this sense what is said by Jacob in the *Prayer of Joseph*: "For having read in the tablet of heaven what will happen to you and to your sons."[12] And indeed also "Heaven shall be rolled up like a book" (Isa. 34:4) demonstrates that the words contained, in so far as they signify future events, are to be

completed and, so to speak, fulfilled, just as it is said that prophecies are fulfilled when the events take place. And thus the stars will
become "for signs" according to the verse we have been discussing:
"Let them be for signs" (Gen. 1:14). Jeremiah – recalling us to
ourselves and banishing fear of things we may suppose to be signified, including, no doubt, things understood to be signified by the
stars – says: "Do not be afraid because of the signs of heaven" (Jer.
10:2).

16   Let us look at a second argument, showing how the stars
cannot be agents, but are perhaps indicators. From a very large
number of horoscopes it is possible to grasp the affairs of one man.
We say this hypothetically, conceding that it is possible for the
knowledge of such things to be comprehended by men. Let us take
an example: they claim that they can tell from a certain person's
horoscope that he will undergo a certain fate and die after falling
among robbers and being murdered and that, if he were to have
brothers and sisters, they could tell the same from each of theirs.
For they suppose that the horoscope of each of these would include a
brother who had died because of robbers, likewise from those of his
father, mother, wife, children, servants, and friends, and likewise
from those of the murderers themselves.

But how could the man whose destiny is determined by so many
horoscopes, even conceding the possibility, be under the control of
one particular configuration of stars rather than of the others? It is
implausible to affirm that the configuration on his own birth date
has produced these events in his life but the configurations on the
other birth dates have not produced them but have only signified
them. Moreover, it is absurd to say that the horoscopes of all the
others contain in each case a cause for his having been murdered, so
that in fifty horoscopes, let us say, are contained the murder of this
one man.

I do not know how they can square with their account the fact
that in Judaea, almost all men must have a configuration at his
birth which causes them to be circumcised on the eighth day, so
that the tip of the penis is cut off, then subject to ulcers, inflamma-
tions, and wounds, so that, as soon as they enter life, they already
need a physician, but for the Ishmaelites in Arabia the configurations are such that all men are circumcised at the age of 13, for this
is what is told about them, or again that for some in Ethiopia, the
configurations are such that their kneecaps are removed, or that, for
the Amazons, one of their breasts. How is it that the stars are

responsible for such things among the nations? I think that if we were to reflect, we could not establish any truth to such claims.

With so many purported means of foreknowledge, I do not know how men have been so inconsistent as to admit that auguries from birds and sacrifices, even auguries from shooting stars, do not contain the efficient cause but are indications only, while making horoscopes a special case.[13] If, therefore, it is known – conceding such knowledge for the sake of the argument – that events can occur because of the means by which they are known, why should they occur because of stars but not, say, because of birds, or because of sacrificed entrails or because of shooting stars? These arguments will suffice for the moment to refute the idea that the stars are responsible for human affairs.

17 It is now, indeed, time to examine the validity of the very matter which we had conceded since it did not affect our argument: namely that it is humanly possible to comprehend heavenly configurations and signs and to know what they signify.

Those who concern themselves with these things say that someone who intends to understand accurately the science of horoscopes must know, not just in which of the twelve signs of the zodiac the star in question is found, but the degree and minute of its position in the zodiac. More rigorous astrologers would specify the second as well. And they say that it is necessary to do this for each of the planets, examining its position with respect to the fixed stars. In addition, it will be necessary, they say, to see not just which sign of the zodiac is on the eastern horizon, but which part of that sign to the closest degree, minute, or even second.

How then, since an hour, broadly speaking, includes half of a sign of the zodiac, can someone grasp the minute without having an analogous division of hours, so that one could say, for example, that a man was born at the fourth hour, plus a half hour, a quarter hour, an eighth, a sixteenth, and a thirty-second?

For they say that indications may be entirely different due to ignorance, not a whole hour, but of a fraction of one. Thus, when twins are born, there is often a slight period of time between them, and the many differences between their destiny and behavior occur, according to astrologers, because of the position of the stars and the part of the sign of the zodiac at the horizon is not observed by those who, they suppose, observe the moment of birth. After all, no one can say that the thirtieth part of an hour does not pass between the birth of one twin and of the other. For argument's sake, let the ability to observe the exact moment be conceded to them.

18   There is a theory demonstrating that the cycle of the zodiac, and likewise the planets, is moved from west to east by one degree in a hundred years, and that this, after a long time, changes the position of the signs of the zodiac.[14] This means that the theoretical concept of a sign of the zodiac is one thing, but its actual form, so to speak, is another. But they say that the results for human destiny are discovered not from the form, but from the theoretical concept of the sign of the zodiac, the very thing that cannot be accurately ascertained.[15]

Let it even be conceded that the theoretical concept of a sign of the zodiac can be ascertained, or that the truth can be ascertained from the form of a sign of the zodiac; astrologers themselves still admit that it is impossible to account adequately for what they call the "combination" of stars in such configurations. Thus a demonstrably bad star can be impaired by its aspect with another star, because that star is in an aspect that might or might not be important with yet another star that is good. By the same token, the impairment of a bad star that would have happened because it is in aspect with a good star is prevented because yet another star, with bad indications, occupies a certain position in the configuration.

I think that, if one were to pay attention to such issues, one would despair of obtaining the sort of information astrologers claim because it is entirely inaccessible to men, and, even at best, does no more than provide signs. Once someone gains experience in these matters, he becomes aware, rather, of what is fallible in the conjectures, both spoken and written, of astrologers, even if they are considered successful. Thus Isaiah, holding that these things cannot be discovered by men, said to the daughter of the Chaldaeans (who, more than anyone else, vouch for this art): "Let them arise and save you, the astrologers of heaven, let them announce to you what will take place" (Isa. 47:13). These words teach us that those most well instructed in these matters are unable to obtain knowledge of what the Lord has willed concerning each nation.

19   At this point, we have interpreted the prophetic text at the verbal level. But Jacob said that he had read in the tablets of heaven what would happen to his son, and someone might contradict us, claiming to prove through the Scripture the opposite of what we have said, since we have said that the signs are humanly incomprehensible, even though Jacob said that he had read something in the tablets of heaven. Our answer is that those among us who are wise, endowed with a spirit exceeding human nature, have learned unspeakable things, not in a human manner, but in a divine manner, as Paul said: "I have heard unspeakable words, which it is not permitted for a man to utter" (2 Cor. 12:4). For they know "alterations of solstices, changes of seasons, cycles of years, and positions of stars" (Wis. 7:18–19) not from men or through men but by the Spirit's having revealed clearly to them and having announced, according to God's will, divine things. And, in fact, Jacob had surpassed the human condition, supplanting his brother and realizing – in the same book from which we have taken the citation "Reading in the tablets of heaven" – that he was the chief commander of the host of the Lord, and that he had already received the name Israel. He realized this while he was serving in the body, when the archangel Uriel reminded him of it.[16]

20   At this point we still need to examine and establish, for those who believe that the luminaries of heaven serve as signs but are disturbed by those who attempt to pry too closely into these matters, why God created these signs in the heaven.

The first thing to say is that believing in the greatness of the whole knowledge of the mind of God – which embraces every existing thing, so that nothing, no matter how ordinary and trivial it may be considered, escapes the notice of his divinity – includes the opinion that God's mind embraces in itself, for all practical purposes, an infinite number of things. This is not, indeed, something capable of proof, but is a corollary to our belief that God's mind is ingenerate and surpasses all nature.[17]

So then this book of heaven is understood experientially by those with superhuman abilities and by holy souls freed from the present bondage, for God has made in heaven those who have learned or will learn to read the signs of God as if they were letters and characters composed by the movements of heaven.

It is not remarkable that God has made certain things for demonstration to the blessed, since Scripture says to Pharaoh: "For this cause I have raised you up, so as to demonstrate my power in you and so that my name might be proclaimed in all the earth" (Rom. 9:17). For if Pharaoh was preserved for the demonstration of God's power and proclamation of his name in all the earth, conceive what sort of demonstration of the power of God the heavenly signs would constitute, all engraved from eternity to the consummation by the excellent book of God in heaven.

Second, I conjecture that the signs are accessible to the powers that manage human affairs,[18] so that those powers may simply know certain things and accomplish other things, just as in books among us some things are written so that we may know about them, such as the matters concerning Creation and certain other mysteries, and others, such as the commandments and ordinances of God, so that, knowing about them, we may act accordingly. It is possible that the heavenly letters, which the angels and the divine powers know how to read well, contain certain things which must be read by the angels and ministers of God so that they may rejoice in knowing them and certain things which they accept like commandments, so as to do them.

21   And we shall not be wide of the mark in saying that heaven and the stars are analogous to matters in the law. But if bad powers different from men do certain things that have been foreknown and signified in heaven, this does not necessarily mean that they have done these things because they were recommended by the letters of God.[19] But just as men who do harm, unaware that God has known in advance the harm that they are going to do, effect the harm they do out of their own wickedness, so the hostile powers, granted that God knows in advance the evil of men and adverse powers who have depraved intentions, accomplish what they do out of their own most shameful choice.

On the other hand, in the case of the holy angels, the ministering spirits sent out to accomplish an assigned task (see Heb. 1:14), it is probable that, like those who receive orders from things written in the law of God, they do good things in an orderly way when they should, as they should, and in so far as they should. It is absurd that they, being divine, should go out at random and with no fixed purpose, so that, for example, they should give some instruction to Abraham, do something for Isaac, deliver Jacob from danger, or be present to the spirit of a prophet. Therefore, so that they may not do these things at random or by chance, they read the book of God and so carry out their assignments.

But as we have already said, whether it is what we do or the things which the adverse powers accomplish against us, we act by means of our own choice, by one which is undisciplined, when we sin, but one that is educated, when we accomplish things well pleasing to God, not without the assistance of the angels, the divine Scriptures, or the holy servants.

COMMENTARY ON JOHN, BOOK 1

Introduction

Origen probably began this work in Alexandria around 231, shortly after completing *Peri Archon*. Book 1, provided in full here, falls into three main parts. Sections 1–89 constitute a preface to the whole intended commentary. It resembles contemporary prefaces to philosophical commentaries.[1] In it Origen examines the relationship of the Gospel of John to the other gospels and to the rest of Scripture and argues that an interpreter must have unmediated access to Jesus Christ, who is the gospel embodied. Aside from a brief conclusion (sections 289–92), the remainder of the book examines the two principal words in the initial phrase of verse 1:1. Sections 90–124 deal with "beginning" (*Archê*) and sections 125–288 with "Word" (*Logos*). In the former Origen identifies "beginning" with God's Wisdom. In the latter Origen criticizes those who make "Word" the sole privileged title for the Son, taking its meaning for granted and neglecting all the other titles in Scripture. Arguing the "Word" can only be understood in relation to the rest of these titles, Origen deals with all the Son's titles in what amounts to his most sustained statement of Christology. Our selections from later books of the *Commentary on John* show how he consistently follows through these interpretations of the titles.

The text illustrates Origen's interest in Christ's divine and human natures and multiple aspects (the *epinoiai* designated by various Christological titles) as they relate to human transformation through participation in Christ. He announces a concern for human transformation by addressing his patron Ambrosius as someone "hastening to be spiritual and no longer human" (section 9). The person thus transformed becomes, like John the evangelist, another Jesus (23), not differing from Christ (65) and knowing the Father as

103

the Son does (92). Such a person no longer needs the Son in those aspects that he assumed in becoming man for the sake of the divine *oikonomia*, but in his original aspects (124). Extending the image of Isaiah 11:1 (as transmitted in the Septuagint), Origen states that such a person no longer encounters Christ as a rod of chastisement, or even as a flower, but as a fruit coming to mature perfection within him (263). Such human transformation derives from and extends the union of the divine and human in Christ (197). The Christ who transforms the individual Christian also transforms Scripture, turning the Old Testament into gospel (36) and, eventually, for those who are spiritually mature enough to comprehend it, turning the New Testament itself into a spiritual gospel (44–5).

The work begins with a complex example of homonymy, in which Origen generalizes from Paul's notion that some are Jews "in secret" to argue that the church as the new people of God is Israel "in secret." As such the church contains, in a hidden and spiritual manner, all the divisions of the Jewish people, including priests and levites consecrated entirely to God's service. Origen goes on to argue that the interpreter of John must be a believer who is, spiritually, like Christ himself, a high priest. Only such a person can, with the assistance of the Holy Spirit, "open up the mystery that is hidden as a treasure in the text" (89).

The translation is from Origène, *Commentaire sur S. Jean*, vol. 1, ed. Cécile Blanc = *SC* 120 bis, Paris, Cerf, 1996, pp. 52–210.

Text

Preface

I 1   Just as, I think, the people once referred to as "of God" (see Num. 27:17) were divided into twelve tribes in addition to the Levitical order – itself composed, for divine service, of many corps of priests and levites – so I consider that, in accordance with "the secret man of the heart" (see 1 Pet. 3:4),[2] the whole people of Christ, entitled Jewish in secret (see Rom. 2:29) and circumcised in spirit, has, in a very mysterious way, the properties of the tribes. This matter may be learned openly from John's Revelation, but, for those who know how to listen, the other prophets are scarcely silent about it. 2   John indeed speaks in this way:

> And I saw an angel ascending from the rising of the sun, having the seal of the living God, and he cried out in a

loud voice to the four angels who were responsible for harming the earth and the sea, saying, "Do not harm the earth, the sea, or the trees, until we have sealed the servants of our God on their forehead." And I heard the number of the sealed: one hundred and forty-four thousand from all the tribes of the sons of Israel, from the tribe of Judah twelve thousand sealed, from the tribe of Reuben twelve thousand sealed.

(Rev. 7:2–5)[3]

3   Then after listing the rest of the tribes except Dan, he adds, in addition:

And I looked, and behold the Lamb seated upon Mount Zion, and with him the one hundred and forty four thousand having his name and the name of his Father written on their foreheads. And I heard a voice from heaven like the voice of many waters, and like the voice of great thunder, and the voice which I heard was like harpers harping on their harps. And they sang a new song before the throne and before the four creatures and the elders, and no one could learn the song except the one hundred and forty four thousand, who were gathered from the earth. These are those who have not sullied themselves with women, for they are celibate. These are those who follow the Lamb wherever he leads, these have been gathered from men as first-fruits to God and to the Lamb, and no falsehood is found in their mouths, for they are blameless.

(Rev. 14:1–5)

4   It can be demonstrated in the following way that these things are said by John about persons who have believed in Christ and who belong in tribes even if their corporeal race seems not to descend from the seed of the patriarchs: " 'Do not,' " he says,

"harm the earth, the sea, or the trees, until we have sealed the servants of our God on their forehead." And I heard the number of the sealed: one hundred and forty-four thousand from all the tribes of the sons of Israel, from the tribe of Judah twelve thousand sealed, from the tribe of Reuben twelve thousand sealed.

5   Note that those from all the tribes of the children of Israel who are sealed on their foreheads are one hundred and forty four thousand in number. Later on these one hundred and forty-four thousand are spoken of by John as those who have the name of the Lamb and of his Father written on their foreheads and who are celibate persons and have not sullied themselves with women.

6   Since in the two cases the forehead is said to bear either the seal or letters comprising the name of the Lamb and the name of his Father, can the seal on the foreheads be anything but the name of the Lamb and of his Father?

7   But if, as we have already shown, those from the tribes are the same as the celibate persons, and if a believer from the Israelites according to the flesh (see 1 Cor. 10:18) is rare, so much so that one would dare to say that those who believe from among the Israelites according to the flesh do not make up the number one hundred and forty four thousand, obviously gentiles who have approached the divine Word must comprise the one hundred and forty four thousand who have not sullied themselves with women. Moreover, one would not stray from the truth in saying that, in each tribe, the celibate are the first-fruits, 8   for it adds "these have been gathered from men as first-fruits to God and to the Lamb, and no falsehood is found in their mouths, for they are blameless."

But it must not be ignored that the discourse concerning the one hundred and forty four thousand celibate persons is open to an elevated sense. At this time it is superfluous and beside the point to cite the prophetic texts teaching us the same thing about those who are from the gentiles.

II 9   "What does all this mean for us?" you say, Ambrosius, on coming across this composition – you, truly a man of God and a man in Christ (see 1 Tim. 6:11 and 2 Cor. 12:2) hastening to be spiritual and no longer human.

The members of the tribes offer to God tithes and first-fruits through the levites and priests, but tithes and first-fruits do not constitute all they have. On the other hand, the levites and priests employ nothing except tithes and first-fruits[4] when they offer tithes to God through the high priest, and I suppose that they offer first-fruits as well. 10   Among us who follow the teachings of Christ, the majority who, for the most part, have no particular purpose in their lives and offer few activities specifically to God may, indeed, be the members of the tribes who have little in common with the priests and rarely cultivate the worship of God. But those who are really dedicated to the divine word and to the worship of God may, because of the excellence of their activities in this regard, be spoken of without absurdity as levites and priests.[5]

11   Indeed those who are more excellent than everyone else, occupying, as it were, the first place in their generations, will be high priests in the order of Aaron rather than in the order of Melchizedek (see Heb. 7:11). For if anyone object to this, reckoning that we court blasphemy by ascribing the high-priestly title to men, since Jesus is often prophesied as our great priest – for we have "a great high priest, who has passed across heaven, Jesus, the Son of God" (Heb. 4:14) – he should be told that the Apostle made a distinction when he said that the prophet said about Christ, "You are a priest forever after the order of Melchizedek" (Heb. 7:17, 5:5; Ps. 109:4 [110:4]) rather than according to the order of Aaron. On this basis we say that that men can be high priests after the order of Aaron but only the Christ of God according to the order of Melchizedek.

12   When, because we are hastening to better things, all our activity and all our life is dedicated to God and when we want to have it entirely as a first-fruit out of many first-fruits, then, unless I am mistaken, what ought to be the subject of my investigation, while we are bodily separated from one another, but the gospel? For one must dare to say that the gospel is the first-fruits of Scripture as a whole. 13   Then should the first-fruits of my activity, since I have returned to Alexandria, be anything else but the study of the first-fruits of Scripture?[6]

We must know that first-fruits and firstlings are not the same: the first-fruits are offered after the rest of the fruit, the firstlings before it. 14   Among the scriptures actually accepted and believed by all the churches to be divine, one would not be mistaken in saying that the law of Moses is the firstlings, but the gospel is the first-fruits. For, after all the fruit of the prophets who preceded the Lord Jesus, the perfect Word has come to fruition.

III 15   But if someone should object to the rationale by which we explain first-fruits, saying that, because the acts and epistles of the apostles actually follow the gospels, our previous exposition of first-fruits – according to which the gospel is the first-fruits of the whole Scripture – is untenable, the response is: we possess in the epistles the mind of men who are wise in Christ and assisted by him, requiring, for credibility, the witness of depositions in the legal and prophetic discourses. Thus that we may say that the apostolic writings are wise, credible, and very cogent, but not to be compared with "The Lord Almighty says these things." 16   In this regard, ask if, when Paul says that "All scripture is divinely inspired and useful" (2 Tim. 3:16), he included his own writings, or if, on the other hand, "I say, not the Lord" (I Cor. 7:12), "I establish this rule in all the churches" (1 Cor. 7:17), "Such things as I have suffered in Antioch, in Iconium, and in Lystra" (2 Tim. 3:11), and similar things written by him from time to time imply apostolic authority but not the absolute authority of words from divine inspiration.[7]

17   In addition it must be added that the old Scripture is not gospel, since it does not disclose but herald in advance "the one who is coming." But all the new Scripture is gospel, not just because it says, near the beginning of the gospel, "Behold the Lamb of God, who takes away the sin of the world" (Jn 1:29), but also because it consists of varied praises and of the teachings of him on whose account the gospel is the gospel.

18   Yet if God has established in the church apostles, prophets, evangelists, pastors, and teachers (see 1 Cor. 12:28), when we examine what is the task of an evangelist – that is not just a matter of recounting how the Savior accomplished miracles as curing a man blind from birth (see Jn 9) and resurrecting a dead man who was already stinking (see Jn 11), but the evangelist is also characterized by exhortations intended to produce faith in the things Jesus accomplished – we shall not hesitate to say that the apostles' writings are in some way gospel.

19   But, as concerns this second explanation, to someone who retorts that we do not appropriately term the entire New Testament a gospel because the epistles are not entitled "gospel," we respond: often the Scriptures use the same term for two or more things even though, strictly speaking, the term applies to only one of them. Thus, even though the Savior says "Do not call anyone teacher on earth" (Mt. 23:8), the Apostle says that teachers are instituted in the church. 20   These are not teachers in the strict sense of the term used in the gospel. In the same way each letter in the epistles is not, strictly speaking, gospel in comparison with the account of Jesus' deeds, sufferings, and words.

Nonetheless, the gospel is the first-fruits of the entire Scripture, and of all things that we intend to accomplish, we shall dedicate the first-fruits to the first-fruits of the Scriptures.

IV 21   For my part I suppose that the evangelists, being four,[8] are, as it were, the elements of the church's faith, from which elements the whole world is constituted in Christ so as to be reconciled to God, as Paul says, "God was in Christ, reconciling the world to himself" (2 Cor. 5:19), the world from which Jesus took away the sin, since it is concerning the world of the church that

Scripture says, "Behold the Lamb of God, who takes away the sin of the world" (Jn 1:29). I also suppose that the first-fruits of the gospel is the one which you have requested us to interpret to the best of our ability, the Gospel according to John, which speaks of the one who is given a genealogy and begins with one who has no genealogy (see Heb. 7:3).[9]

22   For Matthew, writing for the Hebrews awaiting the son of Abraham and David, says, "A book of the generation of Jesus Christ, the son of David, the son of Abraham" (Mt. 1:1) and Mark deliberately writes "the beginning of the gospel" (Mk. 1:1) so that doubtless we may discover his purpose in the Word "in the beginning" of John's gospel, the Word who is God (see Jn 1:1). But Luke also reserves[10] for him who reclined upon Jesus' breast (see Jn 13:25) the better and more perfect discourses concerning Jesus, for none of them revealed his divinity straightforwardly as John did, who presented him saying "I am the light of the world" (Jn 8:12), "I am the way, and the truth, and the life" (Jn 14:6), "I am the resurrection" (Jn 11:25), and in Revelation, "I am the alpha and the omega, the beginning and the end, the first and the last" (Rev. 22:13). 23   Further, if one must be so bold as to say that the gospels are the first-fruits of the entire Scripture, then the first-fruits of the gospels is [the Gospel] according to John. No one can understand[11] this gospel unless he reclines on Jesus' breast and unless he accepts Mary from Jesus as one who has become his own mother. And, in order to become another John, he must become such a person that, like John, he has been designated by Jesus as one who is Jesus. For no one but Jesus was a son of Mary according to those who soundly glorify her,[12] but when Jesus says to his mother, "See, your son" (Jn 19:26), rather than, "See, this man is also your son," it is the equivalent of saying, "See, this man is Jesus whom you bore." For everyone who is perfected "no longer lives, but Christ lives in him" (see Gal. 2:20), and since Christ lives in him, Christ says to Mary concerning him, "See, your son."

24   What also needs to be said about what kind of intelligence we must have to understand fully the discourse stored in the earthen treasure (see 2 Cor. 4:7) of ordinary speech, that is, a letter legible to anyone who chances to read it and audible by the sound of the sensible word to all who attend with their bodily ears? Someone who is going to comprehend it accurately must be able to say with truth, "We have the intelligence of Christ, so that we know the things graciously given to us by God" (1 Cor. 2:16 and 12).[13]

25 It is possible to cite a saying from Paul to the effect that the entire New Testament is gospel, namely "according to my gospel" (Rom. 2:16), for among Paul's writings we do not have a book customarily called a gospel, but everything which he proclaimed or said was the gospel. But what he proclaimed and said, he wrote, so that what he wrote was gospel. **26** But if the writings of Paul were gospel, it follows that Peter's writings were gospel as well as, in a word, all writings which commend Christ's presence[14] and prepare for his advent by producing it in the souls of those who receive the Word of God waiting at the door and knocking (see Rev. 3:20) and wishing to enter into souls.

V **27** It is time to examine what the word "gospel" means and why these books have it as their title. A gospel is a discourse consisting of an announcement of events that, because of the benefits they procure, please those hearing it when they receive the announcement. Such a discourse is no less a gospel if one examines the attitude of the hearer.

Or a gospel is a discourse that itself makes present something good for the one who believes or a discourse promising that the promised good is present. **28** All of the definitions above are appropriate to the writings we entitle gospels.

For each gospel is a collection of benefits announced to the believer producing benefit for the person who does not chance to misinterpret it. It ordinarily produces joy, since it teaches the presence among men for their salvation of Jesus Christ, the firstborn of all creation (see Col. 1:15). But it is also apparent to every believer that each gospel is a discourse teaching the presence of the good Father in those who wish to receive the Son. **29** Without doubt the expected good thing is promised through these books. For John the Baptist was perhaps voicing the concerns of the whole people when he said, in his message to Jesus, "Are you the one who is to come, or are we expecting someone else?" (Mt. 11:3), because the good thing which the people were expecting was the Christ, whom the prophets had announced, so that whoever chanced to be under the law and the prophets had hopes in him, as the Samaritan woman testified saying, "I know that Messiah is coming, the so-called 'Christ.' When that one comes, he will announce all things to us" (Jn 4:25). **30** But Simon and Cleopas also, as they were discussing "among themselves concerning all the things that had occurred" (Lk. 24:14) to Jesus, said to the resurrected Christ himself, whom they did not yet know to have risen from the dead, "Are you the only inhabitant of Jerusalem who does not know the things that have occurred there in these days?" But when he asked, "What things?" they answered,

> The things concerning Jesus the Nazarene, that he was a man who was a prophet powerful in deed and in word before God and all the people, how the high priests and our rulers betrayed him to a condemnation of death and crucified him. But we were hoping that he was the one who was going to deliver Israel.
>
> (Lk. 24:18–21)

31   In addition Andrew, the brother of Simon Peter, finding his own brother Simon, said, "We have found the Messiah, which is, being interpreted, Christ" (Jn 1:41). A little later, Philip, finding Nathanael, says to him, "We have found the one about whom Moses wrote in the law and the prophets, Jesus the son of Joseph from Nazareth" (Jn 1:45).

VI 32   Someone may deem the first definition above unsatisfactory because writings not entitled gospels fall under it, for the law and the prophets are discourses believed to be "consisting of an announcement of events which, on account of the benefits which they procure, please those hearing it when they receive the announcement."

33   One might answer this objection by saying that, because Christ had not yet appeared to clarify their mysteries, before Christ's presence, the law and the prophets did not possess the promise implied by the definition of gospel. Nonetheless, when the Savior became present, acting so as to embody the gospel, he made them all into gospel by the gospel. 34   It would not be irrelevant to cite as an example "A little leaven leavens the whole loaf" (Gal. 5:9). Because * * * removing the veil (see 2 Cor. 2:15) which, in the law and the prophets, hid his divinity from the children of men, he showed the divine character of all the Scriptures, furnishing to all who wished to become disciples of his wisdom what was true in the law of Moses which the ancients worshipped in a pattern and a shadow (see Heb. 8:5) and what was the truth in the events narrated, which happened figuratively to them, but were written for us, on whom the ends of the ages have come (see 1 Cor. 10:11).[15]

35   For every person in whom Christ is present no longer worships God in Jerusalem or on the mountain of the Samaritans, but, knowing that God is spirit (see Jn 4:24), he no longer worships the father and maker of the universe figuratively.

36 Therefore before the gospel, which came about through Christ's presence, none of the old Scriptures were gospel. But the gospel, which is a new covenant, has illuminated with the light of knowledge (see Hos. 10:12) the never-aging newness of the spirit proper to the new covenant, delivering us from the oldness of the letter (see Rom. 7:6).

VII 37 But it must not be ignored that there was a presence of Christ before his fleshly presence, namely an intellectual presence which occurred to those who happened to be more mature – not, that is, infants or still under pedagogues and guardians (see Gal. 4:2) – to whom the intelligible fullness of time (see Gal. 4:4) was present, as it was to the Patriarchs, to Moses the attendant (see Heb. 8:5), and to the prophets who contemplated the glory of Christ.[16]

38 Just as, before the manifest bodily presence, he was present to the perfect, so also, after his advent has been proclaimed, in the case of those who were still infants – because they were under guardians and stewards[17] and had not arrived at the fullness of time – the forerunners of Christ have been present as discourses,[18] reasonably referred to as pedagogues, adapted to childish souls. But the glorified Son himself, God the Word (see Jn 1:1), was not present to them, but was waiting until they should receive the preparation necessary for men of God to appropriate his divinity.

39 And this ought to be known: just as there is a law containing a shadow of good things to come (see Heb. 10:1) clarified by the law promulgated according to the truth, so also there is a gospel, considered to be intelligible to anyone who should chance upon it, that actually teaches the shadows of the mysteries of Christ.[19]

40 But, to those who perceive face to face (see Prov. 8:9) all things concerning the Son of God himself, what John called the "eternal gospel" (see Rev. 14:6), which might appropriately be referred to as the spiritual gospel, reveals clearly both the mysteries concealed in his words and the realities of which his deeds are the enigmatic expression.

From this reasoning it follows that we must conclude that, just as there is someone who is manifestly a Jew and circumcised (see Rom. 2:28), and that there is an obvious circumcision and one which is in secret (see Rom. 2:29), so it is with being a Christian and with baptism. **41** Both Paul and Peter, initially being Jews and circumcised outwardly, later received from Jews the condition of being Jews and circumcised in secret. But for the sake of the salvation of many according to a plan[20] they showed that they were manifestly Jews not only by words but by actions as well. And the same thing must be said concerning their Christianity. 42 And just as it was not possible for Paul to benefit the Jews according to the flesh, unless, when reason persuaded him, he circumcised Timothy (Acts 16:3) and, when it was reasonable, shaved his head and made an offering (Acts 21:24) and, all told, became a Jew in order to gain the Jews (see 1 Cor. 9:20), so it is not possible for what is set forth openly for the benefit of the majority to improve, solely through secret Christianity, those who are receiving elementary instruction in open Christianity and lead them to greater and more elevated things.[21]

43 For this very reason it is necessary to act as a Christian both spiritually and bodily, and where it is appropriate to proclaim the bodily gospel, saying that one knows nothing among carnal persons except Jesus Christ and him crucified (see 1 Cor. 2:2), this must be done. But if one finds persons restored in the Spirit (see Gal. 6:1), bearing fruit in him (see Col. 1:10), and asking for the wisdom of heaven, they should participate in the Word who has returned after being incarnate to what he was in the beginning with God (see Jn 1:2).

VIII 44 We deem that it is not vain to have said these things as we scrutinize the meaning of "gospel" and differentiate the sensible aspect of the gospel from its intelligible and spiritual aspect. 45 And now our task is to change the sensible gospel into the spiritual, for what is interpretation of the sensible gospel unless it is transforming it into the spiritual? It is no interpretation at all, or a trivial one, if anyone who chances on the text can be convinced that he comprehends its meaning. 46 But every kind of struggle confronts us when we attempt to reach the depths of the evangelical sense and to discover the naked truth of the things figuratively expressed in it.

47 If one understands the identity of the good things proclaimed as gospel, the apostles announce Jesus. Even though they are said to have announced the resurrection also as a good thing (see Acts 17:18), the resurrection is, in a way, Jesus as well, for Jesus said, "I am the resurrection" (Jn 11:25). But Jesus himself proclaims as gospel to the saints those things that are set aside for the destitute (see Mt. 11:5), summoning them to the divine promises.

48 The divine Scriptures testify concerning the apostles' evangelism and about that of our Savior. David testifies concerning that of the apostles and indeed also of the evangelists, saying, "The Lord will give utterance to those announcing the gospel with great power, the king of the powers of the beloved" (Ps. 67:12–13 LXX

[68:11–12]), teaching at the same time that it is not the arrangement of discourses, manner of delivery, or studied eloquence that carry conviction, but the assistance of a divine power. 49 For this reason Paul says somewhere: "We shall know, not the discourse of those who are puffed up, but power, for the kingdom of God is not in discourse, but in power" (1 Cor. 4:19), and somewhere else: "And my discourse and my proclamation are not in persuasive words of wisdom, but in the demonstration of the Spirit and of power" (1 Cor. 2:4). 50 Testifying to this power, Simon and Cleopas said: "Were not our hearts burning on the road, as he opened the scriptures to us?" (Lk. 24:32).[22] But the apostles, since there are different degrees of power accorded by God to those who speak, had great power, according to David's words: "The Lord will give utterance to those proclaiming the gospel with great power."[23] 51 But Isaiah – saying "How beautiful are the feet of those who announce good things as gospel" (Isa. 52:7) and recognizing the beautiful and opportune proclamation of those who walk on the way of him who said "I am the way" (Jn 14:6) – praises the feet of those who advance through the intelligible way of Jesus Christ and come into God's presence through the door (see Jn 10:9). For such persons, whose feet are beautiful, announce good things, that is, Jesus, as gospel.[24]

IX 52 Do not be astonished at our having understood a plural term as a proclamation of Jesus. When we understand the things to which the terms for the Son correspond, we shall realize that Jesus is, in a way, many "good things" which they whose feet are beautiful announce as gospel.

53 One good thing is life, and Jesus is life (see Jn 14:6). Another good thing is the "light of the world" (see Jn 8:12), a light which is the "true light" (Jn 1:9) and the "light of men" (Jn 1:4), all of which the Son of God is said to be.

In terms of aspect,[25] "truth" is still another good thing alongside "life" and "light," and yet a fourth is the "way" which leads to truth, all of which the Savior teaches us that he is by saying "I am the way, and the truth, and the life" (Jn 14:6).

54 And how is not a good thing when someone who is dead shakes off the dust and rises again, something accomplished by the Lord who is the resurrection, for he says "I am the resurrection" (Jn 11:25)?

And is not the door through which one enters high blessedness also a good thing, and Christ says "I am the door" (Jn 10:9).

55 What is to be said about wisdom, whom "the Lord created in the beginning of his ways for the purpose of his works" (Prov. 8:22),

in whom her Father rejoiced, delighted by her highly variegated intelligible beauty, seen only by intelligible eyes, which summons to heavenly love one who meditates the divine beauty? For the "wisdom of God" (see 1 Cor. 1:24) is a good thing that, along with all the above good things, those whose feet are beautiful announce as gospel.

56 We must also count the "power of God" (see 1 Cor. 1:24), which is Christ, as an eighth good thing.

57 But God the Word who is with the Father of the universe must not be passed over in silence, for this good thing is inferior to none.

Therefore blessed are they who receive such good things, obtaining them from those evangelists whose feet are beautiful.

58 However, if someone is one of those Corinthians among whom Paul chose to know nothing except Jesus Christ and him crucified (see 1 Cor. 2:2), he obtains, when he learns about him, the one who became man for our sakes. This enables such a man to be "in the beginning" of good things, becoming a man of God by virtue of the man Jesus and dying to sin by virtue of his death, for Jesus is the one who "in that he died, died to sin once and for all." 59 But by virtue of his life – since Jesus "in that he lives, lives to God" (Rom. 6:10) – everyone conformed to his resurrection receives the ability to live to God.

But who will doubt that justice itself is a good thing, along with sanctification itself and redemption itself? These very things those who announce Jesus as gospel announce as gospel, saying that he has become for us justice from God and wisdom, sanctification, and redemption (1 Cor. 1:30).

X 60 It is possible from these countless Scriptural references to him to demonstrate how Jesus is a multitude of good things and to guess at things not contained in Scripture that subsist in him in whom the fullness of the godhead was well pleased to dwell bodily (see Col. 1:19; 2:9). 61 Why do I say "in Scripture" when John says concerning the whole world: "I do not think that the world itself could contain the books written" (Jn 21:25)?

62 It is therefore the same thing to say that the apostles announce the Savior as gospel and that they announce good things as gospel. Jesus is indeed the one who receives the ability to be good things from the good Father, so that everyone who receives Jesus or who receives good things through him finds himself in the midst of good things.

63   The apostles, whose feet are beautiful, and those who emulate them would not be able to announce good things as gospel if Jesus had not first been announced to them as gospel, as Isaiah says:

> I, the one speaking, am present with you as a season upon the mountains, as the feet of one who announces peace as gospel, as the one announcing good things as gospel, because I shall make your salvation heard, saying "Zion, your God will reign."
>
> (Isa. 52:6–7)

64   What are the mountains on which he avows to be present unless they are those who are inferior to none of the loftiest and greatest things upon earth? Such must be sought by servants adequate to the new covenant (see 2 Cor. 3:6), so that they may keep the commandment that says: "Go up to a lofty mountain, you who announce the gospel to Zion, lift your voice with strength, you who announce the gospel to Jerusalem" (Isa. 40:9).
65   It is not surprising that Jesus announces good things as gospel to those who are going to announce good things as gospel, because they do not differ from him, for the Son of God announces himself to those who are capable of understanding him without intermediaries. But he who climbs the mountains and announces good things as gospel to them – after being instructed by the good Father who makes the sun rise upon the evil and the good and rain fall on the just and the unjust (Mt. 5:45) – does not despise those whose souls are destitute. 66   For to them he announces the gospel, as he himself testifies when he takes Isaiah and reads, "The Spirit of the Lord is upon me, because he has anointed me to announce the gospel to the destitute. He has sent me to proclaim release to the captives and renewal of sight to the blind." Closing the book, and handing it back to the assistant, he sat down and, while all were looking intently at him, he said: "Today this scripture is fulfilled in your ears" (Lk. 4:18–21; see Isa. 61:1–2 and 58:6).
XI 67   One must know that every good deed done for Jesus is included in such a great gospel. An example is the action of the woman who had once done evil deeds but had repented. By authentically abandoning vice she was empowered to pour perfume on Jesus (see Lk. 7:37) and to produce throughout the house an odor which all in it could perceive (see Jn 12:3). 68   Therefore it is written: "Wherever, among all nations, this gospel is proclaimed,

what she has done shall also be spoken of in memory of her" (see Mt. 26:13).

It is evident that things accomplished for those who are his disciples apply to Jesus, for in referring to cases where persons have received good treatment, he says to those responsible: "What you have done for these, you have done for me" (Mt. 25:40). Thus every good deed we achieve for a neighbor is noted in the gospel, namely the one inscribed on tablets in heaven[26] and read by all who have been made worthy of the knowledge of all things.

69   But, by the same token, the sins committed against Jesus are a part of the gospel in order to denounce those who have committed them. 70   Judas's betrayal and the cry of the impious people saying "Remove such a one from the earth" (Acts 22:22) and "Crucify, crucify him" (Jn 19:15), the mockery of those who crowned him with thorns (see Mt. 27:29) and similar deeds are included in the gospels. 71   Consequently, we must understand that every betrayal of Jesus' followers amounts to a betrayal of Jesus. Thus he said to Saul, while still persecuting, "Saul, Saul, why are you persecuting me?" and "I am Jesus whom you are persecuting" (Acts 9:4–5). 72 Who are those who have thorns, with which they derisively crown Jesus? Those who are stuffed by the cares, the wealth, and the pleasures of life so that, after they have received the word of God, they do not reach maturity (see Lk. 8:14). 73   Therefore we ourselves must be on guard not to be recorded among those who crown Jesus with their own thorns and to be read as such by those rational and holy ones who learn, by and through all things, how Jesus is anointed with myrrh, entertained at dinner and glorified, but also how he is dishonored, derided, and beaten.

74   This discussion is necessary to show how our good deeds and the sins of those who stumble are included in the gospel, either for life eternal or for eternal infamy and shame (see Dan. 12:2).

XII 75   But if there are, among men, some who have been honored with the ministry of evangelists and if Jesus himself announces good things as gospel and announces the gospel to the poor, it is not necessary to exclude from being evangelists those angels who have been made spirits by God and the servants of the Father of the universe who are flames of fire (see Heb. 1:7 and Ps. 103:4 [104:4]).

76   Thus it is actually an angel who stands before the shepherds and, as he makes glory shine about them, says: "Do not be afraid, for see, I announce to you as gospel great joy which shall be to all the people, for a Savior had been born for you today, who is Christ

the Lord, in the city of David" (Lk. 2:9–11). Since men did not yet understand the mystery of the gospel, greater beings, God's heavenly host, say in praise of God: "Glory to God in the highest places and on earth peace to men with whom he is well pleased" (Lk. 2:14). 77   And when they had said this, the angels departed from the shepherds into heaven, leaving it for us to understand how the "joy" announced as gospel to us through the birth of Christ is "glory" "to God in the highest places" when those who had been humbled to the ground have turned back to their rest (see Ps. 114:7 [116:7]) since they are going to glorify God through Christ in the highest places.[27] 78   But the angels also marvel at the peace that exists through Christ on the earth, this place of warfare, to which Lucifer, who rises at dawn, fell from heaven (see Isa. 14:12) so as to be crushed by Jesus.

XIII 79   In addition to what I have just said, this must be known about the gospel: it belongs primarily to Jesus Christ, the head of the whole body of the saved, as Mark says: "The beginning of the gospel of Jesus Christ" (Mk. 1:1), but that it also belongs to the apostles, for Paul says: "According to my gospel" (Rom. 2:16). 80   But the beginning of the gospel (for it has magnitude, including a beginning, a continuation, a middle and an end) is either the whole Old Testament, of which John is the type, or, by virtue of the connection between the Old and the New, it is the end of the Old represented by John.

81   Mark himself says:

> The beginning of the gospel of Jesus Christ, as it was written in Isaiah the prophet "See, I send my messenger [angel][28] before my face, who shall prepare my way. The voice of one crying in the wilderness 'Prepare the way of the Lord, make his paths straight.'"
>
> (Mk. 1:1–3)

82   Therefore it shocks me how the heterodox can attach the two Testaments respectively to two gods,[29] since they are reproved by no less an authority than this text itself.

For how could he be the beginning of the gospel, as they suppose, if John belonged to a different god, a man belonging to the demiurge and ignorant, by their account, of the new divinity?

XIV 83   The angels are entrusted with an evangelizing ministry not limited to just one announcement to shepherds. Thus, at the end-time, an angel flying through the air, having a gospel, will announce the gospel to every nation, because the good Father will not entirely abandon those who have fallen away from him. 84 Therefore John the Son of Zebedee says in Revelation:

> And I saw an angel flying in the midst of heaven, having an eternal gospel to announce as gospel to those left on the earth, and to every nation, tribe, language and people, saying in a loud voice "Fear God and give him glory, because the hour of his judgment has arrived, and worship him who made heaven and earth, the sea and the springs of waters."
>
> (Rev. 14:6–7)

XV 85 We have posited that that entire Old Testament, symbolized by the name of John, is, according to one explanation, the beginning of the gospel. In order to show that this explanation is not without warrant, we appropriate from Acts the passage concerning Philip and the eunuch of the queen of the Ethiopians. It says, "Philip, beginning with the scripture from Isaiah, 'As a sheep is led to the slaughter, and as a lamb is dumb before its shearers,' announced the Lord Jesus as gospel to him" (Acts 8:32). How could he have announced Jesus as gospel by beginning with the prophet, if Isaiah did not belong to the beginning of the gospel? 86 We are now in a position to confirm what we have already said about all of divine Scripture's being a gospel: if anyone who evangelizes "announces good things as gospel," and if all those who preceded Christ's bodily presence announce the one who is, as we have shown, "good things," in one way or another the discourses of all of them are part of the gospel.

87 Since what is called the gospel has been spoken of in the whole world (see Mk. 16:15), we can infer that it has been announced in the whole world, not, that is, this earthly place alone, but in the entire system of heaven (or heavens) and earth.

88 But why should we delay any longer discussing the meaning of "gospel"? What we have said suffices and those not lacking in skill can, along the same lines, gather similar passages from the Scripture so as to see the real glory of the good things in Jesus Christ according to the gospel ministered by men and angels, and also, I suppose, by principalities, powers, thrones, dominations, and every name that is named not only in this age but also in the age to come (see Eph. 1:21), since it is ministered by Christ himself. We shall therefore stop our introduction at this point.

89   We now ask God to assist us through Christ in the Holy Spirit to open up the mystical sense hidden as a treasure in the text.

In the beginning . . .

XVI 90   The Greeks are not alone in giving the term "beginning" many meanings.[30] But if one observes how the word is used by taking examples from every side, and if one wishes to understand it by examining carefully for what purpose they are employed in each place in Scripture, one will find that it has multiple meanings even in divine discourse.

91   One of these meanings refers to a commencement, as in the beginning of a road or distance, which is evident in "The beginning of the good way is to do just things" (Pr. 16:7 LXX). Because the "good way" is very long, it must be understood that the first things involve practical life, the very thing proposed by "do just things." The remainder is contemplation,[31] whose issue and purpose is, I think, in the so-called "restoration"[32] (see Acts 3:21), when no enemy will remain – if "For he must reign until he puts all his enemies under his feet, but the last enemy to be destroyed is death" (1 Cor. 15:25) is actually true. **92**   Then there will be one activity, the apprehension of God, for those who have come to be with God through the Word who is with God. Thus, by being transformed by knowledge of the Father (see Gal. 4:19), just as now only the Son knows the Father, they will all become "sons" in the strict sense of the word. **93**   If one should investigate diligently when it will happen that those will actually know the Father to whom the Son, who has known the Father, reveals him (see Mt. 11:17) and when it will happen that he will see who now sees what he sees "through a mirror in a enigma" (1 Cor. 13:12), not yet knowing "as he ought to know" (1 Cor. 8:12), he would not be mistaken in saying that no one, should he even be an apostle or prophet, has seen the Father, except whenever they have become one, as the Son and the Father are One (see Jn 17:21).

94   If it appears that, in the process of ascertaining one sense of "beginning," we have digressed from our subject, it must be shown that the digression is necessary and useful for our subject.

If "beginning" is understood as a commencement of a road and of a distance – "The beginning of the good way is doing just things" (Prov. 16:7 LXX) – it is possible to see if every good way somehow has "doing just things" as its beginning, if it has contemplation as a further stage, and, in that case, what sort of contemplation.

XVII 95 There is also a "beginning" in the sense of coming into existence attested in "In the beginning God made the heaven and the earth" (Gen. 1:1). I believe that this sense is indicated even more clearly in Job where it says: "This is the beginning of the Lord's fashioning, made as a sport for his angels" (Job 17:19 LXX).

96 Someone might assume that "heaven and earth" were made "in the beginning" of those things that existed when the world came to be, but it is better to say, as in our second citation, that of the many things that came to be in bodies, the first of those in the body was the so-called "dragon," also named somewhere "great whale," which the Lord subdued (see Job 3:8; 2 Pet. 2:4).

97 And we must ask if, since the saints in blessedness live an entirely immaterial and incorporeal life, the so-called "dragon" deserved, by falling away from pure life, to be the first to be attached to matter and a body, so that for this reason the Lord, speaking oracularly through the whirlwind and clouds, said, "This is the beginning of the Lord's fashioning, made as a sport for his angels."

98 Possibly the dragon is not in an absolute sense the beginning of the Lord's fashioning, but since many beings were created in the body as a sport for the angels, he is the beginning of those things only, leaving open the possibility that some others are in the body for a different purpose. For the soul of the sun is in a body,[33] and so is all of creation, concerning which the Apostle says: "All creation groans and is in birth pangs until now" (Rom. 8:22).

99 And doubtless it is for this latter purpose that "the creation has been subject to vanity, not willingly, but through the one who subjected it in hope" (Rom. 8:20), since bodies and bodily actions, which are necessary for one in the body, are vain * * * The one who is in the body does not willingly do the things of the body, therefore the creation was unwillingly subjected to vanity.

100 The one who unwillingly does the deeds of the body does what he does through hope, as if we should say that Paul wished "to remain in the flesh" not willingly but through hope. Even though he preferred, for his own sake, "to be dissolved and to be with Christ," it was not irrational "to remain in the flesh" (see Phil. 1:23–4) in order to be of benefit to others and to further, not only his own progress in things hoped for, but the progress of those whom he benefited.

101 This will enable us to grasp the meaning of a "beginning" of coming into existence and what is said by Wisdom in Proverbs: "God created me in the beginning of his way for his work" (Prov.

8:22). But this passage, "God created me the beginning of his way," can also refer to our first meaning, "beginning" as of a road.

102   But it is not absurd to say that the God of the Universe is evidently a beginning [or principle] on the grounds that because the Father is the beginning of the Son, the artisan[34] of the things fashioned, God is also, in an absolute sense, the beginning of existing things. This is proved by "in the beginning was the Word," understanding the Word as the Son, so that as a result of his being in the Father, he is said to be "in the beginning."

103   Third is the sense of "beginning from which," as in beginning from underlying matter. This is proposed by those who believe that matter is ingenerate,[35] but not by us who believe that God made the things that are from things that are not, as the mother of the seven martyrs in Maccabees (2 Mac. 7:28) and as the angel of repentance in Shepherd taught (Hermas, Mand. 1,1; Vis. 1.1.6).[36]

104   In addition a principle [beginning] is that in accordance with which something is, that is, in accordance with its form. So, if indeed the first-born of all creation is "the image of the invisible God" (Col. 1:15), the Father is his principle. But similarly Christ is the form of those who have come to be in accordance with the image of God. 105   Therefore, if men are created "according to the image" (see Gen. 1:26–7), the image itself is "according to the Father." The principle in accordance with which Christ is is the Father, but the principle in accordance with which human beings are is Christ, because they have come to be not in accordance with the one of whom he is the image, but in accordance with the image. "In the beginning was the Word" is consistent with the same example.[37]

XVIII 106   There is also a "principle" of instruction according to which we say that the letters [= elements] are the principle of writing. According to this meaning the Apostle says: "Even though by this time you ought to be teachers, you need someone to teach you what are the elementary principles of the oracles of God" (Heb. 5:12). 107   "Principle" of instruction can be regarded in two ways, by nature, and as it relates to us. If we should say that Christ's principle by nature is divinity, in relation to us – who, because of his grandeur, cannot begin with the truth concerning him – that principle is his humanity. This is why "Jesus Christ," and he "crucified" (see 1 Cor. 2:2), is proclaimed to infants (see 1 Cor. 3:1). Accordingly it is possible to say that Christ is a principle of instruction by nature, in so far as he is the wisdom and power of God (see 1 Cor. 1:24), but in relation to us, "the Word became flesh" so as to make his dwelling among us (see Jn 1:14), since only thus are we initially capable of receiving him. 108 And indeed for this reason he is not just the first-born of all creation but "Adam," which is interpreted "man". That he is Adam, Paul says in "the last Adam is a life-giving spirit" (1 Cor. 15:45).

There is also a "principle" of an action, in which action there is a certain end which follows from the principle. And consider if wisdom, the beginning of God's deeds, can be understood to be a principle in this sense.

XIX 109 Since in this discussion there are so many meanings included in "beginning," we shall investigate in which sense we ought to apprehend "In the beginning was the Word."

It is obvious that it does not refer to the commencement of a road or of a distance, and it is clear enough that it does not refer to coming into existence. 110 Nonetheless, it may refer to the principle "by which" a thing is as it is, since God "commanded and they were created" (Ps. 148:5). For Christ is in some way the artisan by whom the Father says "Let there be light" (Gen. 1:3) and "Let a firmament come into existence" (Gen. 1:6). 111 As "beginning," Christ is an artisan, in as much as he is Wisdom; because he is Wisdom, he is called "beginning." For Wisdom says in Solomon: "God created me, the beginning of his ways, for his work" (Prov. 8:22) so that "in the beginning" – that is, "in wisdom" – "was the Word." This is because "Wisdom" is understood as the structure of a theoretical consideration of the universe and of designs by which it is constituted, and "Word" is understood as the communication to rational beings of things theoretically considered.[38]

112 And it is not surprising if, as I have already said, the Savior being many conceivable good things, he should have in him some first, some second, and some third. John accordingly bore witness, saying of the Word: "that which came to be in him was life" (Jn 1:4). Life therefore came to be in the Word, and the Word is none other than Christ, God the Word, who is with the Father, through whom all things came to be, nor was life anything other than the Son of God, as it says, "I am the way, and the truth, and the life" (Jn 14:6). Just as life came to be in the Word, so the Word was in the beginning.

113 Let us determine if it is possible to interpret "In the beginning was the Word" in terms of this meaning: that all things came to be according to Wisdom and according to the patterns of the system of designs[39] in the Word.

114   For I think that, just as a house or a ship is built or constructed according to architectural patterns, so that the ship and the house have as a principle the patterns and rational formulas[40] of the builder, so everything came into existence according to rational formulas of future things made plain in advance in wisdom by God "For he made all things in wisdom" (Ps. 103:24 [104:24]).

115   And it must be said that God, having, so to speak,[41] created a living Wisdom, delegated it to supply to beings and to matter, from the patterns included in it, structure, shape and, I conjecture, even existence.

116   It is not difficult to say that the Son of God is more or less the principle [= beginning] of existing things who says, "I am the beginning and the end, the alpha and the omega, the first and the last" (Rev. 22:13). But it is necessary to know that he is not a principle according to all his titles. 117   For how can he be a principle in so far as he is life, the life that came to be in the Word (see Jn 1:4), which is evidently its principle? And it is clearer still that the "first-born from the dead" (Col. 1:18) cannot be a principle.[42]

118   And if we studiously examine each of his aspects, he is principle only in so far as he is Wisdom, not in so far as he is Word, since the Word was "in the beginning," so that one may boldly say that "beginning" is the oldest of all the attributes revealed by the titles of the first-born of all creation.

XX 119   God is therefore entirely one and simple, but the Savior, on account of the many –since God "designated" him "in advance as a propitiation" (Rom. 3:25) and first-fruits of all creation – has become many and is doubtless all things that every created being, capable of liberation, has need of from him.

120   Therefore he became the light of men, because men darkened by evil required the light shining in the darkness and not overcome by the darkness (see Jn 1:5), but, if men had not been in darkness, he would not have become the light of men.

121   Something similar should be understood concerning his being the first-born from the dead. For if, hypothetically, the woman had not been deceived and Adam had not fallen, the man created for incorruptibility would have grasped that incorruptibility, Christ would not have gone down "to the dust of death" (Ps. 21:16 [22:15]) or died, since that sin on account of which he had to die out of love of humanity[43] would not have existed, and, if Christ had not done those things, he would not have been "the first-born from the dead."

122   It should be investigated if he would not have become a shepherd if man were not comparable to "the beasts without understanding nor made similar to them" (Ps. 48:13 [49:12]). For if "God preserves men and beasts" (Ps. 35:7 [36:6]), he preserves the beasts whom he preserves by providing a shepherd to those who cannot receive a king.

123   Therefore gathering together the Son's titles, one must investigate which of them came into existence afterwards, since, had the saints remained in their original blessedness, he would not have become so many things. Indeed he would have remained Wisdom alone, or Word, or Life, certainly Truth, but not any of the others that he assumed for our sake.

124   And blessed are those requiring the Son of God who have become such that they need him no longer as a physician healing the infirm, as a shepherd or as a redeemer, but as Wisdom, Word, and Justice, or something else for those who, by their perfection, are able to receive the best from him.

This will suffice for "In the beginning."

... was the Word.

XXI 125   Let us look very carefully at what "Word" is.

Reflecting on the things said about Christ by certain persons wishing to believe in him, I have often been astonished at how they rush silently past the greater part of the countless names ascribed to our Savior. But even if one should recall one such name at some point, they imagine that the expression is used not in its proper sense, but figuratively. They do not pause except for the one title, "Word" – as if, as far as they were concerned, the Christ of God were simply "Word" – and they do not think that "Word" requires interpretation as other names do.

126   What astonishes me with regard to the many – I will make myself clearer – is this. The Son of God says somewhere, "I am the light of the world" (Jn 8:12), and in other places, "I am the resurrection" (Jn 11:25), and again, "I am the way, and the truth, and the life" (Jn 14:6); it is written "I am the door" (Jn 10:9) and he also says, "I am the good shepherd" (Jn 10:11); and when the Samaritans said to him, "We know that the Messiah is coming, who is called Christ, and when that one comes, he shall announce all things to us," he answered, "I, the one speaking to you, am he" (Jn 4:25–6). 127   Besides these, when he washed the disciples' feet, he confessed himself their teacher and lord when he said:

"You call me 'teacher' and 'lord' and you speak well, for so I am" (Jn 13:13). **128** But he clearly proclaims himself to be the Son of God when he says, "Do you say concerning him whom the Father has sanctified and sent to the world 'You blaspheme' because I said 'I am the Son of God'?" (Jn 10:36) and "Father, my hour has come, glorify your son, so that your son may glorify you" (Jn 17:1). **129** We find him also proclaiming himself king, as when, in response to Pilate's question "Are you the king of the Jews?" he says, "My kingdom is not of this world, if my kingdom were of this world, my followers would put up a struggle, so that I might not be betrayed to the Jews, but now my kingdom is not from here" (Jn 18:33, 36). **130** We also read, "I am the true vine, and my Father is the vinedresser" (Jn 15:1), and again, "I am the vine, you are the branches" (Jn 15:5). **131** One could add to these, "I am the bread of life," and again, "I am the living bread, which came down from heaven" (Jn 6:35, 51), and "giving life to the world" (Jn 6:33).

These are citations from the gospel that come to mind at the present time, since the Son of Man says them about himself.

XXII **132** But also in the Revelation to John he says, "I am the first and last and the living one, who was dead and behold I am alive for ever and ever" (Rev. 1:17–18), and again, "I have become the alpha and the omega, the first and the last, the beginning and the end" (Rev. 22:13).

133 There are also no few comparable passages in the holy books which the attentive reader could find in the prophets, like "chosen arrow." And he calls himself "servant of God" and "light of the nations." **134** For Isaiah says,

> He has called me from my mother's womb and he has made my mouth like a sharp sword, he has hidden me under the shelter of his hand, he has placed me as a chosen arrow and has hidden me in his quiver and he has said to me: "You are my servant, Israel, and in you I shall be glorified."
>
> (see Isa. 49:1–3)

135 And shortly later,

> And God will be strength for me. And he said to me: "This is a great thing for you, to be called my servant, to establish the gates of Jacob, and to gather again the dispersion of

Israel, behold, I have placed you as a light of the nations, so
that you may be for salvation to the end of the earth."

(Isa. 49:5–6)

But also in Jeremiah he is compared to a lamb in these words: "I am
like an innocent lamb led to the slaughter" (Jer. 11:19).

136   He thus says these, and other similar things, about himself,
but it is also possible from the gospels, from the apostles and from
the prophets to collect thousands of such titles, by which the Son of
God is addressed, either by the gospel writers setting forth their
own understanding about who he was, or the apostles glorifying
him by what they had learned about him, or by the prophets
proclaiming in advance his future arrival and announcing things
concerning him with diverse terms.

137   Thus John announced him as "Lamb of God," saying,
"Behold the Lamb of God, who takes away the sin of the world" (Jn
1:29) and as "man" in: "This is he about whom I said that after me
comes a man who was before me, because he was prior to me, and I
did not know him" (Jn 1:30–1).

138   In the catholic epistle John says that he is an "advocate" for our
souls with the Father, saying, "If any one sins, we have an advocate
with the Father, Jesus Christ the righteous" (1 Jn 2:1). 139   He
adds, "and he is the propitiation for our sins" (1 Jn 2:2), which Paul
takes up in similar terms when he calls him a "propitiatory sacrifice,"
saying, "Whom God has foreordained as a propitiatory sacrifice
through faith in his blood for the remission of sins already committed
during God's time of forbearance" (Rom. 3:25).

140   He is also proclaimed, according to Paul, to be wisdom and
power, as it says in Corinthians that Christ is the power and the
wisdom of God (see 1 Cor. 1:24), and, in addition to these, that he
is "sanctification" and "redemption" (1 Cor. 1:30), for it says, "Who
became for us from God wisdom, justice, sanctification, and
redemption."

141   But he also teaches us that he is the great high priest, writing
to the Hebrews: "Having therefore a great high priest who has
passed through the heavens, Jesus the Son of God, let us be firm in
our confession" (Heb. 4:14).

XXIII 142   Besides these, the prophets also address him by other
names. In his blessing of his sons, Jacob called him Judah:

Judah, may your brothers praise you, your hands are on the
back of your enemies, Judah, lion's whelp, you have arisen,

my son, from a shoot, falling down you have fallen asleep
like a lion, and like a whelp, who shall awaken him?

(Gen. 49:8–9)

* * * It is not possible at this time to explain in detail how the
things said to Judah apply to Christ. 143 But an objection that
may reasonably be offered to "A ruler shall not be lacking from
Judah and a leader from his loins" shall be resolved more appropriately in another context.

144 Isaiah knows that Christ is called "Jacob" and "Israel" when
he says:

> Jacob, my servant, I shall assist him, Israel, my chosen, my
> soul has received him. He shall proclaim judgment to the
> nations. He shall not contend or cry out, nor shall his voice
> be heard in the streets. He shall not break a bruised reed
> nor quench a smoking flax, until he produces judgment
> from victory, and in his name shall the nations hope.

(Isa. 42, 1–4, LXX)

145 Matthew shows clearly in the gospel that it is Christ
concerning whom these things are prophesied, partially citing the
passage, "That the saying might be fulfilled, 'He shall not contend
or cry out,'" etc. (Mt. 12:17–19).

146 Christ is also called "David," as when Ezekiel, prophesying to
the shepherds, offers, in the person[44] of God, "I shall raise up my
servant David, who shall shepherd them" (Ez. 34:23), for David the
Patriarch will not arise in order to shepherd the saints, but Christ.

147 Isaiah also calls Christ "branch" and "flower" in

> A branch shall arise from the root of Jesse, and a flower
> shall come up from the root and the spirit of the Lord shall
> rest upon him, the spirit of wisdom and understanding, the
> spirit of counsel and strength, the spirit of knowledge and
> piety, and he shall be full of the spirit of the fear of the
> Lord.

(Isa. 11:1–3 LXX)

148 And our Lord is thus called "stone" in the Psalms: "The stone
which the builders rejected, that one has become the keystone. This
was on the Lord's part, and it was marvelous in our eyes" (Ps.
117:22–3 [118:22–3]).149 Luke shows in his gospel and in Acts

that the stone is none other than Christ; in the gospel: "Have you not read, 'The stone which the builders rejected, that one has become the keystone'? All who fall on that stone shall be crushed, and he on whom that stone falls will be smashed" (Lk. 20:18; Mt. 21:42–4). 150   In Acts Luke writes: "This is the stone which was rejected by you builders, which has become the keystone" (Acts 4:11).

In fact one of the names attributed to the Savior – not one of those spoken by him but registered by John – is also "The Word which was in the beginning next to God, God the Word" (see Jn 1:1).

XXIV 151   It is worthwhile to attend to those who dismiss so many of the names and employ this one as their preferred name. They seek explanations for the others, if one mentions them to them, but imagine in this case that it is clear just what "Word" means when applied to the Son of God, especially since they cease-lessly employ "My heart has belched a good word" (Ps. 44:2 [45:1]). They suppose that the Son of God is a fatherly utterance expressed, as it were, in syllables, and so if we examine their position precisely, it does not accord him a distinct existence and does not clearly define his essence.[45] 152   It is indeed impossible, at the outset, to understand how a word proclaimed can be a son. Let them proclaim to us as God the Word a word having its own life; either it is not distinguished from the Father, and for this reason does not have a distinct existence and cannot be a son, or it is so distinguished and is endowed with its own essence.[46]

153   This must then be said. Just as, with each of the above names, we must disclose the meaning of the term employed in that title and we must also provide a demonstration of how the Son of God can be called by that name, the same procedure is required when "Word" is used as a name. 154   What an absurdity it is not to halt at the term itself in each other case – but to seek, for example, how we must allow him to be a "door" and how he is a "vine" and why he is a "way" – but to abandon his procedure in one case alone, when he is called "Word"!

155   In order to give better consideration to a very difficult matter – what is to be said about the Son's being the Word of God – we must start with the names for him that we have already put forward. 156   We are aware that some will consider such an exer-cise is utterly beyond the scope of our concern. But, for someone paying attention, it will be quite germane to our subject to examine closely the senses according to which the names are given and an

understanding of the objects of the names given will in turn be profitable.

157   Moreover, once we have taken up theology about the Savior, we must necessarily understand him fully, as far as an attentive examination makes possible, not just as Word, but as the rest of his titles.

XXV 158   He said that he was "the light of the world" (Jn 8:12, 9:5), and we must examine similar titles, since it seems to us that some are not just similar, but the same. 159   There are "the light of men," "true light," and "light of the nations." He is "light of men" at the beginning of the present gospel, for it says, "That which came into being, in it was life, and the life was the light of men, and the light shines in darkness, and the darkness has not overwhelmed it" (Jn 1:4–5). Farther on in the same passage it is recorded: "He was the true light, who enlightens every man, coming into the world" (Jn 1:9). "Light of the nations" is found in Isaiah, as we have already said in citing, "Behold, I have placed you as a light to the nations, so that you may be for salvation to the end of the earth" (Isa. 49:6).

160   The sun is the light of the sensible world and, in turn, it is not appropriate for the moon and the stars to be designated by the same term. 161   But even though they are sensible light, they are said to have come into existence, according to Moses, on the fourth day (Gen, 1:14–16). Because they enlighten the things on earth, they are not the true light, but the Savior is the light of the intelligible world, illuminating those beings that are rational and endowed with a guiding principle, so that their minds may see the things proper for them to see – I speak of the rational souls in the sensible world and any others besides these which together fill the world – to which the Savior tells us he belongs, and, indeed because his role is the most commanding and distinguished, he can be said to be the sun that is the maker of the great day of the Lord (Rev. 16:14). 162   With regard to that day he says to those who participate in his light: "Work while it is day, for the night comes when no one can work. While I am in the world, I am the light of the world" (Jn 9:4–5).

Yet he said to his disciples: "You are the light of the world" (Mt. 5:14) and "Let your light so shine before men" (Mt. 5:16). 163   We understand the bride, the church, and the disciples to be in a position analogous to the moon and the stars. In each case they possess their own proper light acquired from the true sun in order to enlighten those who cannot construct in themselves a source of light. So we call Paul and Peter "the light of the world," but ordinary people who are called into discipleship by them, who are enlightened but cannot enlighten others, are the "world" of which the disciples are the "light of the world."

164   The Savior, being the "light of the world," does not enlighten bodies but, by an incorporeal power, he enlightens the incorporeal mind, so that, just as each of us is enlightened by the sun, we are enabled to see other intelligible things. 165   Just as, when the sun is shining, the ability of the moon and stars to shine is dimmed, those illuminated by Christ and receiving his beams do not require the ministrations of any apostles or prophets or – one must dare to tell the truth – angels, or, I add, any of the greater powers, since they are trained as disciples by the first-begotten light himself. 166   The holy ones ministering to those who do not receive Christ's solar rays supply an enlightenment much inferior to Christ's direct enlightenment to those scarcely able to accept even that enlightenment and be filled by it.

XXVI 167   But possibly Christ, as the light of the world, is the true light in contrast to the sensible, since nothing sensible is true.[47] But it does not follow that, because the sensible is not true, the sensible is false, for the sensible can bear an analogy[48] to the intelligible, for it is not reliable to categorize as false everything that is not true.

168   I investigate whether "the light of the world" is the same as "the light of men" and I think that a greater power is presented by the light when it is proclaimed "the light of the world" than when it is "the light of men," for "world," on one interpretation, is not just "men." 169   And Paul presents the world as something greater and other than men in First Corinthians, saying: "We have become a spectacle to the world and to angels and to men" (1 Cor. 4:9).

170   But do you ask whether, according to one interpretation, "world" is the creation freed "from the bondage of corruption into the liberty of the glory of the children of God" (Rom. 8:21) of which the "earnest expectation waits patiently for the revelation of the sons of God" (Rom. 8:19)? 171   I have added "do you ask" because "I am the light of the world" can be interpreted alongside what Jesus said to the disciples, "You are the light of the world." 172   There are some who presume that those men who are trained as disciples by Jesus, who have become so as a result of rational conduct characterized by a most difficult struggle, are actually better than other created beings so trained, who have become so by

nature. 173   For the toil is great and life is precarious for those in flesh and blood compared with those in an ethereal body. Indeed the luminaries in the heavens, were they to assume earthly bodies, would not pass through the life here without peril and entirely without sin.[49] 174   For "As I and you are one, so may they be one" (Jn 17:21) and "Where I am, there will my servant also be" (Jn 12:26) are clearly recorded concerning men, but concerning the creation it is recorded that it shall be freed "from the bondage of corruption into the liberty of the glory of the children of God." And they add that it does not, if it is liberated, already share in the glory of the children of God. 175   They shall not forbear to mention that the firstborn of all creation became man because of the honor in which he held man above everything else, but he did not become any living thing belonging to heaven. But that which had been fashioned of the second rank, as servant and slave of the knowledge of Jesus, the star appearing in the East (see Mt. 2:2), is either like the rest of the stars, or indeed greater, because it has become the sign of him who is distinguished above all.

176   And if the saints' boast is in afflictions, knowing "that affliction produces endurance, and endurance character, and character hope, but hope is not deceived" (Rom. 5:3–5), an unafflicted creation would not have the same endurance, character, and hope as it does, since "the whole creation was subjected to futility, not willingly, but by him who subjected it in hope" (Rom. 8:20).

177   He who does not dare to ascribe such dignity[50] to man will say, on coming to terms with the issue, that the creation subjected to futility is afflicted and groans even more than those who groan by virtue of being in this tent (2 Cor. 5:4), since it is enslaved to futility for such a long time that a great many human struggles could occur. 178   Why does it do this "unwillingly"? No doubt because it is against its nature to be subjected to futility and not to retain its original status, which it will resume when it is liberated at the destruction of the world and released from the futility of bodies.

179   But since we are speaking about a great issue beyond our subject, let us go back to the beginning: remembering why the Savior is called "the light of the world," "true light," and "light of men." We have, in fact, explained that because of the sensible light of the world he is called "true light" and that "light of the world" is the same as "light of men" or an explanation is expected of how they are not the same. 180   But, necessarily, because of those who have not comprehended that the Word is the Savior, these things are investigated. Thus we are determined, on the one hand, not to halt

arbitrarily at the concept and title "Word" without providing a possible paraphrase and, on the other hand, to furnish an allegorical interpretation of the term "light of the world" and the many other terms we have cited.

XXVII 181 Thus because of his function of enlightening and illuminating the governing faculties of men and all rational beings in general, he is "light of men," "true light," and "light of the world." By the same token, because he makes possible the expulsion of all death and because he produces growth, he is properly called "life," and because those who have really received him are raised again, he is called "resurrection" (Jn 1:25). 182 He is not only making this possible in the present for those who can say "We have been buried together with Christ through baptism" and we have been raised together with him, but much more when someone who has completely expelled all death, even that of the Son, walks "in newness of life" (Rom. 6:4) – "we bear about the death of Jesus everywhere here below in our bodies," when we are extraordinarily assisted, "so that the life of Jesus may be manifest in our bodies" (see 2 Cor. 4:11).

183 But the walk in wisdom, also involving practical activity, of those who are saved in him – a walk which they make by following commentaries on the truth in the divine discourse[51] and by acting in accordance with true justice – enables us to understand how he is the "way" (Jn 14:6), on which way one ought not to take anything, either purse or cloak, and on which it is unnecessary to hold a staff or to have sandals tied on one's feet (see Mt. 10:10). 184 For this way is self-sufficient and requires no provisions, for everyone who journeys on this road needs nothing, since he is dressed in clothing fitting for someone departing for the wedding feast (see Mt. 22:11), and no obstacle can obstruct this way. For, according to Solomon, it is impossible to find the ways of a serpent upon a rock (Prov. 24:54 LXX [30:19]) but I say that no wild beast shall ever be there.[52] 185 Therefore there is no need for a staff on the road which has no trace of adversaries and is inaccessible on account of its hardness – for which reason it is called rock – to those who are evil.

186 The only-begotten is called "truth" because he understands everything about the universe according to the will of the Father with a reason[53] of complete clarity, and, in as much as he is truth, transmits it to each according to his worthiness. 187 If someone asks whether our Savior knows absolutely everything that has been known by the Father according to the depth of the wealth of his wisdom and knowledge (Rom. 11:33) and, on the pretext of glorifying

the Father, will declare that certain things are known by the Father of which the Son is ignorant, so that he does not[54] have a comprehension equal to that of the ingenerate God, he must reflect on the Savior's being Truth. It must also be added that, if truth is perfect, nothing true is beyond its knowledge, so that truth may not be handicapped by things that it does not know, which are, according to persons who think this way, only in the Father. Or let such a person demonstrate that there are things known that do not belong to the category of truth, but are superior to it.[55]

188 It is clear that the pure source of life in the strict sense of the word, unadulterated by anything else, is in the firstborn of all creation. Taking from this source, those who participate in Christ live life truly. As for those who reckon that they live outside him, just as they lack the true light, they lack true life.

189 And since one cannot come to be in the Father without having first ascended from below to the divinity of the Son, from which one can be led to the paternal blessedness, the Savior is presented as "door" (see Jn 10:7).

190 Since he is a lover of humanity,[56] accepting the impulses of souls inclined in any way toward improvement – even if they do not hasten toward the Word, but are like cattle, having a nature that is tame and gentle even if incapable of discursive thought – he becomes the "shepherd" (Jn 10:11), "for God preserves men and beasts" (Ps. 35:7 [36:6]) and Israel and Judah are sown not only with the seed of men but of beasts (Jer. 38:27 LXX [31:27]).

XXVIII 191 After this one ought to inspect first of all the title "Christ" along with "king" so as to understand the difference between them by juxtaposing them. It is said in Psalm 44 that he who beyond his companions had loved justice and hated lawlessness (Ps. 44:8 [45:7]) received his anointing because he pursued justice and hated injustice. This means that he did not receive anointing along with existence as an ordinary property of creation. Anointing is, among generate beings, the symbol of royalty or sometimes priesthood. Is then the royalty of the Son of God something acquired or is it innate? **192** And how is it possible that the firstborn of all creation, without being king already, became king later because he loved justice, even though he is justice (see 1. Cor. 1:30)? Have we not forgotten that he is Christ as a man – understanding him in terms of the soul which, on account of humanity, was disturbed and became afflicted – but that he is king in terms of his divinity?[57] **193** I support this from Psalm 71, where it says: "O God, give your judgment to the king and your justice to the king's son, to judge your people in justice and your poor in judgment" (Ps. 71:1–2 [72:1–2]). Clearly the Psalm, attributed to Solomon, prophesies concerning Christ. 194   It is worthwhile to see how the prophecy prays for judgment to be given by God to a certain king and justice to a certain son of a king. 195   I think therefore that "king" refers to the preeminent nature of the firstborn of all creation, in as much as judgment is given to him on account of his superiority, and "king's son" to the man, whom that nature assumed, formed in accordance with justice and modeled by that nature. 196   And I am led to admit that this is so because the two are united in a single utterance and the remainder of the passage no longer proclaims two such figures, but one. 197   For the Savior has made "the two one" (Eph. 2:14), having indeed made one the first-fruits of the two that were to become one in him before all things. The "two," I say, also concerns men, in so far as each one's soul is blended with the Holy Spirit and each of those who are saved become spiritual.

198   Just as there are some who are herded by Christ, as we have already said, because they are gentle and tame, even if irrational, so there are some who are reigned over by him because they have dedicated themselves more rationally to piety.[58] 199   And there are differences between those who are reigned over; either they are reigned over in a manner that is more mystical, ineffable and worthy of divinity or in an inferior manner. 200   I would say that those who have contemplated things extracorporeal – called "invisible" and "not seen" by Paul (see Col. 1:18; Rom. 1:20; 2 Cor. 4:18) – having, in reason,[59] got beyond everything sensible, are reigned over by the preeminent nature of the only-begotten. But those who have arrived only so far as reason concerning sensible things, and through those sensible things glorify the one who made them, are also reigned over by Christ as they are reigned over by reason.

Let no one stumble over our distinguishing the aspects of the Savior, thinking that we make such distinctions with regard to his essence.[60]

XXIX 201   Even on a superficial view it is clear how our Lord is the teacher and tutor of those who are exerting themselves in piety and a slavemaster of those who "have the spirit of slavery to fear" (Rom. 8:15). But for those who are making progress, hastening toward wisdom and becoming worthy of it – since "the slave does not know what his master wishes" (Jn 15:15) – he does not remain master but has become a friend.[61] 202   He himself teaches this, even though those listening to him were still slaves. He says: "You refer to me as teacher and master and you do well, for I am" (Jn 13:13), but "I no longer call you slaves, for the slave does not know what is the desire of his master, but I say that you are friends" (Jn 15:15) because you have remained steadfast "with me in all my trials" (Lk. 22:28). **203** Therefore those living by fear – fearing that God takes revenge on those who are not good slaves, as we read in Malachi, "If I am the Lord, where is my fear?" (Mal. 1:6) – are slaves of the master who is called their Savior.

204 Through all these the nobility of the Son is not clearly presented, but "You are my son, today I have begotten you" (Ps. 2:7) is said to him by God to whom "today" is eternity.[62] But I consider that there is no evening in God, nor any morning, but time coextensive, so to speak, with his unbegotten and eternal life, in which the Son was begotten, so that there is no identifiable beginning to his generation nor any date for it.

XXX 205 To be discussed in addition to the above is how the Son is the "true vine" (Jn 15:1). This will be clear to those who understand in a way worthy of the prophetic grace the words "wine that gladdens the heart of man" (Ps. 103:15 [104:15]). **206** If the heart is our discursive intellect, what gladdens it is the most palatable Word, withdrawing it from human concerns, making it divinely inspired and drunk with a drunkenness which is not irrational but divine, the one with which Joseph made drunk his brothers (see Gen. 43:34), so that it is reasonable for the vine that produces the wine that gladdens the heart of man to be the "true vine." It is "true" because it has truth as a fruit and the disciples as branches, imitating him and themselves bearing the truth as fruit. **207** To establish the difference between bread and vine involves toil, since it says not only that he is the vine, but that he is the bread of life (Jn 6:48). **208** Bread nourishes and strengthens and is said to support the heart of man, but wine sweetens, gladdens, and relaxes. See if, in the same way, on the one hand, ethical disciplines, which maintain life in the one who learns and practices them, are the bread of life; one would not refer to them as the fruit of the vine. On the other hand, things that gladden and produce enthusiasm, unspeakable and mystical acts of contemplation, arise for those who delight in the Lord and desire not just to be nourished but also to be delighted. These, coming from the true vine, are called "wine."

XXXI 209 In addition to these, how he is recorded as "the first and the last" (Rev. 22:13) in the Apocalypse must be explained, being first is different from being "alpha" and "beginning," and being last is not the same as "omega" and "end."

210   I therefore believe that rational beings are characterized by
many forms, and a certain one is first, another second, another third,
and so on to the last. 211   And to say accurately who is the first
and who the second, and who is truly the third and so on to reach
the final one is not at all humanly possible, but is beyond our
nature. But we shall attempt to stay and discuss this topic in so far
as we are able.
212   There are gods of whom God is God, as the prophets say:
"Confess the God of gods" (Ps. 135:2 [136:2]) and "The God of
gods, the Lord, has spoken, he has summoned the earth" (Ps. 49:1
[50:1]). God, according to the gospel, "is not a god of the dead, but
of the living" (Mt. 22:32), and the living are the gods of whom God
is God. 213   Even the Apostle, writing in a letter to the
Corinthians, "Just as there are many gods and many lords," has, in
accordance with the prophetic writings, understood the term "gods"
as referring to existing beings.
214   There are, besides the gods, of whom God is God, certain
others who are called "thrones" and others called "dominions, principalities and powers" (see Col. 1:16) and others besides them.⁶³
215   On account of "above every name which is named not just in
this age but in the age to come" (Eph. 1:20), it must be believed
that there are other rational beings besides these which we are not
at all accustomed to naming, of which one is the race which the
Hebrew called "Sabai," from which "Sabaoth" is formed, which
means their ruler, who is none other than God.⁶⁴ After all these
comes man, a mortal rational being.
216   Therefore the God of the universe has created a certain
rational race first in honor, which, I think, are those called "gods" –
the second, let us for the present call "thrones," and the third
doubtless "dominions." Thus one must descend rationally to the last
rational being, which happens, indeed, to be none other than man.
217   Therefore the Savior, in a more divine manner than Paul, has
become "all things to all" so that "he might gain" or perfect "all"
(see 1 Cor. 9:22), and clearly he has become a man for men and an
angel for angels. 218   No believer doubts his having become a
man. We are convinced that he became an angel on observing the
appearances and words of angels, when he appears with the power of
angels in certain places in Scripture when angels are speaking, as in
"An angel of the Lord appeared in the fire of a bush of flame and
said 'I am the God of Abraham, Isaac, and Jacob'" (Ex. 3:2). And
also Isaiah said, "His name shall be called 'Angel of Great Counsel'"
(Isa. 9:6 LXX).⁶⁵ 219   The Savior is therefore "first and last" not

because he is the extremes with nothing in between, but in order to show that he has become all things. It is a question whether man is the "last" or those beings called infernal, to which all or some of the demons belong.[66] 220　It should be investigated in what circumstances the Savior said through the prophet David, "And I have become like a man without assistance, free among the dead" (Ps. 87:5 [88:4–5]), just as he was superior to men by virtue of his virgin birth and the rest of his life in prodigies, so, among the dead, he was superior by being the only free one there, for his soul was not abandoned in Hades (see Acts 2:27; Ps. 15:10 [16:10]). So therefore he is "the first and the last."

221　If there are letters of God, as there are, which the saints read, saying that they are reading in the tablets of heaven,[67] these letters, which exist so that heavenly things may be read through them, are concepts about the Son of God dispersed all the way from alpha through omega (see Rev. 1:8). 222　Again he is both the beginning and end, but he is not the same with respect to various aspects. For he is beginning, as we have learned in Proverbs, in so far as he is Wisdom, as is thus written: "God created me, the beginning of his ways, for his work" (Prov. 8:22). But in so far as he is Word, he is not beginning, for "In the beginning was the Word" (Jn 1:1). 223　His aspects then have a beginning and a second after that, a third and so on to the end, as if he were to say, "I am beginning in so far as I am wisdom," but second, if such were the case, "in so far as I am invisible", and third, "in so far as I am life" since "that which came to be in him was life" (Jn 1:4).

224　If someone has the capacity to see, by investigating the sense of Scripture, he will indeed find much concerning [these titles'] order and purpose, but I do not think he will find everything. But it is most evident "beginning" and "end" seem, by ordinary usage, to refer to a unified whole, as when the beginning of a house is the foundation and the end is the cornice. 225　And because Christ is the "cornerstone" (see Eph. 2:20) this must be reconciled to his being the pattern of the whole unified body of the saved. The only-begotten is indeed "all in all" (1 Cor. 15:28) since he is the beginning in the man he assumed, the end in the perfection of the saints and also in every intermediate stage, manifestly being also in those in between, or since the beginning is in Adam and the end in his earthly presence, according to the saying "the last Adam in life-giving spirit" (1 Cor. 15:45). This explanation will also serve for the definition of "the first and the last." 226　Examining what has been said concerning "first and last" and concerning "beginning and end," wherever we have referred the discourse to forms of rational beings or to various aspects of the Son of God, we have discovered the difference between "first' and "beginning" and between "last" and "end" and we have dealt with "alpha" and "omega."

227 Nor is it hard to see how he is "living" and "dead" and, after being dead, he lives for ever and ever (see Rev. 1:18). For when we are in sin and we derived no benefit from his excellent life, he descended to our mortality, so that, when he had died to sin, "carrying about Jesus' death in the body" (see 2 Cor. 4:10), we might, in due order, be able to partake after death in his life for ever and ever. For those who always carry about Jesus' death in the body will also have Jesus' life manifest in their bodies.

XXXII 228 This will suffice for the things that are said about him by himself in the New Testament.

In Isaiah it says that "his mouth" has been made into "a sharp sword" by the Father and that he has been hidden in the shelter of his hand. He is likened to a chosen arrow hidden even in the quiver of the Father, servant of the God of the universe and called by him "Israel" and "light of the nations" (Isa. 49:2, 3, 6). 229 The mouth of the Son of God is indeed a sharp sword, since "the Word of God is living and effective and sharper than any two-edged sword, penetrating to the juncture of soul and spirit, of joints and marrow, judging the desires and thoughts of the heart" (Heb. 4:12) and he also comes not to bring peace to the earth – that is, to bodily and sensible things – but a sword (see Mt. 10:34). According to the prophetic discourse his mouth is a sword or like a sharp sword cutting off, so to speak, harmful friendship from the soul and body, so that the soul giving itself to the spirit which wars against the flesh (see Gal. 5:17) may become friendly to God. Also seeing so many wounded by divine love – like her who professes to have undergone this in the Song of Songs in the words "because I have been wounded by love" (Song 2:5) – the arrow wounding so many souls in the love of God is discovered to be the same one as "He has placed me as a chosen arrow."

230 But still everyone who is conscious how, to those who have become disciples, Jesus has become not "as one who sits at table but as one who serves" (Lk. 22:27) – the Son of God taking the form of a servant for the sake of the liberation of those in bondage to sin (see Phil. 2:7) – will not be ignorant why the Father said to him "You are my servant" and a little farther on "This is a great thing for you, to be called my servant" (Isa. 49:3, 6). 231 Indeed one must dare say that Christ's goodness appears greater, more divine and truly in

the image of the Father, when 'he humbled himself, becoming subject even to death, death on a cross" than if he had "considered being equal with God a thing to be grasped" (Phil. 2:8, 6) and had not desired to become a servant for the sake of the world's salvation. 232 Wishing to teach us that becoming a servant is a great gift he had received from the Father, he therefore says, "And God will be strength for me. And he said to me, 'This is a great thing for you, to be called my servant'" (Isa. 49:5, 6). For if he had not become a servant he would not have reestablished the tribes of Jacob or brought back the dispersed of Israel, nor would he have become a light of the nations in order to be a salvation as far as the ends of the earth (see Isa. 49:5, 6).

233 And it is a modest thing for him to become the servant, even if the Father calls it a great thing, in comparison with his becoming an "innocent sheep" and a "lamb." For he has become like an innocent sheep led to the slaughter, so that he might take away "the sin of the world" (see Isa. 53:7; Jn 1:29), he who furnishes everyone with reason is likened to a sheep dumb "before the shearers" because, by his death, he has purified us all, offered, for those who desire to receive the truth, as a sort of drug[68] against the adverse powers and against sin. For the death of Christ has made weak the powers fighting against the human race and, by means of an ineffable power, life has emerged from sin in each of those believing. 234 Since, until each enemy, the last of which is death (see 1 Cor. 15:26), shall be annihilated, he takes away sin, so that the whole world may be without sin, John said, pointing to him, "Behold the Lamb of God, who takes away the sin of the world." He is not "he who will take it away but is not already taking it away," nor is he "he who has taken away but is not still taking it away." 235 The taking away is operative in every single being in the world, until the sin of the entire world shall have been taken away and the Savior hands over to the Father a kingdom prepared – ready, because no sin remains – to be reigned over by the Father and again to receive, through its whole extent, all things from God, when the saying is fulfilled, "God shall be all in all" (1 Cor. 15:28).

236 But also in addition to these titles he is called the "man coming after John, who is now ahead of him, and was before him" (see Jn 1:30), so that we are taught that the man belonging to the Son of God, the one combined with his deity, existed before the birth from Mary; this is the man about whom the Baptist said, "I did not know him" (Jn 1:31).[69] 237 But how is it that he who started for joy as an infant still in the womb of Elizabeth "did not

know" when "Mary's voice of greeting came to the ears" of Zechariah's wife (Lk. 1:41, 44)? **238** Ask then if possibly the "I did not know" refers to what was before the body. Because, if he did not know him before he came in the body, but he already knew him when he was in his mother's womb, he indeed learned something different about him from what he had known, namely that him on whom the Spirit would descend and remain "is he who baptizes in the Holy Spirit and in fire" (see Jn 1:33; Mt. 3:11). **239** For if he knew him even when he was in his mother's womb, he did not know everything about him, and indeed he did not know that this "is he who baptizes in the Holy Spirit and in fire" when he beheld "the Spirit descending and remaining on him." Only, at first, John did not know that he was a man.[70]

XXXIII **240** None of the above titles manifests his advocacy for us before the Father, interceding and making propitiation for human nature as the "intercessor," "propitiatory victim," and "mercy-seat". The "intercessor" is mentioned in the Epistle of John: "If anyone sins, we have an advocate with the Father, Jesus Christ the righteous, and he is the propitiatory sacrifice for our sins" (1 Jn 2:1–2); "propitiatory sacrifice" is mentioned in the same epistle: "and he is the propitiatory sacrifice for our sins"; and "mercy-seat" likewise in Romans: "whom God predestined as a mercy-seat through faith" (Rom. 3:25). There is a shadow of the mercy-seat in the innermost holy of holies, the golden mercy-seat, placed on the two cherubim (see Ex. 25:17–19).

241 How could he become intercessor, propitiatory sacrifice, and mercy-seat unless the power of God, poured out in the souls of the faithful, eliminated our weakness? A power is ministered to us by Jesus, who is its original, since he is the power of God himself, through whom one can say, "I can do all things in Christ, who strengthens me" (Phil. 4:13). **242** Therefore we know that Simon Magus, promoting himself as "the power of God which is called great," went, with his money, to ruin and destruction (Acts 8:10, 20). Truly confessing Christ to be "the power of God," we are convinced that all who are ever in any way empowered participate in him, in so far as he is "power."

XXXIV **243** Let us not neglect to say that he actually is "the Wisdom of God" (see 1 Cor. 1:24) and so spoken of for that reason. For his wisdom has its substance not in mere mental images of the God and Father of the universe, on the analogy of mental images in human reflection. **244** But if it were possible to conceive of an incorporeal substance of various objects of contemplation embracing

the rational principles of the universe, a substance living and, as it were, ensouled, one would know the Wisdom of God above all creation, as it well describes itself saying: "God created me in the beginning of his ways for his work" (Prov. 8:22). Through this Wisdom creation is made possible and all creation subsists, a creation with the capacity to receive the divine Wisdom by which it has come to be. For, according to David, God made everything in wisdom (see Ps. 103:24 [104:24]). 245 But many things have come into existence by participation in Wisdom without apprehending the Wisdom by which they were created, and few indeed comprehend Wisdom, not just in relation to themselves, but to many other things, it being understood that Christ is all Wisdom. 246 Each of the wise participates in Christ, because He is Wisdom, to the extent that he receives wisdom, just as each of those possessing superior power has been in relationship with Christ, because He is power, to the extent that he has obtained power.
247 Something similar must be understood concerning sanctification and redemption, for he is sanctification, by which the saints are sanctified, and Jesus has also become redemption for us; each of us are sanctified by that sanctification and redeemed by that redemption. 248 Ask if the Apostle did not add "for us" superfluously when he said: "Who became for us from God wisdom, justice, sanctification, and redemption" (1 Cor. 1:30). If it were not the case that in other places Christ, in so far as he is wisdom and power, is referred to without qualification – "Christ the power of God and the wisdom of God" – we might infer that he is not absolutely the wisdom and power of God but only "for us." But now, with regard to "wisdom" and "power," they are recorded both with the addition of "for us" and unqualifiedly, but this is not so with "sanctification" and "redemption."
249 Therefore, since "he who sanctifies and those who are sanctified are all from one" (Heb. 2:11), see if the Father is not the "sanctification" of our sanctification himself, as the Father is the head of Christ himself, who is our head (see 1 Cor. 11:3). 250 Christ is our redemption because we have been taken captive and need redemption; I do not seek a redemption for him, since he shared all of our experience except for sin and so was never reduced to slavery by the adverse powers.
251 Having already established the distinction between "for us" and an absolute statement, we have noted that "sanctification" and "redemption" are "for us" and not absolute, but "wisdom" and "power" are both "for us" and absolute, so we must not neglect to

examine what it says about "justice." That Christ is "justice" "for us" is evident from "Who has become for us from God wisdom, justice, sanctification, and redemption." 252 If we do not find him to be "justice" absolutely, as we do in the case of "wisdom" and "power of God," it must be verified if, just as the Father is "sanctification" for Christ, the Father is also "justice," for there is no injustice in God, but he is just and holy and his judgments are in justice (see Rev. 16:5, 7), and being just he governs all things justly. XXXV 253 A misconception impels adherents of heresy to say that there is a just god who is not the same as a good god, supposing as they do that the creator is just, but the Father of Christ is good. I think it possible after a rigorous examination to say that the Father and the Son are each both just and good, since the Son who had received authority to execute judgment is Justice, because he is the Son of Man (Jn 5:27) and judges the world in justice (see Acts 17:31), while it is the Father who shows kindness, after the reign of Christ, to those disciplined in the Son's justice – proving by his deeds that he is "good" – when God will become "all in all" (see 1 Cor. 15:28).

254 And indeed by his justice the Savior prepares all things to receive for themselves at the end the goodness of the Father. In this he uses favorable opportunities, his word, order, chastisements, and what can be called spiritual healing remedies. Aware of this, when someone addressed the only-begotten saying "good teacher," he said, "Why do you call me good? There is no one good except God alone?" (Mk. 10:18). 255 We have demonstrated a similar principle elsewhere concerning there being someone greater than the creator, considering Christ as the creator and the Father as the one greater than he.

In his capacity as "intercessor," "propitiatory sacrifice," and "mercy-seat" – and as one who empathizes with "our infirmities" by having experienced all things human "without sin," just as we have (Heb. 4:15) – he, then, is the "great high priest" who, by his oblation of himself "except for God he tasted death on behalf of all" (Heb. 2:9), offers himself as a sacrifice once and for all (see Heb. 9:28), not on behalf of men alone, but of all rational beings. In certain manuscripts of Hebrews, this reads "by God's grace." 256 But, if the reading is "apart from God he tasted death on behalf of all," it was not just for men but for the rest of rational beings as well. If it is "by God's grace he tasted death on behalf of all," he still died apart from God on behalf of all, "for by God's grace he tasted death on behalf of all." 257 It would indeed be outlandish to say that he tasted death on behalf of men because of their sins, but not on behalf of any being that had become involved in sins other than man, not, for example, on behalf of the stars, since the stars are not entirely pure in God's sight, as we read in Job: "but the stars are not pure in his sight" (Job 25:5), if this is not said hyperbolically.[71] **258** He is therefore a "great high priest," since he has restored all things to the Father's kingdom, arranging[72] to fill up the defects in each generate being so that they can receive the paternal glory.

259 This high priest, according to another aspect already discussed, is named "Judah," so that those who are Jews in secret (see Rom. 2:29) – who do not derive their name from Judah the son of Jacob, but from him – are his brothers and praise him, receiving in turn the freedom with which they have been freed by him, having been rescued from enemies, since he has placed his hands on their back and brought them into submission (see Gen. 49:8).

260 But because he has supplanted the adverse power, because he alone has seen the Father and because he became a man, he is "Jacob" and "Israel." So that, just as we have become light, because he is the light of the world, so we are "Jacob," because he was called Jacob, and "Israel," because he was called Israel.

XXXVI 261 Yet again he is doubtless addressed as "David" because he takes over the kingdom from a king whom the children of Israel had caused to reign over them – since they had established him in power without God's involvement and without paying attention to God (see Hos. 8:4)[73] – fighting the Lord's battles (see 1 Sam. 25:28), he prepared peace for his son, a people. After this he is addressed as "rod" for the benefit of those who need harsh and stern direction and have not offered themselves to the Father's love and gentleness. **262** Therefore, if he is called "rod," he will come forth (Isa. 11:1), because he does not remain in himself, but seems to come forth from his previous situation. **263** Coming forth and having become a "rod," he does not remain a rod, but after being a rod becomes a "flower" springing up, and the purpose of his being a rod is so that he may reveal himself a flower to those prepared by his visitation as one who had become a rod. For God will visit "with a rod," that is, with Christ, "the lawless deeds" of those whom he will visit. But he will not withdraw his mercy from him (see Ps. 88:33–4 [89:33–4]), for he has mercy on him, since the Father has mercy on those whom the Son wishes to have mercy. It is also possible to understand that he does not become "rod" and "flower" for the same persons, but that he is "rod" for those who need punishment and "flower" for those who are being saved. Of these alternatives I think the first is better. 264 Besides it must be added in relation to this topic, that doubtless at the end, if he has become "rod" for someone, he will be completely "flower" for that person; in the case of someone for whom he has been "flower," it does not follow that he will become completely "rod" for that person, unless – since one flower is more perfect than another flower, and since those plants that never bear mature[74] fruit are still said to flower – the perfect receive from Christ what comes beyond the flower, but those who are prepared by his rod do not partake of his perfection along with the rod but rather of the flower that precedes the fruit.

265 Finally, before discussing "Word," Christ was a "stone" rejected by the builders that has been established as the "cornerstone" (Ps. 117:22 [118:22]; Mt. 21:42). Indeed since the living stones (1 Pet. 2:5) are built upon the foundation of other stones, "the apostles and prophets, Jesus Christ" our Lord "himself being the chief cornerstone" (see Eph. 2:22) – because he forms a part of the building of living stones in the "land of the living" (Ps. 141:6 [142:5]) – he is entitled "Stone."

266 We have said all these things out of a desire to prove the arbitrariness and lack of consideration of the many who, when so many names are attributed to him, pay attention only to the title "Word," without examining why the Son of God was ever recorded to be the Word of God in the beginning with the Father, through whom all things came into being (see Jn 1:1–3).

XXXVII 267 Moreover, just as by the activity of illuminating the world, of which he is the light, he is entitled "light of the world" (Jn 9:5), and because he enables those who genuinely belong to him to discard death, rising again to life, he is called "resurrection" (Jn 11:25) – and "shepherd," "teacher," "king," "chosen arrow," and "servant" in accordance with other activities, and in addition "intercessor," "propitiation," and "mercy-seat" – so also he is called "word [*logos*]," because he rescues us from all irrationality [*alogon*] and confirms in truth rational creatures [*logikoi*] who do everything, even eating and drinking (see 1 Cor. 10:31), to the glory of God, accomplishing by means of reason [*logos*][75] life's ordinary activities as well as its more perfect ones.

268 If by means of participation in him (see Heb. 3:14) we are raised again and illuminated – but indeed we are shepherded or reigned over – it is clear that we become rational beings in a divinely inspired manner, when he destroys what is irrational and

dead in us, in so far as he is "word" and "resurrection."
269   Consider if all men somehow participate in him, in so far as
he is reason. Therefore the Apostle teaches us that, by those who
have chosen to find him, he is not to be sought outside those
seeking, saying,

> Do not say in your heart, "Who shall ascend into heaven?"
> that is to bring Christ down, or "Who shall descend into
> the abyss?" that is to bring Christ up from the dead, but
> what does the scripture say? "The word is very near you, in
> your mouth and in your heart,"
>
> (Rom. 10:6–8)

since Christ himself is both the word and the one sought.
270   But when the Lord himself says: "If I had not come and
spoken to them, they would not have had sin, but now they have no
excuse concerning their sin" (Jn 15:22) one can only understand one
thing: the Word says that in those whom he has not yet fully filled
there is no sin, but that those are responsible for sin who, while they
already participate in him, act contrary to the conceptions by which
he fully fills us, and only in this sense is it true that "If I had not
come and spoken to them, they would not have had sin."[76]
271   Try to interpret this text as referring to the visible Jesus, as
the many suppose. How is it true that they to whom he had come
do not have sin? In that case all who lived before the advent of the
Savior will be excused from every sin, since the Jesus who is seen in
a fleshly manner had not yet arrived. 272   But in addition all those
who have never received the news about him will not have sin, and
it is clear that, since they do not have sin, they will not be subject
to judgment.
273   But the reason in men, in which the human race has been
said to participate, is spoken of in a twofold manner, either to the
fullness of conceptions, which occurs in all who have passed out of
childhood, once marvels have been set aside,[77] or to the summit,
which is reached among perfect men alone. 274   In the first sense
one must receive the words, "If I had not come and spoken to them,
they would not have had sin, but now they have no excuse
concerning their sin," but according to the second, "All who came
before me are thieves and robbers, and the sheep did not listen to
them" (Jn 10:8). 275   In fact, before the maturation of reason[78]
everything in men is reprehensible because of deficiencies and omissions, and because the irrational faculties in us do not obey

perfectly, they are spoken of symbolically as "sheep." And doubtless according to the first meaning "the Word became flesh" (Jn 1:14) and according to the second "the Word was God."[79]

276   Following this we must investigate if any intermediate state is evident in human affairs[80] between "the Word became flesh" and "the Word was God." In such a state the Word would be reconstituted after becoming flesh and gradually lightened, so to speak, until he becomes again what he was in the beginning, God the Word, the one next to the Father. This is the Word whose glory John saw truly as that of the only-begotten of the Father (see Jn 1:14).

XXXVIII 277   The Word can be Son because of his announcing the secrets of his Father, who, on the analogy of the Son's being word, is mind. For just as among us the word is the messenger of the things seen by the mind, so the Word of God, knowing the Father, when no generate being can approach him without a guide, has revealed the Father whom he knows. 278   "For no one knows the Father except the Son and he to whomsoever the Son should reveal him" (Mt. 11:27), and, in so far as he is Word, he is the "angel [messenger] of great counsel" and "the government" has come to be "on his shoulder" (Isa. 9:6 LXX),[81] for he reigns because of having suffered the cross (see Phil. 2:9).

In the Revelation the faithful and true Word is said to sit on a white horse (Rev. 19:11), showing, I think, the clarity of the voice that was possessed by the Word of truth coming to us. 279   It is inopportune at this time to demonstrate that the term "horse" is often used to designate "voice" in Scripture, including the passage just cited, through which we hear divine teachings for our benefit. Only one or two must be mentioned, "A horse is false for salvation" (Ps. 32:17 [33:17]) and "Some in chariots and some in horses, but we magnify ourselves in the Lord our God" (Ps. 19:8 [20:7]).

280   We must not leave unexamined, "My heart has belched a good word, I say, 'my works are for the king'" (Ps. 44:2 [45:1]), recorded in the forty-fourth Psalm and continually cited by the many as if they understood it. Let it be the Father who says this. 281   What then is his heart, so that it may appear consistent with "good word"? If indeed, as they understand, "word" does not require explanation. neither does "heart," which is absurd, for it is clear that God does not, like us, have a heart as a part of his body. 282   But they must be reminded that just as in references to God's hand, arm, or finger, we do not let our understanding be based on the mere letter, but we examine how these things ought to be

understood sanely and in a manner worthy of God, so also God's heart must be understood to be the intellective and planning power of his mind concerning the universe, and his "Word" as the messenger of the things in it. **283** Who announces the will of the Father to those who have become worthy, having become present to them, if it is not the Savior?

But indeed "belched" is intentional, for their are many other things that might have been said instead of "belched" – "my heart set forth a good word," "my heart spoke a good word" – but perhaps just as the belch is the outlet into the open of some hidden breath of the person belching, as if he were breathing, so the Father, not withholding intuitions of truth, belches and makes their representation in the Word, and therefore he is called "the image of the invisible God" (Col. 1:15).

And we have demonstrated these things concerning the Father's saying "My heart has belched a good word" in order to accommodate ourselves to the interpretation of the many.[82]

XXXIX 284 But it should not at all be conceded to them that, by common consent, these words are pronounced by God. Why is it not possible that the prophet is speaking, filled with the Spirit and putting forth a good word concerning prophecy about Christ, unable to withhold "My heart has belched a good word, I say, 'my works are for the king'. My mouth is the plume of an accomplished scribe. He is handsome with a beauty beyond that of the sons of men" and then addressing Christ, "Grace is spread out over your lips" (Ps. 44:2–3 [45:1–2])? **285** How, if the Father were speaking, did he add to "Grace is spread out over your lips" the words "therefore God has blessed you forever" (Ps. 44:3 [45:2]) and a little later "therefore God, your God, has anointed you with the oil of gladness beyond your peers" (Ps. 44:8 [45:7])?

286 Someone wishing the word in the Psalm to be pronounced by the Father might bring up in turn, "Listen, daughter, see, and incline your ear, forget your people and your house and your father" (Ps. 44:11 [45:10]) for it is not the prophet who thus speaks to the church. **287** It is not difficult to demonstrate from other Psalms that changes of person speaking often occur, so that it is possible that, beginning with "Listen, daughter," it is the Father speaking.

288 It must be added with reference to the interpretation of "Word" that also "By the word of the Lord the heavens were made firm and by his spirit all their host" (Ps. 32:6 [33:6]). Some consider this to refer to the Son and the Holy Spirit, so that this text proves that the Word of God made firm the heavens, as if we should speak of the heavens' coming to be by the Word of God as a house comes to be by the architect's word or a ship by the ship-wright's word. So therefore the heavens came to be by the Word of God – having a more divine body called "firmament" because it lacks the fluid and unstable constitution of the inferior remainder of creation – it was made firm and because of its excellence was the foremost product of the divine Word.

Conclusion

289 Our proposal was to see clearly "In the beginning was the Word." As for "beginning," it has been demonstrated according to the testimonies of Proverbs (see Prov. 8:22) that Wisdom is spoken of and that the notion of wisdom precedes the word that announces it. So it must be understood that the Word always exists in the beginning, that is, in Wisdom. Since he is in Wisdom, which is called "beginning," he is not hindered from being "with God" and he is God, and he is not simply "with God," but, being "in the beginning" in Wisdom, he is "with God." 290 John adds and says, "This one was in the beginning with God"; he could have said, "This one was with God," but just as he was "in the beginning," so he also was with God in the beginning. And "all things came into being through him" since he was "in the beginning," for, according to David, God created all things "in wisdom" (see Ps. 103:24 [104:24]).

291 In addition, to demonstrate that the Word has its own indi-viduality, in so far as it lives on its own, one must also speak about powers – not just about a power for "thus says the Lord of powers"[83] often occurs, certain rational beings being termed divine living powers – of whom the highest and best was Christ, addressed just as God's wisdom but also his power (1 Cor. 1:24). 292 Just as there are many powers of God, of which each has an individuality which differs from the Savior, so also Christ is understood through our previous argument to be the Word – even if for us a word has no individuality apart from us – who had his own individual existence in the beginning, in Wisdom.

This will suffice for now concerning "In the beginning was the Word."

COMMENTARY ON JOHN,
BOOK 13.3–192

Introduction

Origen probably wrote Book 13 of his *Commentary on John* during his earlier years in Caesarea, most probably in the 230s. He interprets Jacob's well as a symbol of Scripture and the Samaritan woman as a heretic who cannot find lasting satisfaction in a shallow interpretation she mistakenly takes to be profound. In John's story she finally discovers in Scripture the truly profound and inexhaustible understanding open to those who encounter Jesus himself and, through him, gain access to a knowledge transcending Scripture (27–30). Such an understanding enables those who have progressed spiritually beyond the normal human condition to worship God in a way that is more confident as well as more contemplative than ordinary Christians can (98–100), even if they still await an eschatological perfection (113). With characteristic attentiveness, Origen notices that, although the woman uses the word "well" (*phrear*), Jesus uses a different word, "spring" (*pēgē*), indicating a continuous supply of fresh water (23). Origen is also attentive, as Jean-Michel Poffet's recent study has shown, to the actual dynamic of John's story and to its larger context.[1] Thus, in order to place the story in its historical setting, he investigates how, precisely, a Samaritan would understand Messiahship (154–62). We also see Origen being characteristically attentive to spiritual life when he argues that we do not gain benefits from God unless we ask for them (5).

Here Origen argues with an alternative interpretation, that of the second-century Gnostic Heracleon, a follower of Valentinus, whose approach has much in common, superficially at least, with his. Thus, for example, like Origen, Heracleon interprets the text as dealing with the relationship between the Old and New

Testaments. While giving Heracleon credit where he feels it is due, Origen criticizes him (with good cause, in Poffet's view) for lacking *akribeia*, "accuracy." Heracleon, Origen argues, imposes an interpretation determined by his own heterodox theology rather than by the logic of the text itself. [2] Exampes are Heracleon's arbitrary interpretations of "you" in verse 4:22 as "Jews and gentiles" (102–3) and of the water-jar in verse 4:28 as "aptitude to receive life and mindfulness of the power which comes from the Savior" (187–9).

The translation is from Origène, *Commentaire sur S. Jean*, vol. 3, ed. Cécile Blanc = *SC* 222, Paris, Cerf, 1975, pp. 36–136.

Text

Jesus answered and said to her: "Everyone who drinks from this water will thirst again, but whoever drinks from the water that I shall give him, there shall be in him a spring of water leaping to eternal life" (Jn 4:13–14).

I 3   This is Jesus' second response to the Samaritan woman; the first was when he said, "If you knew the gift of God, and who it is who is saying to you 'Give me something to drink,' you would have asked him and he would have given you living water" (Jn 4:10). And now, to encourage her to ask for living water, he says the words just cited. 4   In response to his first question, the Samaritan woman did not ask for it but instead raised an objection to his comparison of one water with another, but after the Lord's second response, accepting what he said, she says, "Give me that water" (Jn 4:15).

5   Perhaps there is some requirement that no one receives a divine gift except those who ask for it. In a Psalm, the Father even encourages the Son himself to ask so that he may give to him, as the Son himself teaches, saying: "The Lord has said to me: 'You are my Son, ask of me and I shall give you the nations as your inheritance, and the ends of the earth as a possession'" (Ps. 2:7–8). The Savior also says: "Ask and it shall be given to you, everyone who asks receives" (Mt. 7:7–8; Lk. 11:9–10) . 6   Nonetheless, the Samaritan woman – who is, as I have already said,[3] an image of the outlook of the heterodox when they study the divine Scriptures – is persuaded to ask for Jesus' water, when she had heard about his comparison of the two kinds of water. 7   And see how, in her experience, when she drank from what she supposed to be a deep well, she was not refreshed nor was her thirst assuaged.

II 8   Let us therefore see what is signified by "Everyone who drinks from this water will thirst again." From a bodily perspective "thirst" and "hunger" can signify two things; one is that we lack nourishment, and after being deprived of it, we desire food or drink as a result of dehydration, the other is when often the poor and those deprived of basic needs are said to be consumed by hunger or thirst.

9   An example of the first is in Exodus when,

> lacking food on the nineteenth day of the second month after they had departed from the land of Egypt, the whole assembly of the children of Israel grumbled against Moses and Aaron, and the children of Israel said to them, "It would have been better if we had died, stricken by the Lord in Egypt, when we sat by pots full of flesh and ate bread and were filled, since you have led us out into this desert in order that all this assembly may die of famine." The Lord said to Moses "See, I shall rain down for you bread from heaven, and the people shall go out and collect it day after day, until I test them, whether they will walk in my law or not."
>
> (Ex. 16:1–4)

10   Such words are those of men who are hungry and lack necessary nourishment. Those deprived of water and thirsty also grumbled against Moses "what shall we drink?" when Moses cried to the Lord, and the Lord showed him wood, and he threw it into the water and the water became sweet (see Ex. 15:24–5). 11   And a little later, when they had come to Rephidim, it is written that "The people thirsted there for water, and the people grumbled there against Moses" (see Ex. 17:1–3; Amos 8:11).

12   An example of the second usage may possibly be in Paul when he says: "Up until this time we have hungered, we have thirsted, we have been naked" (1 Cor. 4:11).

The first kind of hunger and thirst necessarily happens to those with healthy bodies, the second happens to those who are impoverished.

III 13   It must be investigated what sort of thirst is intended in "Everyone who drinks from this water will thirst again." The first sense is perhaps as it is from a bodily perspective, when someone is assuaged for the moment, but when the drink has passed through, the one drinking it experiences the same craving, that is, he thirsts again, having been restored to the same situation in which he began. 14   Therefore he added: "but whoever drinks from the water that I shall give him, there shall be in him a spring of water leaping to eternal life." For who could ever thirst if he had a spring inside himself?

15 Nonetheless, the principal sense must be the following: the person partaking in what he considers to be a doctrinal profundity is refreshed for a short time, having accepted the ideas deduced as very profound and thinking that he had discovered them. Nonetheless, on reflecting on them a second time, he has his doubts about the ideas in which he had earlier found refreshment, because what he had accepted as something he supposed to be profound could not provide a clear and distinct perception of the things investigated. 16 Therefore, someone who is inveigled into assent to specious reasoning later finds he has the same predicament which he had before he had learned those things. But I have doctrine[4] of such a kind that what I have announced will be a spring of living refreshment in the person who accepts it. And the person who receives my water will experience such a great benefit that there will gush forth in him a spring of waters leaping upwards capable of discovering everything investigated, when his intelligence is leaping and flying swiftly, as a consequence of that highly mobile water, bearing him upwards by its leaping and bounding into eternal life. 17 He says that somehow the purpose of the leaping water is eternal life, just as Solomon says about the bridegroom in the Song of Songs: "See, that one comes leaping on the mountains, bounding over the hills" (Sg 2:8). 18 Just as there the bridegroom leaps over the most noble and most divine souls, called "mountains,"[5] and bounds over the inferior souls, called "hills," so, here, in the person who drinks from the water which Jesus will give, the spring which comes to be in him will leap to eternal life. 19 Doubtless it will also leap, after eternal life, to the Father who is above eternal life.[6] For Christ is life (see Jn 14:6), but the one who is greater than Christ (see Jn 14:28) is greater than life.

IV 20 Then he who drinks from the water which Jesus will give will have in himself the spring of water leaping to eternal life, when the promise is fulfilled that those who hunger and thirst for justice will be made happy. 21 For the Word says: "Happy are they who hunger and thirst for justice, for they shall be fed" (Mt. 5:6). 22 And perhaps, since one must hunger and thirst before being fed, we are to induce hunger and thirst in order to be satisfied, so as to say, "Just as the stag languishes for springs of water, so my soul languishes for you, God. My soul has thirsted for the strong, living

God, when shall I come and see the face of God?" (Ps. 41:2–3 LXX [42:1–2]).

23 Therefore when we thirst, it is good to drink first from Jacob's spring, which should not be referred to, as the Samaritan did, as Jacob's well. For in fact the Savior, even in responding to her statement, did not say that the water was from a well, but said simply: "Everyone who drinks from this water will thirst again." **24** If it were not beneficial to drink from the spring, Jesus would not have sat on the well (see Jn 4:6), nor would he have said to the Samaritan woman, "Give me something to drink". **25** It should then be added that when the Samaritan woman also asked Jesus for water, he promised somehow to offer it to her in a particular place, beside the spring, saying to her, "Go, call your husband, and come here" (Jn 4:16).

V 26 We shall still seek to understand if it is possible to show a difference in kind between the benefit gained by those who converse with the truth himself and live with him and the benefit[7] supposed to come to us from the Scriptures, even when we understand them accurately. The difference is that he who drinks from Jacob's spring will thirst again, but he who drinks from the water which Jesus will give will have a spring in himself able to leap to eternal life. **27** Indeed, considering the most important and most divine of the mysteries of God, there are some that Scripture does not contain and others that human speech – following the conventional meanings of words – or human language cannot contain, "For there are many other things, which Jesus did, which, if I were to write them one by one, I do not think that the world itself could contain the books written" (Jn 21:25). **28** And when John was going to write what the seven thunders said, he was prohibited (see Rev. 10:4). And Paul says that he had heard unspeakable words, which it was not possible to utter, for it was possible to speak them to angels, but it was not possible to men, for all things are possible, but not all things are expedient (see 1 Cor. 6:12). **29** Now the unspeakable words that he had heard, it is not possible, he says, to utter to a man (see 2 Cor. 6:12).[8] **30** I think that, in relation to knowledge as a whole, the Scriptures as a whole are to be understood as most meager elements and the briefest introductions, [9] even when they are understood entirely accurately.

31 See, then, if Jacob's spring, from which Jacob once drank, but no longer drinks now, and from which his sons also drank, but now have a drink superior to it, and from which his beasts had drunk, cannot be the whole of Scripture, and Jesus' water the things above

Scripture (see 1 Cor. 4:6). **32** It is not possible for all to discover what is above Scripture, unless they become similar to those things,[10] so that they may not be shocked by hearing, "Do not investigate things that are too difficult for you, and do not discover things that are too hard for you" (Sir. 3:21).

VI 33 If we speak of what is above Scripture, we do not say that these things are knowable by the many, but they could have been known by John, who heard such things as the words of thunder without being given permission to write them (see Jn 12:29), learning that it was in order to spare the world that he did not write them, for he thought that the whole world could not contain the books written (see Jn 21:25). **34** But the "unspeakable words" which Paul had learned are also above Scripture (if we concede that it was men who had spoken the things written as Scripture). And things which eye has not seen are above Scripture, and it is not possible to write as Scripture things which ear has not heard. **35** And the things which have not entered into the heart of a man (see 1 Cor. 2:9) are better than Jacob's spring. These things have been manifested by a spring of water leaping up to eternal life to those who no longer have the heart of a man, but can say, "We have the mind of Christ" (1 Cor. 12:16) "so that we may know the things graciously given to us by God, which we speak, not in words taught by human wisdom, but in words taught by the Spirit" (1 Cor. 2:12–13).

36 And understand, if it is possible to call "human wisdom" not false doctrines, but the elementary principles of truth that concern those who are still human, as opposed to "teachings of the Spirit," which are doubtless the spring of water leaping up to eternal life. **37** The Scriptures, therefore, are introductions, from whose exact understanding, called here the spring of Jacob, one must ascend to Jesus, so that we may be graciously given the spring of water leaping to eternal life. **38** But everyone does not draw in the same way from Jacob's spring. For if Jacob, his sons, and his beasts drank from it, the Samaritan woman, when she was thirsty, also came to it and drew. Did not Jacob drink with his sons in a distinct way and with intelligent understanding in contrast to his beasts, who drank in a simpler, animal way, and the Samaritan woman in a still different way from Jacob, his sons, and his beasts? **39** Those who are wise about the Scriptures drink as did Jacob and his sons; the so-called "flock of Christ" (see Jn 10:2–5) drink as did Jacob's beasts; but those who abuse the Scriptures and compose blasphemies on the pretext of understanding them drink as the Samaritan woman drank before believing in Jesus.

The woman says to him, "Lord, give me that water, that I may not thirst nor come here to draw" (Jn 4:15).

VII 40   This is already the second time the Samaritan woman has addressed Jesus as "Lord," the first being when she said, "Lord, you do not have a water-jar and the well is deep" (Jn 4:11) and sought from where he had living water and if he were greater than Jacob, whom she supposed to be her father (see Jn 4:11–12), and then now when she also asks him for the water that will become in the one drinking it a spring leaping to eternal life. 41   And if "You would have asked him and he would have given you living water" (Jn 4:10) is actually true, clearly, when she said, "Lord, give me that water," she received the living water, so that she might no longer be baffled as someone thirsting nor come to Jacob's well to draw, but, away from Jacob's water, she might be able to contemplate the truth as the angels do and in a superhuman way. For the angels do not require Jacob's well that they may drink, but each one has in himself a spring leaping to eternal life, a spring brought about and revealed by the Word himself and Wisdom herself.

42   But no one can receive another water, not given by the Word from Jacob's spring, without taking great care because of thirst to go to there and draw. For this reason many things are lacking to the many who do not exert themselves very vigorously to draw from Jacob's spring.

He said to her, "Go, call your husband, and come here." The woman answered and said "I do not have a husband" (Jn 4:16–17).

VIII 43   We have said above that the law is the soul's ruler, so that, for each person submitted to it, the law is the soul's husband. Now, as a testimony to this, we cite the Apostle in the Epistle to the Romans who says: "Are you ignorant, brothers – for I speak to those under the law – that the law has dominion over a man for as long as he lives" (Rom. 7:1). But who "lives"? If we take "law" in its ordinary sense, it is the law. 44   He adds immediately: "So the married woman is bound to her husband as to a law," as if he were saying, "To her living husband, and the husband is the law." 45   Then again he says: "But if the husband should die, she is set free from the law of the husband" (Rom. 7:2), as if the woman were freed by the death of the law and no more accomplishes the duties of a wife to her husband. 46   Then he says: "Indeed, while he is living she is considered an adulteress if she should belong to another man, but if her

156

husband should die, she is free from the law, so as not to be an adulteress with another man" (Rom. 7:3).

47 For the law according to the letter has died, and the soul will not be an adulteress should it belong to another husband, the law which is according to the Spirit. For when the husband has died to the wife, it may somehow be said that the wife has died to the husband, so we can interpret "So, my brothers, you also have been put to death with respect to the law through the body of Christ, so you may belong to another, the one who has been raised from the dead, so that we may bear fruit for God" (Rom. 7:4). 48 Assume that the husband is a law and the Samaritan woman has a certain husband, having submitted herself, by abuse of healthy doctrines, to a certain law according to which each of the heterodox wish to live. Here the divine Word desires that the heterodox soul, having been confounded by the comparison with the law ruling her, should despise it, because it is not a legitimate husband, and seek another husband. Thus she will belong to another, the Word who will rise from the dead, who is not to be refuted or put to death, but will remain eternally (see Isa. 40:8; 1 Pet. 1:25), reigning, and subduing all enemies (see Ps. 8:7; Eph. 1:22) –"for Christ, being raised from the dead will never die again, death no longer has dominion over him. For what died, died to sin once and for all, but what lives, lives to God" (Rom. 6:9–10) "being at his right hand, until all his enemies are placed as his footstool" (see Heb. 10:12–13; Ps. 109:1 [110:1]).

49 If the woman had not by herself repudiated her husband, where should the Samaritan woman's supposed husband be convinced that he is not a husband, except by Jesus beside Jacob's spring? Therefore Jesus said to her, "Go, call your husband, and come here." 50 Possibly she already has some of the water leaping to eternal life. Because she had said "give me that water" and did not lie to the one who had already announced to her, "You would have asked him and he would have given you living water" (Jn 4:10), the woman answered, accusing herself on account of her relations with such a man, and said, "I do not have a husband."

Jesus says to her: "You have said well 'I have no husband,' for you have had five husbands, and the one you now have is not your husband; you have spoken the truth in this" (Jn 4:17–18).
IX 51 I think that every soul introduced into reverence toward Christ in accordance with the Scriptures, starting from so-called sensible and corporeal things, has five husbands, one husband

corresponding to each of the senses. But if, after having had relations with sensible things, wishing to emerge and turning toward the intelligible, it comes across an unsound doctrine[11] that makes a pretext of allegory and spiritual interpretations, that soul, after the five husbands, submits to another – giving, so to speak, a bill of divorce to the previous five and deciding to cohabit with the sixth.[12] 52   Until Jesus' coming makes us conscious of what sort of man that is, we consort with him. But when the doctrine[13] who is Lord has conversed with us, we renounce that man, saying, "I have no husband," and he praises us, saying, "You have said well 'I have no husband.'"

53   "You have said well" is like a reproach, since the things that she had said earlier were not true. And doubtless it was not true that "Jews have no dealings with Samaritans" (Jn 4:9). 54   Indeed Jesus himself, as we have discussed earlier, had dealings with Samaritans so that he might benefit them. 55   Neither was "You do not have a water-jar and the well is deep" (Jn 4:11) a true statement. 56   Doubtless "Jacob drank from the well and his sons and his beasts" was also not true, if Jacob and his sons and his beasts did not, in fact, drink in the same way as the Samaritan woman. When the Samaritan woman supposes that she had drunk in the same way exactly the same drink as Jacob, his sons, and his beasts, she is clearly mistaken.

X 57   Let us also look at Heracleon's comments on this passage. He says that "this life and its glory have become limp, brief, and flawed, for they are of the world," and he supposes that the reference to Jacob's beasts having drunk from it is proof that it is of the world. 58   We would not blame him for such an interpretation, if what he considers limp, brief, and flawed is knowledge in part (see 1 Cor. 13:9), either that which comes from the Scriptures by comparison with the knowledge of unspeakable things which it is not possible for a man to say (see 2 Cor. 12:4), or all that knowledge which we now see through a mirror in an enigma (see 1 Cor. 13:12) and will be canceled by the arrival of that which is perfect (see 1 Cor. 13:10). However, if this interpretation is intended to slander the Old Testament, he is blameworthy.

59   But when he says "that the water which the Savior gives is from his spirit and power," he is not mistaken. 60   "He shall not thirst until eternity" (see Jn 4:14), he explains in these terms:

> his life is eternal and never corrupted, like the first, that of
> the well, but it abides, for the grace and gift of our Savior

are not to be taken away and are not lost or corrupted in those who participate in them.

61   In holding that the first life is corruptible, if he speaks of that life according to the letter – seeking that life according to the Spirit which comes about when the veil is lifted (see 2 Cor. 3:16) and finding it – he speaks soundly. But if he accuses the Old Testament of being entirely corruptible, he evidently does so because he does not see that these good things have the shadow of things to come (see Heb. 10:1).

62   His explanation of the "leaping" water is unpersuasive: "those who receive part of a gift richly accorded from above, in turn cause those gifts which have been accorded to them to gush out to the eternal life of others."

63   But he also praises the Samaritan woman as "having received an unhesitating faith in accordance with her nature, not hesitating with regard to the things said to her." 64   If he had approved the woman's choice, without hinting that her nature was something distinctive, we would also agree, but if he ascribes the cause of her assent to her natural constitution, as if all did not have such a constitution, his reasoning is to be rejected.

65   I do not know how Heracleon, making an unsubstantiated inference, says concerning "give me that water": "the woman, being stimulated instantly by the Word, hated from then on even the place of this so-called 'living water.'"

66   Yet also concerning "give me that water, that I may not thirst nor come here to draw," he says: "The woman says this indicating how exhausting, hard to obtain, and sterile this water is." Where, however, does he find any indication that Jacob's water is sterile?

XI 67   Again, regarding "He said to her," he says: "It is evident that he was saying something like 'If you want to receive that water, get up and call your husband'" and he supposes that "what the Savior referred to as Samaritan woman's husband was her Fullness,[14] so that being with him in the Savior's presence she might be able to receive from him the power, unity, and amalgamation with her Fullness." For he says "that Jesus did not speak to her concerning a husband of the world, that she might summon him, because he was not ignorant that she did not have a lawful husband."

68   Obviously he forces the text here, saying that "when the Savior said to her 'call your husband, and come here' he was indicating her comrade[15] from the Fullness." If that had been the case, he would have needed to indicate the husband and in what manner he was to

be called, so that he might be with her in the Savior's presence. **69** But since, as Heracleon says, "in intelligible terms, she did not know her own husband, but in simple terms she was ashamed to say that she had a paramour and not a husband," how was it not pointless to give her the order "Go, call your husband, and come here"? **70** Then, with regard to "You have said well 'I have no husband,'" he says: "because the Samaritan woman had no husband in the world, but she did have a husband in eternity."

71 Now we have read "you have had five husbands" but we find in Heracleon "You have had six husbands." **72** And his interpretation is that "by the six husbands is indicated the whole material evil in which she was implicated and to which she was related by fornicating contrary to reason and by which she was abused, rejected, and abandoned." **73** It should be said to him that if indeed the spiritual woman fornicated, the spiritual woman sinned, but if the spiritual woman sinned, the spiritual woman was not a good tree, for according to the Gospel: "A good tree cannot bear wicked fruit" (Mt. 7:18). **74** This clearly eliminates their[16] made-up fables: if it is impossible for a good tree to bear wicked fruit, and if the Samaritan woman, being spiritual, was a good tree, it follows that he would either have to say that her fornication was not a sin or that she did not fornicate.

The woman said to him: "Lord, I behold that you are a prophet. Our fathers have worshipped on this mountain, and you say: 'In Jerusalem is the place where one should worship"' (Jn 4:19–20).

XII 75 This is already the third time that the Samaritan woman addresses our Savior as Lord,[17] and it is also the final time that she is recorded as saying this. But she does not yet suppose that he is greater than the prophets or that he is the one whom they prophesied, but that he is a prophet. **76** Once her first five husbands, along with the one left after them whom she supposed to be her husband, are confuted, the heterodox opinion of those dealing with the Scripture, not being able initially to see who the Word refuting them is, says that he is a prophet, as if he were someone divine who had about him some superhuman quality, but not as great as he actually was. That is why she says, as if somehow looking up and considering herself in a state of contemplation:[18] "I behold that you are a prophet."

77 With regard to "Our fathers" *et cetera*, one must know the difference between Samaritans and Jews concerning what they regarded as a holy place. The Samaritans, regarding the mountain called "Gerizim" as a holy place, worshipped God on it, because Moses mentioned it in Deuteronomy, saying:

> And Moses commanded the people on that day, saying "These are to bless the people on Mount Gerizim after the crossing of the Jordan: Simeon, Levi, Judah, Issachar, Joseph, and Benjamin. And these are to stand in condemnation on Mount Hebal: Reuben, Gad and Assher, Zebulon, Dan and Naphthali.
>
> (Deut. 27:11–13)

78 But the Jews, having regarded Zion as a place that is divine and special to God, suppose that it is the place chosen (see Ps. 131:13 [132:13]) by the Father of the universe, and they say that for this reason the Temple was built on it by Solomon and the whole levitical and priestly cult is carried out there. 79 Following these assumptions, each race considers that their fathers worshipped God on the one mountain or the other.

XIII 80 If ever Samaritans and Jews agree up to this point in their doctrine, each will raise difficulties as to the rest, and the Samaritan will say to the Jew the word attributed here to the woman: "Our fathers have worshipped on this mountain," indicating Gerizim, "and you say: 'In Jerusalem is the place where one should worship.'" 81 But since the Jews – indeed from them salvation comes (see Jn 4:22) – are images of those who approve sound doctrines, while the Samaritans are images of the heterodox, it follows that the Samaritans divinize Gerizim, which is interpreted "separation" or "division," since the historical separation and division of the ten tribes separated from the remaining two happened in the time of Jereboam (see 1 Kings 12), whose own name is interpreted "judgment of people," but the Jews divinize Zion, which is "observatory".

It is likely someone would ask why the blessings of which Moses wrote took place on Mount Gerizim. 82 It must be said in this regard that the word "Gerizim" means both "separation" and "division." One must take "separation" as a reference to when the people were divided by Jereboam and the king lived in Samaria. But one must take "division" as a reference to the blessing, since sages make orderly use of divisions in all of their problems, a procedure required for the understanding of truth.

83 In as much as the hour had not yet come, of which the Savior spoke, when they should worship the Father neither on

this mountain nor in Jerusalem, it was necessary to shun the Samaritans' mountain and worship God on Zion, where Jerusalem is, since Jerusalem is the city which Christ spoke of as that of the great king (see Mt. 5:35). **84** What could be the city of the great king, the true Jerusalem, if it is not the church built of living stones, where there is a holy priesthood, where spiritual sacrifices are offered to God (see 1 Pet. 2:5) by spiritual men and the spiritual law is understood? **85** When the fullness of time has arrived (see Gal. 4:4), then it must no longer be assumed that the true worship and perfect reverence are still carried out in Jerusalem, because one would no longer be in the flesh, but in the Spirit, and no longer in type but in truth, since one has been so constituted as to be assimilated to those worshippers whom God seeks (see Jn 4:23).

XIV **86** "The hour is coming" is written twice, and the first time "and now is" is not added, but the second time the evangelist says, "the hour is coming and now is" (Jn 4:21 and 23) **87** And I suppose that the first indicates the external bodily worship in the process of perfection, the second is the worship of those who in this life have been perfected as much as is possible for human nature to progress. **88** Therefore it is possible to worship the Father both in spirit and in truth when the hour is not only coming but also now is, even if one considers that we remain in Jerusalem on account of those who have come only so far. **89** When it is written, "the hour is coming and now is," it is no longer said, "neither in this mountain nor in Jerusalem will you worship the Father," since this was already said when "the hour is coming" was recorded without "and now is."

90 In saying this the Samaritan woman still has a false opinion similar to that which she expressed concerning what she considered a well. For in that case she said "Are you greater than our father Jacob, who has given us this well and drank of it himself, and his sons, and his beasts?" (Jn 4:12) and in this case "Our fathers worshipped on this mountain."

XV **91** In reference to this passage Heracleon says that "the Samaritan woman had graciously assented to the things spoken by him to her, for, she says, only a prophet could know everything." He speaks falsely on either account, for the angels can know everything, and the prophet does not know everything, for we know in part and we prophesy in part (1 Cor. 13:9) when we do prophesy or know.

92 After this he praises the Samaritan woman for "having acted appropriately in accordance with her nature by neither lying nor affirming outright her disgraceful behavior." He says that, "convinced that he was a prophet, she questions him while indicating the cause of her fornication, namely that through ignorance she neglected God, the worship intended by God, and all things necessary to her life, going through life with no particular purpose, for otherwise," he says, "she would not have gone to the well which chanced to be outside the city." 93 I do not know how he reckoned that the cause of her fornication is indicated or that ignorance was the cause of her transgressions, even ignorance of the worship intended by God, but he seems to have put down whatever came to his mind without any plausibility. 94 He adds to this that, "wishing to learn how and whom she should please, and what God she should worship, so that she might be delivered from fornication, she says 'Our fathers have worshipped on this mountain' *et cetera*." But these statements are extremely easy to refute, for where is it that she wanted to learn whom to gratify so as to give up fornication?

Jesus said to her: "Believe me, woman, the hour is coming when neither in this mountain nor in Jerusalem will you worship the Father" (Jn 4:21).
XVI 95 When Heracleon seemed to have made a very convincing observation on these matters, namely "that earlier he had not said to her, 'Believe me, woman,' but now this is enjoined on her," he then clouds this convincing observation, saying that "the mountain bespeaks the Devil or his world, because the Devil was one part of the whole of matter," he says, "the whole world was a mountain of evil, the desert home of wild beasts, which all before the law and the gentiles worshipped" (see Rom. 1:25), but "Jerusalem bespeaks the creation or the creator whom the Jews worshipped." 96 But, alternatively, he considered the mountain to be the creation which the gentiles worshipped, but Jerusalem to be the Creator whom the Jews venerate. 97 "Therefore," he says, "you, in so far as you are spiritual men, worship neither the creation nor the Artisan[19] but the Father of truth, and he accepts her," he says, "because she is already believing and counted among those who worship according to truth."
98 But we say that what is called reverence by the heterodox, in the ostentation of Gnostic discourses and lofty speculations, is indicated by "neither on this mountain," but the rule[20] followed by the majority in the church – which the perfect and holy man surpasses by worshipping the Father in a way that is more contemplative, more sure, and more divine – is indicated by "nor in Jerusalem will

you worship the Father." **99**　For, just as even the Jews themselves admit, the angels do not worship the Father in Jerusalem, because they worship the Father in a better manner than that practiced in Jerusalem, so those who already have the privilege of being equal to the angels in disposition (see Lk. 20:26) will not worship the Father in Jerusalem, but in a better way than those in Jerusalem, even if, for the sake of those in Jerusalem, they have relations with those in Jerusalem, becoming Jews for the Jews in order to gain the Jews (see 1 Cor. 9:20). But in my opinion Jerusalem must be understood as we have already set forth above, and the Jews similarly. **100**　Assuredly when one worships neither on this mountain nor in Jerusalem, the hour having arrived, he worships the Father with bold confidence, having become a son.[21] Therefore it does not say "nor in Jerusalem will you worship God," but "nor in Jerusalem will you worship the Father."

You worship what you do not know, we worship what we know, because salvation is from the Jews (Jn 4:22).
XVII **101**　The "you," according to the letter, are the Samaritans, but according to an elevated interpretation, those who are heterodox with regard to the Scriptures. The "we," according to what is said, are the Jews, but according to allegory, they are "I, the Word, and those who are formed like me." These have salvation out of the Jewish discourses, for the mystery now manifested (see Rom. 16:25–6) had been manifested through the prophetic Scriptures as well as by the appearance of our Lord Jesus Christ (see 2 Tim. 1:10). **102**　See if Heracleon has not, idiosyncratically and in defiance of the context, explained the "you" as "Jews and gentiles." **103**　Is it possible to say to a Samaritan woman, "You Jews," or to say to a Samaritan woman, "You gentiles"? But the heterodox do not know what they worship, because it is something made up and not truth, a myth not a mystery. But the person who worships the Artisan,[22] especially in the manner of one who is secretly a Jew (see Rom. 2:29) and of the spiritual Jewish discourses, that person knows what he worships. **104**　It would be too long to cite here Heracleon's statements taken from the work entitled *Proclamation of Peter*[23] and to pause to examine whether that book is genuine, illegitimate, or of mixed character. Therefore wishing to postpone such an examination, we report this only, that it represents, as Peter's teaching, that one must not worship as the Greeks do, who admit material things, worshipping wood and stone, nor should one reverence God in the manner

of the Jews because, supposing themselves alone to understand God, they do not know him, offering veneration to angels, months, and the moon. 105   It must indeed be investigated to whom, in truth, the bodily veneration of the Jews accrues, nonetheless, as to their intention, this is clear: it is to offer sacrifices to the Creator of the Universe. 106   But it is worth seeing what is the meaning of the text in the Acts of the Apostles: "God has turned and given them over to veneration of the host of heaven" (Acts 7:42).

I do not know how, when the Savior has plainly said, "Salvation comes from the Jews," the heterodox deny the God of Abraham, Isaac, and Jacob, the fathers of the Jews (see Ex. 3:6). 107   In addition, if the Savior has fulfilled the law (see Mt. 5:17) and if this or that event during his bodily presence occurred so as to fulfill things written in the prophetic books, how is the meaning of "Salvation comes from the Jews" not clear? 108   For the same God is God of Jews and gentiles, "If indeed there is one God, who justifies the circumcision from faith and the uncircumcision by faith" (Rom. 3:30). For we do not abolish the law through faith, but we establish the law through it (see Rom. 3:31).

But the time is coming and now is when the true worshippers will worship the Father in spirit and in truth (Jn 4:23a).
XVIII 109   Those who make no profession at all to worship the Father must not be referred to as worshippers of God, but of all those who do profess to worship the Creator – if it is the case that some are no longer in the flesh but in the Spirit (see Rom. 8:9) because they walk in the Spirit and do not accomplish the lust of the flesh (see Gal. 5:16), but others are not in the Spirit but in the flesh and make war according to the flesh (see 2 Cor. 10:3) – the true worshippers must be those who worship the Father in Spirit and not in flesh, and in truth and not in types, but those who do not behave this way are not true worshippers. 110   The person who is in slavery to the letter that kills – neither sharing in the life-giving Spirit (see 2 Cor. 3:6) nor following the spiritual meanings of the law – that person would be the one who is not a true worshipper, not worshipping the Father in spirit. That man, entirely adhering to types and bodily matters,[24] even when he appears to have fully achieved his purpose, worships God in type and not in truth, and cannot therefore be designated a true worshipper. 111   It may indeed be conceded that the true worshipper, worshipping in spirit and in truth, sometimes reasonably does certain things as types, so that, acting according to a plan,[25] he may liberate those enslaved to

types, leading them out of types to the truth. It appears that Paul did this in his actions in relation to Timothy (see Acts 16:3), and doubtless also in Cenchreae (see Acts 18:18) and in Jerusalem (see Acts 21:23–6), as it is written in the Acts of the Apostles.

112   It must be observed that the true worshippers do not worship the Father in spirit and in truth only in a future time, but in the present as well. But those who worship in spirit, worshipping as they have received, worship in the earnest of the Spirit (see 2 Cor. 5:5) in the present, but they will worship the Father in the entire Spirit, when they have obtained the entire Spirit. 113   If he who sees with a mirror does not see the truth, as has been demonstrated by those who are skillful in the study of optics,[26] but Paul and those like him now see through a mirror, it is apparent that, as he sees, so he worships God. He worships God through a mirror, but when the time comes that will follow the present time, then will come worship in truth, that which is face to face and no longer beholding through a mirror (1 Cor. 13:12).

XIX 114   Nonetheless, Heracleon supposes "we" in "we worship" to refer to one who is in eternity and those who go with him, for, he says, "they know the one whom they worship, worshipping in accordance with truth." 115   But also "It says 'because salvation is from the Jews,'" according to him, "because he was born in Judaea, but not among them, for he was not well pleased with all of them (see 1 Cor. 10:5), and because from this race salvation and the Word went out to all the inhabited world" (see Ps. 18:5 [19:4]; Rom. 10:18). "But," he explains that, "according to an intellectual perception, salvation has come into existence from the Jews because they are images of things in the Fullness itself". 116   But he himself and those of his opinion ought to have demonstrated how everything that belongs to Jewish worship is an image of things in the Fullness, if indeed they do not simply say this for public consumption, but actually consider it to be true.[27]

117   In addition, as an explanation of worshipping God in spirit and in truth, he says that "the former worshippers in the flesh and in error worshipped one who was not the Father, so that," according to him, "all the worshippers of the Artisan were deceived". 118   Indeed Heracleon adds that "they venerated the creation and not the one who had genuinely created it, who is Christ, if, actually, 'All things came into being through him and without him nothing came to be' (Jn 1:3)."

For the Father even seeks such to worship him (Jn 4:23b).

XX 119 If the Father seeks, he seeks through his Son, who has come to seek and save what is lost (see Lk. 19:10; Ezek. 34:16), namely the ones whom, cleansing and educating by his word and by sound doctrines, he prepares as genuine worshippers.

120 Heracleon says that "what belonged to the Father was lost in deep matter[28] belonging to error. It is this which is sought, so that the Father may be worshipped by those who belong to him."

121 If, therefore, he had had in view the account of the lost sheep (see Lk. 15:4–6) or of the son who had abandoned his father's house (see Lk. 15:11–32), we would have accepted his interpretation.

122 But since, making up fables, those of his opinion provide no clear proofs that I am aware of concerning the loss of the spiritual nature, and provide us no distinct teaching concerning the times and ages before its loss, we find such serious objections adequate reason for deliberately dismissing them.

God is spirit, and those worshipping him must worship him in spirit and in truth (Jn 4:24).

XXI 123 Since many persons affirm many things about God and his being, so that some say that he is of subtle and ethereal bodily nature, others of an incorporeal nature, and yet others of a nature exceeding being by dignity and power, it is worthwhile for us to see if we have impulses from the divine Scriptures toward saying anything concerning God's being.

124 Here it is said that his being is in some way "spirit." "For," it says, "God is spirit," but, in the law "fire" – for it is written, "Our God is a consuming fire" (Heb. 12:29; see Deut. 4:24) – and, in John, "light" – for it says, "God is light and there is not any darkness in him at all" (1 Jn 1:5). **125** If, therefore, we attend to these things in a simpler way, not delving beyond the words themselves, it is the time to say that God is a body. What absurdities result from our saying this it is not possible for the majority to know. Few indeed have understood about the nature of bodies, especially those constituted with reason and providence, saying indeed that what exercises providence is broadly of the same being as those things that are objects of providence, but an object of providence can be perfect. But those wishing God to be a body have accepted all the absurdities that accompany their doctrine, because they cannot face up to the evident consequences of their reasoning.[29]

126 I say these things while making an exception for those who say that there is a fifth nature of bodies in addition to the elements[30]. **127** But if each body has a material nature, properly speaking, without qualities – variable, changing, entirely transformable, receiving whatever qualities its artisan wishes to endow it with – it is necessary that God is a material being, variable, changing, and transformable. 128 These men are not even ashamed to say that he is perishable, being a body, but a spiritual and ethereal body, especially as regards his governing faculty, but even though he is perishable, he is not destroyed, because they say there is nothing to destroy him.

129 But if, in disregard for the consequences, we say that he is body and, on account of Scripture, some particular kind of body, namely spirit, consuming fire, and light – not accepting what which necessarily follows from these, like foolish persons who speak against the evidence – every fire is indeed perishable because it requires fuel, and every spirit, if we accept "spirit" in a very simple way, is, being a body, by its very nature subject to a change in density.

130 It is time, therefore, either to accept these absurdities and blasphemies against God by keeping to the words as they are, or to proceed, as we have in many other matters, and examine what can be indicated by saying that God is spirit, fire, or light.

XXII 131 And first it must be said, that, just as when we find it written that God has eyes (Ps. 5:6 [5:5], 31:8 [32:8]), eyebrows (Ps. 10:4 [11:4]), ears (Jas. 5:4; Ps. 115:2 [116:2]), hands (Ex. 15:6; Deut. 33:3; Ps. 37:3 [38:2]), arms (Deut. 15:6; 1 Kings. 8:42; Ps. 70:18 [71:18]) and feet (Mt. 5:335; Acts 7:49), or even that he has wings (Ps. 35:8 [36:7], 90:4 [91:4]), we understand allegorically what is written, despising those who attribute to God a form like that of men, and we do this reasonably, we must act consistently in dealing with the above terms. And this is evident from what is apparently the most practical procedure, "For God is light," says John, "and there is not any darkness in him at all" (1 Jn 1:5).

132 Let us inspect, to the best of our ability, how we must understand most intelligently that he is light, for the word "light" is employed in two ways, corporeally and spiritually, the latter being intelligible, for which the Scriptures say "invisible" and the Greeks use the term "incorporeal". 133 An example of the corporeal usage, approved by all who accept the narrative, is: "There was light for all the children of Israel in all the places where they resided" (Ex. 10:23). An example of the intelligible and spiritual is in one of the Twelve Prophets: "Sow for yourselves in justice, gather for a fruit of life, light for yourselves a light of knowledge" (Hos. 10:12 LXX). 134 Similarly "darkness" can also, by analogy, be read in

two ways. An example of the commoner usage is "And God called the light 'day' and the darkness he called 'night'" (Gen. 1:5); an example of the intelligible is "The people sitting in darkness . . . and in the shadow of death, a light has risen upon them" (Mt. 4:16; see Isa. 9:1).

XXIII 135 In these conditions it is worthwhile to see what it is appropriate for us to understand concerning the God who is called light in which there is no darkness at all. Is it then the corporeal eyes which God illumines as light or is it the intelligible, concerning which the prophet says, "Enlighten my eyes, so that I may not sleep in death" (Ps. 12:4 [13:3])? 136 I consider that it is apparent to all that we cannot say that God does the work of the sun, while leaving it to another to enlighten the eyes of those who should not sleep in death; accordingly God illumines the minds of those whom he judges worthy of his proper enlightenment. 137 But if he illuminates the mind, according to "the Lord is my enlightenment" (Ps. 26:1 [27:1]), it is necessary for us to comprehend that he is its intelligible, invisible, and incorporeal light.

138 Is he not also called "consuming fire" because corporeal fire seems to consume objects such as wood, hay, and stubble (see 1 Cor. 3:12)?[31] If there are intelligible wood, hay, and stubble, is not our God the fire consuming such matter, he who is said to be "consuming fire"? And it is appropriate for the Lord to consume such things and to obliterate evil, so that, when this happens, pain and distress reach, without, I suppose, any physical contact, to the governing faculty, which is the location of that building[32] that deserves to be consumed.

139 God is therefore termed light, so called by using corporeal light as a metaphor for an invisible and incorporeal light, on account of its power to enlighten intelligible eyes, and in the same way he is addressed as consuming fire, so conceived after a corporeal fire consuming a similarly corporeal matter.

140 Such also appears to be the case with respect to "God is spirit." Since we are in the intermediate state ordinarily called "life" we are made alive by the spirit because our own spirit produces what is called, in a very corporeal way, "the breath of life" (see Gen. 2:7). I understand that God, who leads us to the genuine life, has come to be called "spirit" from this spirit. For the spirit is said, according to Scripture, to be "life-giving" (see 2 Cor. 3:6), but evidently it gives not the intermediate life, but the more divine. For the letter kills and brings about death, not the death which consists of the separation of the soul from the body, but the death which is

the separation of the soul from God, the Lord Jesus, and the Holy Spirit.

XXIV 141   Also do we not better comprehend "You remove their spirit, and they perish" and "You send out your spirit and they are created, and you renew the face of the earth" (Ps. 103:29–30 [104:29–30]) in this sense of "spirit," if we understand that he who is deprived of the divine spirit becomes earthy (see 1 Cor. 15:47)? After making himself ready to receive it and accepting it, he will be re-created, and, being re-created, he will be saved. 142   Such would also be the sense of "He blew into his face the breath of life, and the man became a living soul" (Gen. 2:7), so that we can regard spiritually the "blowing." the "breath of life" and the "life" of the soul. 143   Since when the above power finds the soul of the holy person, as it were, an appropriate dwelling, providing a residence for itself in it, so to speak, so it must be supposed that it was written that "I shall dwell in them and walk about among them, and I shall be their God, and they shall be my people" (see Lev. 26:12; 2 Cor. 6:16).

144   However we require fuller exercise in order to be perfected and to have what the Apostle calls "senses exercised" (see Heb. 5:14) so that we can distinguish good things from evil, true things from false, and to understand matters theoretically, so that we may understand in a manner more opportune and more worthy of God, in so far as human nature is capable, how God is light, fire, and spirit. 145   And in Third Kingdoms,[33] when the Spirit of the Lord came to Elijah, it implies something about God:

> For he said "You shall depart tomorrow and you shall stand before the Lord on the mountain. See, the Lord will pass before you, and there will be a mighty wind[34] breaking the mountains, crushing the rocks before the Lord, but the Lord will not be in the wind."

(In other texts we read simply, "before the wind of the Lord.")

> After the wind will be an earthquake, but the Lord will not be in the earthquake, and after the earthquake a fire, but the Lord will not be in the fire, and after the fire a sound of a slight breeze.
>
> (1 Kings 19:11–12)

Doubtless this passage makes evident in what affairs one must participate before comprehending God, a matter not to be explained at the present time.

146   Who was appropriate to tell us who God is except his Son, "for no one knows the Father except the Son" (Mt. 11:27)? So that we know, by the revelation of the Son, how God is spirit, and we endeavor to worship God in the life-giving Spirit and not in the killing letter (see 2 Cor. 3:6), to revere him in truth and not in types, shadows, or tokens. In the same way, angels do not venerate God in tokens and shadows, as men venerate God, but in ways that are intelligible and heavenly, since they have a high priest after the order of Melchizedek as the leader of their service of intercession for those who need salvation and and for their mystical and unutterable contemplation.

XXV 147   However, Heracleon says concerning "God is spirit" "For his divine nature is immaculate, pure, and invisible." 148   I do not know if, by proclaiming these things, he taught how God is spirit, but, considering that he was clarifying "those worshipping must worship in spirit and in truth," he says:

> spiritually in a manner worthy of the one worshipped, not
> carnally, for, being of the same nature with the Father,
> whoever worships according to the truth and not according
> to error is spirit, as also the Apostle teaches, calling such a
> piety a "reasonable veneration" (see Rom. 12:1).

149   Let us discern if it is not extremely impious to say that they who worship God in spirit are of one being[35] with the unbegotten and entirely blessed nature. These are the ones who, by Heracleon's account, are shortly to fall. He says that "the Samaritan woman, even though she is of spiritual nature, had been made a fornicator." 150   But those who say these things do not see that everything which is of the same being is also susceptible to the same things. If the spiritual nature had been allowed to commit fornication, even though of the same being with God, what unholy, godless, and irreverent consequences follow from such a doctrine about God it is not without danger even to imagine! 151   But we are persuaded by the Savior who says: "The Father who sent me is greater than I" (Jn 14:28, see 6:44) and for this reason would not even bear to have the epithet "good" (see Mk. 10:18) applied to him in its proper, true, and perfect sense, but graciously referred it to the Father, finding fault with the person

171

who wished to glorify the Son too much. We say that the Savior and the Holy Spirit transcend all generated beings, not by comparison, but by an absolute transcendence, but that he is transcended as much and more by the Father, as he and the Holy Spirit transcend other beings, not just ordinary ones.

How is it possible even to say what great praise belongs to one who transcends thrones, dominions, rulers, powers, and every name named, not just in this age, but in the age to come (see Eph. 1:21), and in addition the holy angels, spirits, and souls of the righteous? **152** But even though transcending by his being, dignity, power, divinity – for he is the living Word – and wisdom being so many and so great, he can in no way be compared to the Father. **153** For he is the image of his goodness and the emanation not of God, but of his glory and his eternal light, and the exhalation not of the Father, but of his power, and the pure emanation of the glory of the Almighty, and the spotless mirror of his activity (Wis. 7:25–6; Heb. 1:3), the mirror through which Paul and Peter and those like them see (see 1 Cor. 13:12) God, because he said: "He who has seen me has seen the Father who sent me" (Jn 14:9, see 12:45).

The woman says to him: "I know that Messiah is coming, called Christ. When he comes, he will announce everything to us" (Jn 4:25).
XXVI **154** It is worthwhile to see how the Samaritan woman, who accepts nothing beyond Moses' Pentateuch, hopes for the advent of Christ as it is proclaimed by the law alone. Perhaps it is from Jacob's benediction to Judah that they hope that there will be a coming of the one who said "Judah, may your brothers praise you, may your hands be on the back of your enemies, the sons of your father will worship you" (Gen. 49:8), and, a little farther on "a ruler from Judah shall not be lacking and a leader from his loins, until what is laid up for him arrives, and he is the expectation of nations" (Gen. 49:10). **155** Perhaps also it is from the prophecies of Balaam that they hope for the same thing, namely that

> A man shall go forth from his seed and shall rule over many nations, the kingdom of Gog shall be exalted, and his kingdom shall be increased. **156** God has conducted him out of Egypt; his glory shall be like that of the unicorn. He will eat the nations of his enemies and will suck marrow from their stout parts. With his arrows he will shoot down his enemy. When he has lain down, he has rests like a lion

and like a lion's whelp. Who will rouse him? May those who bless you be blessed and may those who curse you be cursed.

(Num. 24:7–9)

157 In what follows, Balaam himself says:

I shall show them, but not now. I shall bless, and he does not approach. A star shall rise from Jacob, and a man shall arise from Israel, and he shall shatter the captains of Moab, and he shall carry away captive all the sons of Seth. And Edom shall be his inheritance and Esau his enemy shall be his inheritance, and Israel will act in strength. And he shall arise from Jacob and he shall destroy what is saved from the city.

(Num. 24:17–19 LXX)

158 You shall examine if it also seems right for the Samaritans to consider Moses' blessing on Judah – the one which goes "Hear, Lord, the voice of Judah, and may you go to his people. May his hands together judge for him, and may you be his help from his enemies" (Deut. 33:7) – as a reference to Christ. 159 Since the Samaritans boast that Joseph is their patriarch, I investigate whether some of them admit that the blessing of Jacob to Joseph and that of Moses are said in view of Christ's advent, but it is possible for anyone who wishes to take these sayings from Scripture itself.

160 And the Savior himself, knowing that Moses had recorded many instances of prophecy concerning Christ, said to the Jews, "If you believed Moses, believe me, because he wrote about me" (Jn 5:46). 161 But nonetheless most of the things it is possible to find recorded about Christ in the law are referred to him as types and enigmatically. At the present time I do not see any examples more obvious and more clear than these.

He is, moreover, called "Messiah" in Hebrew, which the Seventy translated "Christ," but Aquila "Anointed."[36]

XXVII 162 It must also be carefully thought about whether "When he comes, he will announce everything to us" was said by the Samaritan woman from a tradition or from the law. We must not ignore, moreover, that, just as Jesus arose among the Jews, not only saying that he was the Christ, but demonstrating it, so from the Samaritans a certain Dositheus arose, saying that he was the

Christ prophesied, from whom came the present Dositheans, who possess the books of Dositheus and recount certain fables concerning him, such as that he did not taste death but is somehow still in life.[37] This will suffice for the text itself.

163 Nonetheless, heterodox thought[38] – beside Jacob's spring, which she supposes to be a well – terms "Christ" that doctrine[39] which she understands to be more perfect, saying: "When he comes, he will announce everything to us." But he whom she awaited and hoped for, being present, says: "I am, the one who is speaking to you" (Jn 4:26).

164 See also what Heracleon says, for he says: "The church had received Christ and was convinced concerning him, that he alone knew all things."

Jesus says to her: "I am, the one who is speaking to you." And at this point his disciples came and they marveled that he spoke with a woman. However, no one said: "What are you seeking? Why are you speaking with her?" (Jn 4:26–7).

XXVIII 165 It must be investigated if somehow Christ proclaimed good news about himself, and these passages must be compared to one another, namely, "I am the one who testifies concerning myself, and the Father who sent me testifies concerning me" (Jn 8:18), and "If you believed Moses, believe me, for he wrote about me" (Jn 5:46), and any other passage like these in any of the gospels.

166 Besides, at the verbal level, here we also learn from him that he is gentle and humble of heart (see Mt. 11:29), for he does not disdain to discuss such matters with a woman who is a water-carrier, who on account of her great poverty must leave the town and labor in order to draw water. 167 For even the disciples marvel when they come, because they have already contemplated the magnitude of the divinity in him, marveling that such a great person would speak with a woman. But we, under the impulse of boasting and disdain, scorn those who are inferior, forgetting that "Let us make man according to our image, and according to our likeness" (Gen. 1:26) applies to each human being. 168 Not remembering the one who fashioned us in the womb (see Jer. 1:5) and fashioned one by one the hearts of all men (see Ps. 32:15 [33:15]) and who attends to all their deeds, we do not know that he is the God of the humble, the helper of the lowliest, the protector of the weak, the shelter of the hopeless, and the savior of the rejected (see Jdt 9:11).

169 But he used that woman as an apostle to those in the town. She was so inflamed by his words that, abandoning her water-jar and returning to the town, the woman said to the men: "Come, see a man who has told me everything I have done. Is this man not the Christ?" so that "they left the town and began to come to him" (see Jn 4:28–30). And this was the particular time when the Word revealed himself most clearly. So the disciples marveled when they came that even she, a female easily led astray, should have the Word discoursing with her. 170 Nonetheless, persuaded that all things are brought into existence appropriately by the Word (see Jn 1:3), the disciples did not fuss or raise doubts about the questions he asked the Samaritan woman and about his conversation with her. 171 Doubtless they were astounded by the great beneficence of the Word who condescends to the soul who despised Zion and had her faith in the Mountain of Samaria, so that is why it was written: "they marveled that he spoke with a woman."
172 But Heracleon says with respect to "I am, the one who is speaking to you" that

> since the Samaritan woman was persuaded concerning the Christ, that at his arrival he would announce all things to her, he says: "Know that that one, whom you await, I am he, the one who is speaking to you." And when he had confessed that he was the expected one who had come[, he says,] his disciples came to him, on whose account he had come into Samaria.

But why did he come into Samaria on account of the disciples, who were already with him?

The woman therefore abandoned her water-jar and went back into the town and says to the men: "Come, see a man who has told me everything I have done. Is this man not the Christ?" (Jn 28–29).
XXIX 173 It is not in vain, I suppose, that the evangelist has recorded that the woman left her water-jar behind, which the woman did when she went back into the town. According to the text, it indicates the great zeal of the Samaritan woman, who abandoned her water-jar, thinking that such a corporeal and humble duty was not of as great importance as the benefit to many people. For she was moved by most charitable sentiments in desiring to announce the good news of Christ to the townspeople, testifying

about him that he has told her everything she had done. **174** She called them to see a man who had a doctrine[40] greater than a man, for what was visible to her eyes was a man. It is therefore necessary for us, forgetting corporeal realities and abandoning them, to hasten to share with others the benefits in which we have participated, for it is to this that the evangelist invites us, in recording, for those knowing how to read, the praise of the woman.

175 However, we must scrutinize what is, in an elevated sense, the water-jar which the Samaritan woman left behind when she had accepted in some way the words of Jesus; it is doubtless the recipient of the water which she had revered on account of its depth, that is, of the teaching, which she went along with earlier, but which she rejected with disdain when, from something greater than the water-jar she took some of the water that was already becoming in her a source of water leaping to eternal life (see Jn 4:14). **176** For how could she proclaim Christ charitably to the townsfolk without having partaken of this water, marveling that he had announced all that she had done, if she had not partaken, that is, through what she had heard, of the Savior's water?

177 Nonetheless, Rebecca, a virgin beautiful in appearance, also went out with a water-jar on her shoulders, before she encountered the servant of Abraham before he had finished speaking to himself, but she did not draw as did the Samaritan woman. She descended to the spring and filled the water-jar, and on her ascent Abraham's servant ran to her and said: "Give me a little water to drink from your water-jar." **178** Since he was Abraham's servant, he would have liked to receive even a little water from Rebecca's water-jar "and Rebecca hastened and lowered the water-jar to her arm and gave him drink until he stopped drinking" (see Gen. 24:15–18). Therefore it is evidently because Rebecca's water-jar is praiseworthy that she does not abandon it, but that of the Samaritan woman, not being so, is abandoned at the sixth hour (see Jn 4:6).

XXX 179 Here, then, a woman announces the good news of Christ to the Samaritans, but, at the end of the gospels also, a woman who had beheld him before all the rest recounts the resurrection of the Savior to the apostles. **180** Nonetheless, the one was not thanked by the Samaritans for announcing the good news of the faith in its perfection, since they said: "It is no longer through your speech that we believe, for we have heard and know that this is truly the Savior of the world" (Jn 4:42). And the other was not entrusted with first-fruits of contact with Christ, who said to her: "Do not touch me," for Thomas was going to hear: "Place your finger here and see my hands, and lift your hand and put it in my side" (Jn 20:17). **181** But these are all the things which the woman did. She had had intercourse with five husbands and after them stooped to a sixth who was not her real husband. After renouncing him and abandoning her water-jar, she was reverently refreshed by a seventh and recommended the benefit of this to the inhabitants of a town, her own town, founded on her former dogmas and built on unsound doctrines. Then the occasion arose for the inhabitants also to leave the town and come to Jesus.

182 In what follows it is with complete awareness that the Samaritans ask Jesus, not to stay in their town but, "by them" (Jn 4:40), that is, that he come to be in their governing faculties, for doubtless he could not stay in their town, since indeed they acted well in leaving the town and coming to him.

183 That such an interpretation is evidently the most accurate, because the evangelist himself impels us to an elevated meaning, may be determined from this: **184** first it is written "They left the town and came to him," and a little later, "Many of the Samaritans from that town believed in him on account of the woman's discourse,[41] testifying: 'He told me everything I have done,' and then having come to him, the Samaritans asked him to stay with them" (Jn 4:39–40). **185** Therefore the Samaritans first left the town to go to him and subsequently came to him while he was still at Jacob's spring, for he does not seem to have moved from there, and they asked him to stay with them. It is not written after this that they re-entered the town, but "He stayed there two days." **186** But also in what follows it is not said "After two days he departed the town," but "And he departed from there" (Jn 4:43). In so far as the intelligible meaning is concerned, the entire plan of benefits[42] to the Samaritans took place beside Jacob's spring.

XXXI **187** But Heracleon considers the water-jar to be the aptitude to receive life and mindfulness of the power which comes from the Savior. He says that

> she left it by him, that is, having left by the Savior such a vessel, with which she had come to receive living water, she turned back to the world announcing to those called the good news of Christ's advent, for it is through and by the Spirit that the soul is led to the Savior.

188 Let us consider if it is possible that this water-jar is being praised by being completely abandoned, for it says "the woman

therefore abandoned her water-jar." It is not added that she abandoned it "by the Savior." 189   And is it not implausible to
interpret the text as meaning that, after she had abandoned "the
aptitude to receive life and mindfulness of the power which comes
from the Savior" and the vessel in which she had come to receive
living water, she had returned to the world without them in order
to announce to those called the good news of Christ's advent?
190   And how is it also that the "spiritual woman" had not
believed in Christ in a precise way, but says: "Is this man not the
Christ?"?
191   And he explained "They left the town" as "they left their
previous worldly manner of life, and came by faith to the Savior."
192   One should say to him: "How is it that he stays with them
two days?" because he has not taken notice of what we just
explained, namely that it is recorded, not that he was in the town,
but that he had stayed two days.

HOMILY 12 ON JEREMIAH

Introduction

This homily, preached, most likely, in the late 230s, provides a typical example of Origen's extensive surviving preaching on the Hebrew prophets. Here, as in other such homilies, he seeks to inoculate his hearers against being so scandalized by the passage's harsh language as to deny the goodness of the God of the Old Testament. He encourages reading the Old Testament "in a hidden manner," indicating that a literal reading, besides being a stumbling block to the morally sensitive, actually induces other Christians to observe Jewish high holy days. At the same time, he urges his hearers to take seriously the prophet's warning that those who persist in sin will face severe punishment from God. The punishment is, he argues, an aspect of God's *oikonomia* demonstrably necessary both for society as a whole and for sinners themselves. In so far as ecclesiastical authorities participate in God's *oikonomia*, they need to act likewise, exercising a rigorous discipline for the good of the individual sinner and, even more, of the whole community.

The translation is from Origène, *Homélies sur Jérémie*, vol. 2, ed. Pierre Nautin = *SC* 238, Paris, Cerf, 1977, pp. 10–50.

Text

On "And say to the people, 'Thus says the Lord God of Israel, "Every jar shall be filled" ' " to "Your eyes shall drop tears, because the Lord's flock has been crushed" (Jer. 13:12 –17).
1   What the prophet was ordered by God to say ought to be worthy of God. Yet it seems that this is not worthy of God, if we stay at the literal level, inviting someone to say, on the basis of the

179

letter, "These letters are foolishness." This is what the soulish man says, for "The soulish man does not receive the things of the Spirit of God. They are foolishness to him" (1 Cor. 2:14). Look at what the text itself says: "And say this to the people: 'Thus says the Lord God of Israel'" – let what "the Lord God of Israel says" be worthy of the Lord God of Israel – "Every jar shall be filled with wine, and it shall be if they say to you, 'Are we so ignorant as not to know that every jar shall be filled with wine?'" (Jer. 13:12). If those who make this response do so in such a way as to stick to the verbal level, saying that they have known that every jar shall be filled with wine, they speak falsely, for it is not the case that every jar shall be filled with wine. There are, in fact, jars filled with olive oil or other fluids, and some stay empty. Therefore they speak falsely, for it is not the case that every jar shall be filled with wine. Yet the people replied saying, "Are we so ignorant as not to know that every jar shall be filled with wine?" We shall interpret this to the best of our ability as follows. If we regard the different wines and what is said about them, we shall see, following the logical consequences of what is said about wines, that "every jar shall be filled with wine" is true. If there is a jar among the jars that is, so to speak, good, it will be filled with wine according to its goodness, and if there is one that is bad as jars go and in comparison with others, according to its bad quality it shall be filled with bad wine.

How is it possible to learn from Scripture about the different wines? This is written about the worse kinds: "For their vine is a vine of Sodom and their tendrils are from Gomorra, their cluster is a cluster of bile, grapes of bitterness to them; their wine is the wrath of serpents and the incurable wrath of asps" (Deut. 32:32–3), but about the better kinds: "How strong is the cup that inebriates me!" (Ps. 22:5 [23:5])[1] and Wisdom invites to her mixing bowl saying: "Come, eat my bread, and drink wine which I have mixed for you" (Prov. 9:5). Thus there is a wine of Sodom and a wine which wisdom mixes, and again, "My beloved had a vine on a mountain peak in a fertile place" (Isa. 5:1), which was called the vineyard of Sorek, because it is Chosen and Marvelous, and there is the vine of the Egyptians which God struck according to the passage: "God has struck their vine with hail and their little figs with hoar-frost" (Ps. 77:47 [78:47]). 2   Consider then that all men may be regarded figuratively as vessels of wine and call them, accordingly, "jars." I say that the scoundrel is filled with the wine of the "vine of Sodom," filled with the wine of the Egyptians and of the enemies of Israel. But the one who is holy and has been benefited is filled with the wine of the vine of Sorek and the wine of which it is written: "How strong is the cup that inebriates me!" and he is also filled with the wine from which Wisdom makes her mixture.

These things must therefore be interpreted in terms vice and virtue if you are to obtain insight into "Every jar shall be filled with wine." If one also needs to see the consequences of vice and virtue – punishments as the consequence of vice, but blessings and promises as the consequence of virtue – we shall cite from the Holy Scriptures how punishments and promises are referred to as wine. "Take the cup of this unmixed wine and you shall make all the nations drink from it against whom I sent you," God says to Jeremiah and adds: "and they shall drink, and shall vomit, and shall go mad, and shall fall" (Jer. 32:15–16). Does he not here refer to punishments as unmixed wine, which they drink who are worthy of unmixed wine, that is, unmixed punishment? There are others who drink not unmixed punishment, but mixed, indeed "The cup is in the Lord's hand full of a mixture of unmixed wine, and he has poured from the one into the other, except that its lees have not been drained, and all the sinners of the earth shall drink" (Ps. 74:9 [75:8]). If you would like to see the "cup of blessing" (1 Cor. 10:16), which the just drink, this word of Wisdom will suffice: "Drink the wine which I have mixed for you" (Prov. 9:5). See also the Savior approaching the Passover in a large upper room well furnished (see Mk. 14:15) and ornamented, feasting with his disciples and offering them a cup, about which it is not specified that it was mixed. For Jesus, gladdening the disciples, gladdens them with unmixed wine and says to them: "Take, drink, this is my blood, which has been shed for you for the remission of sins. Do this, whenever you drink it, for my remembrance" (Mt. 26:26–8; Lk. 22:20; 1 Cor. 11:25) and "Truly, truly I say to you. I shall not drink from now on until I drink it with you anew in the kingdom of God" (see Mt. 26:29). You see the promise, which is the cup of the new testament (1 Cor. 11:25). You see the punishments – the cup of unmixed wine, and another sort of punishment, the mixed cup – so that for each person it is blended according to the proportion of beneficial activity mixed with evil activity which he drinks. Imagine that the one group, being total strangers to piety and totally unconcerned with themselves, but living heedlessly, are drinking the unmixed wine in the passage from Jeremiah. However, the other group, not entirely renegades and sinners but unworthy of the cup of the new testament – sometimes doing beneficial deeds but at other times the opposite – are drinking a mixture of unmixed wine. For God has poured from the one into the other. Which one? We see two cups according to: "he has poured from the one into the other, except that its lees have not been drained." Imagine that the cup of your good deeds is in one of God's hands. If you allow me to speak so daringly, let the cup of your good deeds be in God's right hand and let the cup of your sins be in God's left hand.[2] You cannot drink only from the cup of good things, since you have not done good deeds only, nor can you drink only from the cup of sins, since you have done some useful things, therefore he "has poured from the one into the other." According to the proportion of your deeds, you will have poured out for you wrath and punishment, so that the mixture of punishment may either be more watered down or more sharp and obnoxious. For, as I have already said, in proportion to the mixture of sin with good deeds, the pain from the cup of wrath will be either tempered or untempered, in so far as it is administered to each of the sins. But if you are entirely good and admirable, you say, "I shall take the cup of salvation, and I shall call upon the name of the Lord" (Ps. 115:4 [116:4]).

According to the discourse about those things here called jars, "Every jar," therefore, either admirable or evil, shall be filled with wine and wine will be poured as it is appropriate to the quality of the jar. Oil or any other fluid will not be poured into the jars, but every jar must be filled with wine. 3   Then he teaches – because of sinners, at the level of the text, in "Jerusalem" and then in "Judah" (Jer. 13:13) – with what sort of wine God is going to fill these jars, that is, sinners. It is written: "if they say to you, 'Are we so ignorant as not to know that every jar shall be filled with wine?' you shall say to them, 'Thus says the Lord, see, I am filling all those who dwell in this land, the kings and the sons of David sitting upon his throne, and the priests'" (Jer. 13:12–13). He who is going to punish shall spare no one. Someone shall not avoid being filled with these threats just because he is called "prophet" but still sins. God does not spare someone just because he is called "priest" and seems to have the superiority of a name more honorable than that of the people, so that he will not be punished when he sins (see Jer. 13:13). But things written about those people, says the Apostle, "were said for our sake, on whom the ends of the ages have come" (see 1 Cor. 10:11, 9:10). If therefore someone sins among the priests here – I indicate our presbyters – or in the levites here who attend the people – the deacons, I say – he shall have this punishment. There are, again, certain priestly blessings which we shall soon, God willing, have occasion to see, when, after we have finished interpreting the prophetic books, the book of Numbers is read,[3] for some things are said there concerning priests.

"And the priests," therefore, "the prophets, Judah, and all the inhabitants of Jerusalem" (Jer. 13:13), says God, "he shall fill with drunkenness and he shall scatter them, each man and his brother, and their fathers and their sons" (Jer. 13:13–14). And we understand this thus: God gathers the righteous, but he scatters sinners. Therefore when men did not stir from the East, God did not scatter them, but when they stirred from the East and "each man said to his neighbor, 'Come, let us build ourselves a city and a tower, the head of which will reach to heaven'" (Gen. 11:3–4), God said concerning them, "Come, going down, let us confuse their speech there" (Gen. 11:7), and each one was confused and scattered to one particular place on the earth. And the people of Israel, as long as it did not sin, was in Judea, but when it sinned, each was scattered to some place in the inhabited world and dispersed everywhere.

Understand that something similar occurs with regard to each of us. There is a certain church of the firstborn registered in heaven (see Heb. 12:23), where Mount Zion and the heavenly Jerusalem, the city of the living God, are located (see Heb. 12:22). The blessed will be gathered there to be together, but the sinners will receive an additional punishment of not being with others. I know that some in this world like, as a punishment, to banish to an island a person disturbing their rule, and, for added torture, scatter that person's family, sending the wife here, one son there, another somewhere else, so that, even in her misfortune, the mother may not take comfort in her son, or one brother in another. Understand that something similar happens to the unrighteous. You, a sinner, must taste something very bitter, being under God's careful management,[4] so that, having been corrected, you may be saved. Just as you do not punish a servant or a slave whom you punish simply out of a desire to torture, but so that, by means of his distress, he may change, so God also punishes, by making them suffer distress, those who have been changed by reason and have not been healed. It is as an instructor that he involves them in such things, as it says: "By every distress and scourge you shall be corrected, Jerusalem" (Jer. 6:7–8). It is so that one who is instructing may increase their distress that those who are distressed are scattered apart from each other, so that one may not be with another, for the intensity of distress would be relieved by their mutual consolation.

4   If I need to add to this discussion another reason for dispersion, I shall put forward this one: when the evil are together, they are concerned only with evil and augment it, just as the good are concerned only with good. The evil intention, which becomes stronger among those who are like-minded, is diluted and dispersed when the bad are scattered from each other. For this reason God plans[5] for the immoral not to be with each other, perhaps acting providentially on their behalf, so that their evil may not increase, but may diminish by being diluted.

This is implied in "I shall scatter them, a man from his brother and fathers from their sons at the same time, says the Lord. I shall not regret, and I shall not spare, and I shall not have pity on them in their destruction" (Jer. 13:14).   5   The adherents of heresies attack such words, saying, "See what sort of being is the creator, the god of the prophets, who says, 'I shall not spare, and I shall have not pity on them in their destruction.' How can he be good?" But take the example of a magistrate who, for the sake of the common welfare, does not have pity, or of a judge who, for good reason, does not have mercy. By this example I can make a persuasive case that it is in order to spare many that God does not spare one. I shall also take the example of the doctor who, for the sake of the whole, does not spare one part of the body.

Assume that a magistrate's responsibility is to foster peace and to establish a beneficial regime for the nation under him. Now assume that a murderer is arraigned before him. Assume that this murderer is handsome and personable. Assume that his mother appeals to the magistrate for mercy, begging him to spare her old age. Assume that the scoundrel's wife petitions for mercy. Assume that his children stand around begging on his behalf. In this case what is appropriate for the common good? Should he have mercy on this man or refrain from mercy? If he has mercy the man will resume his previous behavior; if he does not have mercy the man will die, but the common good will be benefited. Thus if God should spare the sinner and have mercy on him – having such pity as not to punish him – who would not be incited to sin? What wicked persons and sinners, who are restrained only by fear from committing sins, would not be incited to sin and thereby become worse? It is possible to see such things occurring in the churches. Someone sins; he has asked for communion after his sin; if he is treated with mercy prematurely, the community will be incited to sin; the sin of others will be increased. If, after consideration, the magistrate – not merciless or cruel, but concerned about the one man and even more concerned about the many – looks ahead to the harm that would come about to the community from presence among them of the one man and the indulgence of his sin, clearly he will remove the one man, so that many may be safe.

Consider the physician. If he spares to cut what needs to be cut, or forbears to cauterize what needs to be cauterized because of the pains that accompany such therapies, the illness will increase and grow worse. But if, following this example, he proceeds boldly to cutting and cauterization, he heals by withholding mercy, by appearing not to have pity on that man who is to be cauterized and cut. Likewise God manages[6] not just one man, but the entire world. He universally administers matters both heavenly and earthly. Therefore he looks out for what is appropriate for the whole world and all of its beings, and as far as possible he also looks out for the individual, but not in such a way as to procure what is appropriate for the individual at the expense of injuring the world. For this reason eternal fire is prepared (see Mt. 18:8 and 25:41), for this reason *Gehenna* (see Mt. 18:9, 23:33) has been made ready, for this reason there is a certain outer darkness (see Mt. 18:12). These are necessary, not just for the one punished, but, even more, for the community.

6 If you desire Scriptural testimony to the effect that sinners are punished in order to instruct others, even if hope for their own potential healing is abandoned, listen to Solomon saying in Proverbs: "By scourging the troublemaker, the thoughtless will be made more astute" (Prov. 19:25). He does not say that the one scourged will become more acute and thoughtful as a result of the scourging, but he says that the thoughtless will change from thoughtlessness to thoughtfulness by means of the scourges applied to the troublemaker. Is not the punishment of others beneficial to us, if we become worthy of salvation because others have been punished? As the fall of Israel brought about the salvation of the gentiles (see Rom. 11:11), so Israel's punishment brings about the salvation of others. Therefore, being good, God says, "I shall not spare, and I shall not have pity on them in their destruction."

7 Now that we have delineated one passage, let us see what the next one teaches us:

Listen, give ear, and do not be proud, because the Lord has spoken, "Give glory to the Lord your God before the night falls and before your feet stumble upon the dark mountains, and you shall wait for the light. There is the shadow of death, and they are made into shadows. If you do not listen in a hidden manner, your soul will wail before the face of violence, and your eyes shall drop tears because the Lord's flock has been crushed."

(Jer. 13:15–17)

He wishes them to "listen" and "give ear"; it will not suffice only to listen or only to give ear, so it says, "Listen, give ear," and after this he orders them not to exalt themselves and teaches them what must be done. What then is "listen" and what is "give ear"? Let us learn from the words themselves. "Give ear" means "receive in the ear" and "listen," if it is said in contrast to "give ear," means "receive in the mind." Since, among the things said in the Scriptures, some are more ineffable and mystical, but others are immediately useful to those who understand them, I think that "listen" is said concerning the more ineffable and "give ear" is said concerning those that are more immediately useful and able without interpretation to assist those who hear them.[7]

When we interpret the entire Bible, having become "sound moneychangers,"[8] we shall say "listen" to one thing and "give ear" to another thing. Then, when we have listened and given ear, he orders us "do not be proud." For "everyone who exalts himself will be humbled" (Lk. 14:11, 18:14). The Savior also, when he says, "Learn from me, for I am gentle and lowly of heart, and you will find rest for your souls" (Mt. 11:29), teaches us not to be proud. For along with the other human vices, this sin abounds in us. Often enough we pride ourselves entirely irrationally for things no one ought to be proud of, but even when this is not so and we pride ourselves for good reason, it is not healthy to pride ourselves.

8 I shall make my meaning plain: there are some who are proud because they are the children of governors and the offspring of great worldly dignitaries. Such persons, priding themselves because of something involuntary and indifferent, have no plausible reason to make them proud. Some are proud because they have authority to pronounce a capital sentence – they pride themselves on having achieved what they call "progress"[9] to a position where they can chop off human heads. The glory of such persons is in their shame (Phil. 3:19). Others pride themselves on wealth – not the genuine wealth, but the wealth here below. Others pride themselves, for example, on a beautiful house or many fields. None of these things is worthy of consideration; one should not pride oneself on any of these things. The justifiable thing about which to be proud, should

someone be proud, is being wise, and one might pride oneself on the consciousness that one has not engaged in carnal pleasure for ten years or from childhood on, or, again, someone might be proud because he had been imprisoned for Christ's sake. Such things are justifiable grounds for reasonably being proud, but not even because of these things, if one refers to true reason, should one reasonably be proud.

This is why it is not possible to pride oneself reasonably even on these things. Paul had occasion for priding himself on account of visions (2 Cor. 12:1), apparitions (see Acts 16:10, 18:9), marvels and signs (see Rom. 15:19; 2 Cor. 12:12), the labors he accomplished for Christ, and the churches he established in his zeal to found a church wherever Christ was not named (see Rom. 15:20). All these things would be occasions for his being proud, if we must speak about justifiable reasons for being so. To some it might have seemed appropriate for him to be proud, but, nonetheless, since it was not without danger to be proud even on account of such things, the benevolent Father, even as he was endowing him with visions and apparitions, also gave him, as if it were a gift of grace, an angel of Satan, to buffet him, so that he would not be overly proud concerning which three times he entreated the Lord that the angel of Satan, which he had given him by design so that he would not be proud, might depart from him (see 2 Cor. 12:7–8). And the Lord replied to him – for Paul deserved a response – "My grace is sufficient for you, for my power is perfected in weakness" (2 Cor. 12:9). Therefore there is nothing we ought to be proud about, for a fall results from being proud according to: "the heart of a man exalts itself before distress, and it humbles itself before glory" (Prov. 18:12).

Thus we deal with "Listen, give ear, and do not be proud, because the Lord has spoken." 9   But see how after this he commands us to do certain things: "Give glory" he says "to the Lord your God before the night falls and before your feet stumble upon the dark mountains, and you shall wait for the light." He wishes the person who gives glory to the Lord to give glory while it is light, because the glory of the Lord cannot be announced once night has fallen and it is dark. When is it that night falls, and when is it that night has not fallen? "Work while the light is in you" (see Jn. 9:4, 12:35), for the light is in you if you have in you him who said "I am the light of the world" (Jn. 8:12). As long as that light rises for you, glorify God, but know that a certain darkness can occur, and you must not wait for that darkness, but give glory to God before the darkness.

10 Perhaps we shall understand this by employing a gospel text where it is said by the Savior: "Work while it is day, for the night comes when no one can work" (Jn 9:4). Here "day" is the term for this world – it is necessary to add "here," for I know that in other passages other things are meant.[10] "Day" is therefore the term for this world, "darkness" and "night" are its termination by punishments, for "Why do you desire the day of the Lord. It is also darkness and not light" (see Am. 5:18), says the prophet Amos. If you see what the distress will be after the consummation of the world – a distress that will attend to almost the entire race of men who are to be punished for their sins – you will see that the entire environment will be darkened and no one will any longer be able to praise God, so that the Word has even enjoined the just saying: "Go, my people, enter your cellar, lock your door, hide yourselves a little while, until the fury of my wrath has passed" (Isa. 26:20). Notice at the same time, in this passage, if possible, that it says "a little while," but this "little while" is little to God, it is not little to a man; it is necessary to see that it is little or great according to the individual concerned. I shall offer an example to show how it is little or great according to the individual concerned: for each individual animal a certain amount of food may be little by comparison to its structure, or such an amount may be much by comparison, again, to its constitution. Thus what is little for a man may be great for some other animal. What is little, for example, for a man is much for a child. Thus the span of a human lifetime is little, even when it is of an aged person, in comparison with the whole of the present age. If, therefore, it is said: "Go, my people, enter your cellar, lock your door, hide yourselves a little while," the little is to be considered as being said not from the perspective of the one ordered to go and enter into his cellar, but from the perspective of the one commanding these things, to whom a thing is little which is much to that other person. Indeed if, until the fury of God's wrath is past, some must enter into their cellars, but there are some for whom their sins are not forgiven, not only in the whole of this age, but in the whole of the age to come (see Mt. 12:32), it is evident that the "little" lasts as long as I have mentioned.

11 "Give glory," then, "to the Lord our God." How shall we give glory to the Lord our God? It is not by clamor and slogans that I seek to give glory to the Lord our God, it is rather by deeds that one who gives glory to the Lord actually does so. In temperance we shall glorify God, in justice, in well-doing we shall glorify the Lord. Give glory to the Lord in courage and endurance. Give glory to the Lord in well-doing and holiness and the rest of the virtues.[11] If this is the case and in this way someone glorifies God, do not assume that I blaspheme when, similarly, I adduce the witness of the opposite expressions. The temperate person glorifies God; the debauched person dishonors God. Like Nebuchadnezzar he topples the temple of God and defiles the temple of God (see 1 Cor. 3:17) and through the transgression of the Law he dishonors God (see Rom. 2:23). The expression itself is apostolic. Does not the sinner therefore confer dishonor on God, and if doctrines concerning providence are brought into question, so that some doubt if there is a providence, is there any other reason for this than vice? Remove vice, and providence will be no stumbling block for you. Turning the proper order upside-down, those who question providence say such things as "Why are there adulterers?" and "Why are there effeminate men?" (see 1 Cor. 6:9) "Why are there so many godless and impious?" Sinners are the ones who have brought dishonor upon providence, and cavils against God, and blasphemy against the creator of the world.[12] Therefore let some give glory to God. Those who act contrary to the glory of God by sinning do not give glory to God.

12 "Give glory to the Lord your God before the night falls and before your feet stumble upon the dark mountains" (Jer. 13:16). There are certain dark mountains; there are certain bright mountains. Since both of them are mountains, both of them are imposing. The bright mountains are the holy angels of God, the prophets, Moses the minister (Num. 12:7) and the apostles of Jesus Christ. All these are bright mountains, and I think that it is said concerning them in the Psalms: "Their foundations are on the holy mountains" (Ps. 86:1 [87:1]). And what are the dark mountains? "Those lifting up their heights against the knowledge of God" (see 2 Cor. 10:5). The devil is a dark mountain, the rulers of this world who are being destroyed (see 1 Cor. 2:6) are dark mountains, and the epileptic petty demon[13] (see Mt. 17:5) was a mountain, and it was a dark mountain about which the Savior said: "Say to this mountain" (Mt. 17:20). For, regarding the epileptic, when the word was put to him and the disciples were saying, "Why cannot we cast it out?" (Mt. 17:19), the Savior replied: "If you have faith as a grain of mustard seed, you will say to this mountain" (concerning which you are strained, concerning which you are inquiring) "you will say to this mountain, move over there, and it will move" "From where?" From the man. "To where?" To its own familiar place. Those who stumble do not stumble on bright mountains, but on

189

dark mountains, whenever they have come to be with the Devil and his angels, the dark mountains.

"[A]nd you shall wait for the light" (Jer. 13:16). It is possible that "and you shall wait for the light" is connected with "You shall give glory to our God". If you were to "Give glory to the Lord your God before the night falls and before your feet stumble upon the dark mountains" it is obvious that, if the night falls "you shall wait for the light" and the light will come next for you. Another person might say (I do not vouch for the interpretation) that those who stumble on dark mountains will wait beside the dark mountains, awaiting the light of mercy. If someone goes upon dark mountains, we see what is there: "there is shadow of death" (Jer. 13:16). Where there are dark mountains, there is the shadow of death brought about by those dark mountains.

"[A]nd they are made into shadows. 13   If you do not listen in a hidden manner, your soul will wail before the face of violence" (Jer. 13:17) Those who listen "in a hidden manner," listen, but others, even if they listen, do not listen "in a hidden manner." What is listening "in a hidden manner" but "we speak the wisdom of God in a mystery, that which is hidden, which God foreordained before the ages for our glory" (1 Cor. 2:7) and where it is said elsewhere "most of the works of God are in secrets" (Sir. 16:21)? If I listen to the law, either I listen to it in a hidden manner, or I do not listen to it in a hidden manner. The Jew does not listen to the law in a hidden manner. Therefore he is outwardly circumcised, not knowing that "he is not a Jew, who is one outwardly, nor is circumcision that which is outward, in the flesh" (Rom. 2:28). But he who listens about circumcision in a hidden manner, is circumcised in secret (Rom. 2:29). He who listens to the things ordained in the law concerning the Passover in a hidden manner eats Christ the Lamb, for Christ our Passover has been sacrificed for us (1 Cor. 5:7), and knowing what sort of thing the flesh of the Word is,[14] and knowing that it is genuine food, he partakes of it, for he has understood the Passover in a hidden manner. The ordinary Jew therefore killed the Lord Jesus and is today responsible for the murder of Jesus because he did not listen either to the law or to the prophets in a hidden manner. Whenever you read about the unleavened bread, it is possible to listen in a hidden manner; it is possible to listen outwardly to the commandment. As many among you as celebrate the unleavened bread, the bodily unleavened bread[15] – for the Passover is near – do not listen to the commandment that says, "If you do not listen in a hidden manner, your soul will wail." Also regarding the Sabbath there are women who, not having listened to the prophet, do not listen in a hidden manner, but listen outwardly, not washing themselves on the day of the Sabbath, returning to the poor and weak elements (see Gal. 4:9), as if Christ has not come among us, he who has perfected us and conveyed us from the legal elements to the gospel perfection.

Therefore we are careful, in reading the law and the prophets, never to fall subject to the prophecy: "If you do not listen in a hidden manner, your soul will wail before the face of violence." As many of you women who observe the Jewish feast because of not understanding the day of propitiation (see Lev. 25:9) after the advent of Christ do not listen to propitiation in a hidden way, for to listen to propitiation in a hidden way is to listen to how God offered Jesus as a propitiation for our sins (see Rom. 3:25) and he is the propitiation for our sins, and not for ours only, but for the sins of the whole world (1 Jn 2:2). Also if the gospel parables are read, and there is one who listens to things externally, he does not listen to them in a hidden way, but if the listener is an apostle or one of those who enter into the house (Mt. 13:16) of Jesus, he approaches Jesus and asks about the obscurity of the parable, and Jesus interprets it. Then he becomes a listener to the gospel, listening to it in a hidden way, so that his soul may not wail, for the soul wails of those who do not listen in a hidden way.

Why, surprisingly, does it not say "You shall wail, if you do not listen in a hidden way" but "your soul shall wail"? There is a certain wailing when only the soul wails, and perhaps the Savior teaches us about that wailing when he says: "There is wailing" (Mt. 8:12) and when he says: "Woe to you who laugh now, for you shall mourn and wail" (Lk. 6:25). He speaks of that wailing with which the prophet threatens us here saying: "If you do not listen in a hidden manner, your soul will wail before the face of violence" – for when you have experienced violence, you wail –"and your eyes shall drop tears because the Lord's flock has been crushed" (Jer. 13:17). If you should now see the Jewish condition and compare them with their condition in past times, you will see how "the Lord's flock has been crushed." For that was once the Lord's flock and since "they judged themselves unworthy, the Word was turned towards the Gentiles" (see Acts 13:46). Since that flock of the Lord was crushed, should not we, the "wild olive, engrafted contrary to nature on the cultivated stock" (Rom. 11:17) of the patriarchs, be all the more fearful that this flock of the Lord not sometime be crushed? For it is going to be crushed sometime according to what was said by the Savior, when "because of increase of lawlessness, the love of many will grow cold" (Mt. 24:12). To whom does this discourse apply? Is not "the love of many will grow cold" said about so-called Christians? About whom is the word: "When he comes, will the Son of Man find faith on the earth?" (Lk. 18:8)? Is it not about us? Therefore let us be sure to do all things so that this flock of the Lord may daily improve, that it be healthy, that it heal itself and that all tribulation stay away from our souls, so that we may be perfected in Jesus Christ "to whom be glory and power for ever and ever. Amen" (1 Pet. 4:11).

HOMILIES 19 AND 20 ON LUKE

Introduction

These two homilies were preached at Caesarea, around 242 according to Nautin or about ten years earlier by a different chronology.[1] In them Origen deals with Luke's story of Christ's childhood. Origen found problematical the implication that Jesus shared the limitations of human children in Luke's testimony that Christ "progressed," not just "in age," but also "in wisdom" and "in grace with God and men" (Lk. 2:53). To explain how the incarnate Word could actually grow, he appeals to Christ's self-emptying in the so-called "kenosis hymn" of Philippians 2.[2] In his condescension to humanity, the Logos deliberately puts his wisdom and power aside, gradually and partially taking them back up as he matures physically. In the nineteenth homily the child Jesus, like Origen himself as depicted in the *Address*, teaches Socratically, asking questions rather than lecturing. The twentieth includes a fascinating, if double-edged, discussion of the obedience due to ecclesiastical authority and an application of the principle of homonymy, in this case to physical and spiritual maturity.

The translation is from Origène, *Homélies sur S. Luc*, ed. Henri Crouzel, François Fournier, and Pierre Périchon = *SC* 87, Paris, Cerf, 1962, pp. 272–86.

Text

Homily 19

1   Because some, who appear to believe the Holy Scriptures, deny the divinity of the Savior, alleging as a pretext the glory of Almighty God,[3] it seems right to me to teach them, by the

authority of the same Scriptures, that something divine has entered a human body, and not just a human body, but also a human soul. However, if we carefully examine the sense of the Scriptures, we note that his soul had a property not shared by other souls; every human soul, before attaining virtue, is defiled by vices, but Jesus' soul was never soiled by sin's filth. Even so, before he was 12 years old, the Holy Spirit says of him in Luke's gospel: "The boy indeed grew, became strong and was filled with wisdom" (Lk. 2:40). It is not a property of human nature to be filled with wisdom at 12 years of age. Having a share of wisdom is one thing, but being filled with wisdom is another. 2   There is therefore no doubt that something divine appeared in Jesus' flesh, something exceeding not only human nature, but the nature of any rational creature.

And it says "he grew." For he humbled himself, taking the form of a servant, and by the same power by which he humbled himself, he grew. He appeared weak, when he assumed a weak human body, and on its account he became strong. The Son of God emptied himself (Phil. 2:7) and on this account he was again filled with wisdom. "And God's grace was with him" (Lk. 2:40). It was not when he reached adolescence or when he taught openly, but when he was a child that he had God's grace, and because everything about him is marvelous, his childhood also was marvelous, as he was filled with God's wisdom.

3   "His parents then went to Jerusalem, according to their custom, to the feast day of the Passover. And he was twelve years old" (Lk. 2:42). Observe carefully that, before he was 12 years old, he was filled with the wisdom of God and the other things that are written concerning him were fulfilled. When therefore, as I have said, he was 12 years old, the feast concluded and his parents were returning, but "the child stayed in Jerusalem without the knowledge of his parents" (Lk. 2:43). Understand that here there is something that surpasses human nature. It was not just a matter of his staying while his parents did not know where he was. I think here that the child stayed in Jerusalem and his parents did not know where he stayed in a similar manner to the incident in John's gospel when the Jews laid an ambush for him and he escaped out of their midst and disappeared (see Jn 8:59 and 10:39). Do not be shocked that they are called parents, because they deserved to be called mother and father, the one by giving birth to him, the other by caring for him.

4   It continues: "We have searched for you sorrowing" (Lk. 2:48). I do not think that they were sorrowing because they thought that

the child was lost or dead. It is impossible that Mary, who knew that she had conceived by the Holy Spirit by the testimony of the angel's speaking, the shepherds' hastening to the stable and Simeon's prophesying, should fear that the child was missing because he was lost. Reject that opinion altogether when it comes to Joseph, who had been instructed by an angel to take the child and flee to Egypt (Mt. 2:13) and who had heard the words: "Do not fear to take Mary as your wife, because that which is born in her is from the Holy Spirit" (Mt. 1:20). They could not have feared that the child was lost when they knew him to be divine. The text hints at a different sorrow and searching than what the simple reader would understand.

5 Just as, when you read the Scriptures, you search for the meaning with sorrow and anguish, not because you think that the Scriptures are in error or contain anything absurd, but because you cannot find the true word and intention that they must contain, so they searched for Jesus, anxious that he might have departed from them, either because he had departed to go to another place or – as I suppose is more likely – because he had returned to heaven so that he might descend again at an appropriate time. Therefore they searched for the Son of God sorrowing. And when they found him, they did not find him among their relatives, for the Son of God can admit no human relation. They did not find him among their acquaintances (Lk. 2:44), for the great divine power was beyond human acquaintance and knowledge. Where, then, did they find him? They found the Son of God in the temple (Lk. 2:46). When you yourself are searching for the Son of God, search first in the temple, go there, where you will find Christ, the Word and Wisdom, that is, the Son of God.

6 Because he was really a little child, they found him in the midst of the teachers sanctifying and instructing them. Because he was a little child, they found him in the midst of them, not teaching them, but asking them questions (Lk. 2:46), and that on account of the appropriate behavior for his age, so that he may teach us what is appropriate for a child, even those who are wise and learned, and that they would do better to listen to their teachers, when they wish to teach them, than to engage in vain ostentation. He asked the teachers questions, I say, not to learn something, but to instruct them by asking questions. Asking questions and answering wisely flow from the same source of teaching, and it belongs to the same knowledge to know what questions to ask and how to answer. It was necessary for the Savior as a teacher to instruct us initially in what

questions to ask, so that later we might answer the questions according to the word and reason of God to whom be glory and power for ever and ever. Amen (1 Pet. 4:11).

Homily 20

1   Mary and Joseph were searching for Jesus among those close and did not find him; they were searching for him among companions and could not find him. They searched for him in the temple and not simply in the temple, not simply among the teachers, but in the midst of the teachers instructing (Lk. 2:46). There they found him. Wherever there are teachers, there Jesus is found in the midst of the teachers, provided that the teacher sits in the temple and never leaves it.

Jesus profited his teachers and those who saw him asking questions; he taught them speaking in their midst, and somehow stimulating them to search for what they did not know and to investigate things that, until then, they could not know whether they understood or not.

2   Therefore Jesus is found in the midst of the teachers and, when he is found, he says to those who had been searching for him: "Why were you searching for me? Did you not know that I must be in my father's [place]?" (Lk. 2:49). Initially, understanding this passage simply, let us arm ourselves against the irreverent heretics, who say that the Creator and the God of the law and the prophets is not Christ's father. See, here the God of the temple is declared to be Christ's father. Let the Valentinians blush when they hear Jesus saying: "I must be in my father's [place]." Let all the heretics blush, who accept the Gospel according to Luke and despise what is written in it.[4] This, as I have said, is the simpler sense.

3   But when, in fact, it added "they did not understand what he said," let us diligently uncover the meaning of the text. Were they so dull and stupid that they did not understand what he said, because what he said "I must be in my father's [place]" meant "in the temple"? Or did it mean something more profound, which would better edify its hearers, namely that each of us, if he is good and perfect, belongs to God? Generally speaking, therefore, the Savior teaches each of us that he abides only in those who belong to God the Father. If any of you belong to God the Father, he has Jesus in his midst. Let us then believe in what he said: "I must be in my father's [place]." And I think that we have a temple that is more rational, alive, and true than the one that was built as a symbol by

worldly manufacture. Just as Jesus' presence in the temple has a figurative meaning, so does his departure. For he left the earthly temple (Mt. 24:1) saying, "See, your house is left to you deserted" (Mt. 23:38), and leaving that temple came to the dominion of God the Father, that is, the churches spread out over the whole world, and said: "I must be in my father's [place]." Therefore they did not then understand the word that was spoken to them.

4   At the same time attend to this: as long as he stayed in his Father's dominion, he was above, and because Mary and Joseph did not yet have full faith, they could not reside above with him, so he is said to have descended with them (Lk. 2:51). Often Jesus descended with his disciples, nor did he always go about on the mountain or stay endlessly on the summit. Further, because those who suffer under various infirmities do not have the strength to climb the mountain, he therefore descended and came (see Mt. 8:1) to those who were below. Therefore it is written: "he descended with them and went to Nazareth and was subject to them" (Lk. 2:51).

5   Learn, children, to be subject to our parents. The greater was subject to the lesser. Because he recognized Joseph's seniority, Jesus paid him the honor due to parents, giving all children an example to be subject to their fathers and, if they have no fathers, to be subject to those who have a father's position. Why should I speak of parents and children? If Jesus the Son of God was subject to Joseph and Mary, shall I not be subject to the bishop, who has been made a father to me by God? Shall I not be subject to the presbyter set over me by the Lord's choice? I suppose that Joseph knew that Jesus, who was subject to him, was greater than he, and knowing the one subject to be greater, he reverently moderated his authority. Let anyone see that often an inferior person is placed in authority over better persons, so that he who is subject is better than he who seems to be placed in authority. When he who is higher in rank understands this, he is not puffed up with pride because of his higher rank, but knows that someone subject to him may be his better, as Jesus was subject to Joseph.

6   Then follows: "But Mary kept all these words in her heart" (Lk. 2:51). She suspected something more than human, so she kept all these words in her heart, not as if they were those of a 12-year-old child, but as those of him who was conceived by the Holy Spirit, whom she saw progress in wisdom and in grace with God and men (Lk. 2:52). Jesus progressed in wisdom and year by year appeared more wise. Was he not wise to begin with, if he progressed in

wisdom? But because he emptied himself, taking the form of a servant (Phil. 2:7), he recovered that which he had lost. Did he regain and fill himself again with powers, which earlier he seemed to have left behind when he assumed a body? He progressed, therefore, not in wisdom, but in age. For there is a progress in age. Scripture speaks of two ages: one of the body, which is not within our power but in that of natural law; the other of soul, which is actually in our power, in which, if we wish, we can grow daily 7 and arrive at perfection, so that we may no longer be little children, tossed and borne about with every wind of doctrine (Eph. 4:14), but, ceasing to be little children, we begin to be men and say "when I became a man, I destroyed those things which belonged to a child" (1 Cor. 13:11). As I have said, progress in this age, which involves growth in soul, is in our power. If this testimony is not enough, we can take another example from Paul: "Until we all come," he says, " to the perfect man, to the measure of the age of the fullness of the body of Christ" (Eph. 4:13). It is therefore in our power to come to the measure of the age of the fullness of the body of Christ, and, if it is in our power, let us struggle to put away the little child and destroy it and arrive at the other ages, so that we may also hear these words: "You have gone in peace to your fathers, having been brought up to a good old age" (Gen. 15:15), a spiritual one that is, which is truly a good old age, a white old age which arrives at its end in Jesus Christ to whom be glory and power for ever and ever. Amen (1 Pet. 4:11).

HOMILY 5 ON 1 SAMUEL

Introduction

Origen delivered this homily, perhaps around 240, most likely at Jerusalem.[1] 1 Samuel 28 was controversial among both Jewish and Christian interpreters throughout Antiquity.[2] At issue was whether the necromancer actually raised Samuel's soul from the dead or if what Saul saw was a demonic apparition. Eustathius of Antioch would later write an extensive treatise to refute Origen's interpretation in this homily.[3] Although he finds it problematic for a great prophet to be at the beck and call of a necromancer and, by implication, of a petty demon, Origen concludes that the narrative indicates that Samuel did appear to Saul. He then justifies Samuel's presence in Hades as a continuation of his earthly ministry, preparing departed souls for the coming of Christ, whose soul also descended into Hades at his crucifixion.

The translation is from Origène, *Homélies sur Samuel*, ed. Pierre et Marie-Thérèse Nautin = *SC* 328, Paris, Cerf, 1986, pp. 174–208.

Text

1   A very long passage has been read, consisting of four pericopes, which I must summarize. First was read the rest of the story of Nabal the Carmelite (1 Sam. 25). There followed the story about David's hiding himself among the men of Ziph and being betrayed by them. After this, Saul came with the intention of taking David, but, once arrived, lost the opportunity, but David came to Saul while he and his guards slept and took his sword and a gourd of water and, after giving this proof, he reproached the guards who were entrusted with guarding him but slept (1 Sam. 26). After this, the third story is about how David fled to Achish, son of Maoch, the

king of Gath and how David found favor with him after numerous exploits, so that he said: "I shall make you the head of my guards" (1 Sam. 27:1–28:2). Then there is the famous story of the necromancer and Samuel, where it appears that the necromancer brought Samuel back up and that Samuel prophesied to Saul (1 Sam. 28:3–25).

Since there are four pericopes, each one of which contains no small number of events, which, for persons able to expound the passage, could occupy hours and not just one but several gatherings, will the bishop please choose one of the four, so that we may occupy ourselves with that one?

"Expound the one on the necromancer," he says.

2   There are stories that do not touch us, and there are others that are a necessary basis for our hope. I say "stories," because we have not yet arrived at elevated interpretations useful to every person who knows how to make them or who hears them. Among stories there are some that are useful to everyone, some not to everyone. Take, for example, the story of Lot and his daughters (Gen. 19:30–8): if it teaches something useful in an elevated sense, God knows, as does that person who has received the gift of grace to expound these matters. As for the usefulness of the story itself, it would take quite a search to find it! Indeed, what profit can I find from the story of Lot and his daughters? In the same way, what profit could I gain from simply reading the story of Judah and Tamar and what happened to her (Gen. 38:1–30)? But, nonetheless, because the story of Saul and the necromancer touches all of us, it contains necessary truths at the level of the story. Who, after departing from this life, would care to be under the control of a demon? This would seem to be our situation if a necromancer could summon up, not just any believer, but the prophet Samuel. Concerning him, God said through Jeremiah: "Even if Moses and Samuel were before my face, I would not heed them" (Jer. 15:1–2); concerning him the prophet says in the hymns: "Moses and Aaron among his priests, and Samuel among those who call upon his name, they called upon the Lord and he heeded them, in the column of cloud he spoke to them" (Ps. 98:6–7 [99:6–7]); and elsewhere: "If Moses and Samuel appeared before me and besought me," and so on (Jer. 15:1)? What, then, if such a person was under the earth and the necromancer summoned him, did a demon have authority over a prophet's soul? What is there to say? Are these things in Scripture? Is it true or is it not? To say that it is not true encourages faithlessness, and it will come back to haunt those who

said so, but if it is true, it is a problem that requires investigation.

3 We know very well that some of our brothers look askance at the Scripture and say: "I do not believe the medium; when the medium says that she had seen Samuel, she lies. Samuel was not summoned. Samuel does not speak. Just as there are false prophets who say 'Thus says the Lord' and the Lord has not spoken, so this petty demon is lying when it promises to bring up the man Saul asked for, saying, 'Whom shall I summon for you?' when he says, 'Summon Samuel for me' (1 Sam. 28:11)." This is what is said by those who say that this story is not true: "Samuel in hell? Summoned by a necromancer? Samuel, the exceptional prophet, who was devoted to God from birth (see 1 Sam. 1:11); who from before his birth was destined to be in the Temple; who had worn the ephod since he was weaned and had been invested with the double mantle as a priest of the Lord (1 Sam. 1:22–3; 2:18–19); to whom, even as an infant, the Lord spoke oracularly (1 Sam 3:4–14)? Samuel in hell, Samuel in the underworld, the one who succeeded to Eli when he was condemned by Providence on account of the sins and lawless acts of his children (1 Sam. 2:31–6)? Samuel in hell, the one whom God heeded in the time of grain harvest when he granted rain coming from heaven (1 Sam. 12:17–18)? Samuel in hell, who could have asked freely for whatever he wanted, if covetousness overtook him? He did not take a calf, he did not take a cow, he judged and condemned the people while staying poor himself, and never coveted taking anything from such a people (see 1 Sam. 12:1–5). Why should Samuel be in hell? Look at what follows if Samuel is in hell; Samuel is in hell, why not Abraham, Isaac, and Jacob in hell? Samuel in hell, why not Moses, who is linked with him in the saying, 'Even if Moses and Samuel were before my face, I would not heed them'? Samuel in hell, why not Jeremiah in hell, who was told: 'Before I formed you in the womb, I knew you, and before you came out of your mother, I sanctified you' (Jer. 15:1)? Why not Isaiah in hell along with Jeremiah, and all of the prophets in hell?"

4 These things are what they say, those who do not want to accept the struggle of explaining how Samuel was summoned. But since one must remain faithful in heeding the Scriptures, since the matter has been bruited about and can really annoy and disturb us, let us see whether or not the person who does not accept the Scripture ever understood it or whether, undertaking his interpretation with good intentions, he speaks the opposite of what is written.

What is written? "And the woman said, 'Whom shall I summon

for you?' (1 Sam. 28:11)" Whose persona[4] says "And the woman said"? Is it, in fact, the persona of the Holy Spirit, by whom Scripture is believed to be recorded, or is it the persona of someone else? For the narrative persona everywhere, as they know who study any kind of discourse, is the persona of the author, but the author of these discourses is not believed to be a man, but the Holy Spirit is the author who has moved men.

Does not then the Holy Spirit say "And the woman said, 'Whom shall I summon for you?' and he said 'Summon Samuel for me'"? Who says, "And the woman saw Samuel and cried out with a loud voice, saying . . . " (1 Sam. 28:12)? We respond to those who have been bruiting it about and saying that Samuel was not actually in hell: " 'The woman saw Samuel,' the narrative voice says this."

> And the woman cried with a loud voice and said to Saul: "Why have you tricked me? You are Saul!" and the king said: "What is wrong? Do not be afraid, whom have you seen?" And the woman said to Saul: "I have seen gods ascending from the earth." And he said to her: "What form do they have?" And she said to him: "An old man is ascending, and he is wearing a double mantle."
>
> (1 Sam. 28:12–14)

It says that she had seen the priestly vestment. I know that the Scripture says, to the contrary: "Do not be surprised, I myself have seen Satan transformed into an angel of light. It is not therefore a great thing, if his ministers are transformed into ministers of justice" (2 Cor. 11:14–15). But what is it that the woman saw? Samuel. Why did it not say: "The woman saw a demon who was taking on the appearance of Samuel"?

But it is written: "Saul knew that it was Samuel" (1 Sam. 28:14). If it was not Samuel, it ought to have been written: "Saul thought that it was Samuel." But what actually was written was "Saul knew," and no one knows something that does not exist.

"Saul knew," therefore, "that it was Samuel and he fell on his face to the ground and worshipped" (1 Sam. 28:14) and again the persona of Scripture says: "And Samuel said to Saul 'Why have you troubled me by summoning me?'" (1 Sam. 28:15).'Scripture says "said" and we ought to believe that Samuel said to Saul: "Why have you troubled me by summoning me?" Saul answers: "I am in great anguish. Foreigners make war on me, and God has abandoned me and has not answered by the hand of the prophets or in dreams to tell me what I should do" (1 Sam. 28:15), and again Scripture gives no indication but that Samuel himself said: "And why should you inquire of me, when even the Lord himself has abandoned you?" (1 Sam. 28:16). Does it speak the truth or does it lie in saying this?

"The Lord has abandoned you and has come to be against you and he has made himself another, as he spoke through my hand, and he will tear the kingdom from your hand" (1 Sam. 28:17). And does a demon prophesy about the kingdom of Israel? What does the opposing argument say? See, what a great struggle there is in the word of God, a struggle requiring hearers capable of hearing holy doctrines, namely the great and ineffable ones concerning our departure from this place, since at the place where we are now in our discussion, objections have arisen against the first interpretation [that Samuel did not actually appear to Saul], but the second [that Samuel did appear] is by no means clear. But the text is still to be expounded, 5   even though I say that the story and its interpretation are necessary if we are to see what awaits us after our departure.

"[H]e has spoken through my hand, and the Lord will tear the kingdom from your hand and will give it to your neighbor, David" (1 Sam. 28:17) – a demon would not be able to know that David had been consecrated king by the Lord (1 Sam. 16:1–13) – "because you have not heeded the voice of the Lord, you have not executed his wrath against Amalek" (1 Sam. 25:18). Are not these God's words? Saul really did not do the will of the Lord, but he honored King Amalek by letting him live (1 Sam. 15:9), so that Samuel reproached Saul before his own sleep and when Saul was about to depart (1 Sam. 15:16–23, 28:16–19).

"And for this reason the Lord has made this sentence against you in this day, and the Lord will even give Israel over into the hands of foreigners" (1 Sam. 28:18–19). Could a demon prophesy about the whole people of God and say that the Lord was going to hand over Israel?

"Indeed, the Lord will give the camp of Israel into the hands of foreigners. Hasten, Saul, tomorrow you and your sons will be with me" (1 Sam. 28:19). Is this something that a demon would be able to know, that David had been consecrated with prophetic oil and that the following day Saul would depart life and his sons with him – "Tomorrow you and your sons will be with me"?[5]

6   These things clarify that what is recorded is not false and that Samuel is the one who was summoned. What, then, is the necromancer doing here? What does the necromancer do to summon the soul of a just person? This is what the earlier argument sought to

avoid. For, so as not to experience the struggle concerning so many other matters that might be investigated in this place, it says: "It is not Samuel, the demon is lying, since Scripture cannot lie." But these are the words of Scripture, they are not from the persona of the demon itself, but from Scripture's persona: "And the woman saw Samuel" and "Samuel said" what was said by Samuel.

How, then, can we present a real solution to the necromancer's behavior in this place? I ask the person mentioned earlier who upheld the argument "Samuel in hell?" and so on that he answer this question: Who is better, Samuel or Jesus Christ? Who is better, the prophets or Jesus Christ? Who is better, Abraham or Jesus Christ? Here no one who has once come to know that Jesus Christ is the Lord previously prophesied by the prophets will dare to say that Christ is not better than the prophets. Therefore when you confess that Jesus Christ is better, did Christ come to be in hell or did he not? Is it not true what was said in the Psalms, interpreted by the apostles in their Acts as referring to the Savior's descent into hell? For it is written that he is the one referred to in Psalm 15: "For you did not leave his soul in hell, nor did you give your holy one to see corruption" (Ps. 15:10 [16:10] in Acts 2:27–31). Then Jesus Christ was in hell and you are afraid to say that he descended there for the very purpose of prophesying and to go to the other souls?

If, then, you answer that Christ did descend into hell, I ask, when Christ descended into hell, what did he do: did he go to defeat death or to be defeated by it? And he descended into those places not as a servant of those there, but as a lord going to fight, as we have just said in explaining Psalm 21: "Many calves have encircled me, fat bulls have surrounded me, they have opened their mouths against me, like a rapacious, roaring lion, they have put my bones out of joint" (Ps. 21:13–15 [22:12–14]). Let us remember, if we do remember the Holy Scriptures, I remember these things spoken about Psalm 21.[6]

The Savior descended, then, in order to save. Did he descend there after being announced beforehand by the prophets, or not? But here he was announced beforehand by the prophets. Did he descend to some other place without making use of prophets? Even Moses announced his advent to the human race, so that it is justly said by our Lord and Savior: "If you believed Moses, believe me, because he wrote about me, but if you do not believe his writings, how can you believe my sayings?" (Jn 5:46–7, referring to Deut. 18:15–18). Christ made his advent in this life, and it was announced beforehand that he was to make his advent in this life, but if Moses announced him here, why do you not want him to descend there also – so that he might prophesy Christ's coming? Why then? Moses, yes, but the rest of the prophets, no? But Samuel, no? Why is it absurd for physicians to descend to the ill? Why is it absurd for even the chief physician to descend to the ill? They are many physicians (see Mk. 5:26), but my Lord and Savior is the chief physician. For inward desire, which cannot be cured by others, he cures. She could not be cured by any of the physicians (see Lk. 8:43), but Jesus Christ himself cured her. Do not fear (see Mk. 5:36), do not be amazed.[7]

Jesus came to be in hell, and the prophets were before him and they announced in advance the Christ's advent. 7 Then I want to speak about something else from the Scripture itself. Samuel ascends, but, see, the woman does not say that she has seen Samuel, she does not say that she has seen a soul, she does not say that she has seen a man. What does she see? "I have seen gods," she says, "ascending from the earth" (1 Sam. 28:13). And perhaps Samuel had not ascended alone and prophesied to Saul, but, possibly, as here on earth, "one sanctifies oneself with a holy man, one becomes innocent with an innocent man, and one becomes chosen with a chosen man" (see Ps. 17:26–7, LXX [18:25–6]), it is possible here to see holy persons associating with the holy, but not the holy with sinners, unless indeed the holy are associating with sinners in order to save the sinners. So doubtless you will also investigate if, when Samuel ascended, some holy souls of other prophets ascended with him. Or doubtless you will investigate if they were angels set over their spirits – a prophet says: "The angel speaking in me" (Zech. 1:9) – or they were angels who had ascended with the spirits? The universe is full of those needing salvation and they are all ministering spirits sent for service because of those who are going to inherit salvation (Heb. 1:14).

Why are you afraid to admit that every place has need of Jesus Christ? Someone who needs Christ needs the prophets. For it is not possible that he needs Christ, but he has no need for those who prepare the coming and advent of Christ. And concerning John, than whom no one was greater among those born of women, according to our Savior's own testimony, when he said: "No one among those born of women is greater than John" the Baptist (Lk. 7:28), do not be afraid to admit that he descended into hell in order to announce my Lord in advance, in order to say in advance that he was coming down. That is why, when he was in prison and knew that his departure was imminent, he sent two of his disciples and asked, not "Are you the one who is to come?" – indeed he knew that – but "Are you the one who is to come, or do we await another?" (Lk. 7:20). He had seen his glory (Jn 1:15); he had spoken many things concerning his marvelous character; he had first borne witness to him (Lk. 9:32; Jn 1:14; Acts 7:55): "He who is coming after me, was before me" (Jn 1:15, 30); he saw his glory, the glory as of the only son of the Father, full of grace and truth (Jn 1:14); after seeing such things concerning Christ, he hesitated to believe, he doubted but did not say: "Say to him, 'Are you the Christ?'" (Mk. 14:61).

Now there are some who, not understanding what had been spoken, say: "John, as great as he was, did not know the Christ; the Holy Spirit had abandoned him". And he did know him, to whom he bore witness before his birth by leaping when Mary came to him, as his mother bore witness, saying: "For, see, as the voice of your greeting came to my ears, the baby leapt out of joy in my womb" (Lk. 1:44). This John, then, who had leapt before he was born, is the one who said: "This is he of whom I spoke, 'He who is coming after me, was before me'" (Jn 1:4) and "He who sent me said to me 'The one on whom you see the Spirit descend and remain, that one is the Son of God'" (Jn 1:33). He, do they say, did not know that Jesus was the Christ? Indeed he knew him already in the womb.

But through his consummate glory Christ did something similar to what he did with Peter. Which was? Peter knew something great about Christ: "Who am I? Who do men say that I am?" and he said this and that, "But you, what? You are the Christ, the Son of the living God" in which he was blessed "because flesh and blood had not revealed" it to him "but the Father in heaven" (Mt. 16:13–17). Because he had heard great things about Christ and comprehended them, but had not accepted the divine exclamation to him: "See, I am ascending to Jerusalem, and it will be completed" (Lk. 18:31) and "The Son of Man must suffer many things and be rejected by the chief priests and elders and die and on the third day rise again" (Lk. 9:22), he said: "Not for you, Lord" (Mt. 16:22). He knew great things about Christ, but he did not want to accept the humbler things about him. It seems to me that John was in a similar situation. He was in prison knowing great things about Christ – he knew about the heavens opening (Mt. 3:16), he knew the Holy Spirit descending on the Savior and remaining on him (Mt. 3:16), he had seen such a great glory (Jn 1:14) – but he doubted and perhaps disbelieved that one so glorious would descend to hell and to the abyss (see Rom. 10:7). Therefore he asked: "Are you the one who is to come, or do we await another?"

8   I have not made a digression, nor have I forgotten our subject, but we want to establish that, if all the prophets descended into hell before Christ as forerunners of Christ, Samuel also descended there, not in the ordinary way, but as a holy person. Wherever a holy person is, he is holy. Is Christ no longer Christ because he was once in hell? Was he no longer the Son of God because he was in an underground place so that every knee might bow at the name of Jesus Christ, things above the earth, on the earth, and under the earth (Phil. 2:10)? Just as Christ was Christ even when he was below, so that, in a manner of speaking, while he was in the place below, he was above with respect to self-determination. In the same way the prophets as well, including Samuel, when they descended where the souls are below, could be below with respect to place, but not below with respect to self-determination. But I ask: "Did they prophesy supercelestial things?" For my part, I cannot allow a demon such great power as to prophesy concerning Saul and the people of God, and to prophesy about David's kingship that he was about to reign. Those who say such things [i.e. that a petty demon could prophecy concerning God's plan] will come to recognize the truth about the passage by finding no way to explain how a physician should come for the salvation of those who are ill to the place where the ill are. Let physicians go to the places where soldiers suffer and enter the place of their stench and wounds; this is what medical benevolence[8] inspires. So the Word has inspired the Savior[9] and the prophets to come here and to descend into hell.

9   But this consideration must be added to our discourse: if Samuel was a prophet and, when he departed, the Holy Spirit abandoned him and prophecy abandoned him, the Apostle would not have spoken the truth in saying, "Now I prophesy in part and I know in part, but when the perfect comes, then the partial will disappear" (see 1 Cor. 13:9–10). The perfect comes, in fact, after this life. Although even Isaiah, when he prophesied, prophesied with assurance (see Acts 4:29) "in part," Samuel's testimony here concerning David actually achieves "the perfect" in prophecy.[10]

But Samuel did not reject the prophetic gift of grace. Since he did not abandon it, did he make use of it like those speaking with tongues, so as to say: "My spirit prays, but my mind is unfruitful" (1 Cor. 14:14)? Now he who speaks in a tongue does not build up the church, even though Paul says that he who prophesies builds up the church, saying so in the phrase "the one prophesying builds up the church" (1 Cor. 14:4). But if the one prophesying builds up the church and Samuel had the prophetic gift of grace – for he had not lost it, not having sinned – for he alone loses the prophetic gift of grace who has done things unworthy of the Holy Spirit, so that it leaves him and deserts his governing faculty.[11] This is what David feared when, after his sin, he said: "And do not take your Holy Spirit from me" (Ps. 50:13 [51:11]). But if the Holy Spirit prophesies and Samuel was a prophet who, in prophesying, builds up the church, whom was he to build up? Was he to prophesy in heaven? To whom? To the angels who do not need it, for those who are well do not have need of physicians, but those who are ill (see Mt. 9:12)? There are some who need his prophecy; indeed the prophetic gift of grace is not barren – no gift of grace remains barren in a holy person. The souls of those who have fallen asleep are, I dare say, those who need the prophetic gift of grace. Israel here needed the prophet, but also the Israel that had fallen asleep, having left this life, needed prophets, so that the prophets might again proclaim to that Israel Christ's advent.

In addition, before the advent of my Lord Jesus Christ, it was impossible for anyone to pass to the place where the tree of life is, for it was impossible to pass by those posted to guard the way to the tree of life for he posted cherubim and a turning fiery sword to guard the way of the tree of life (see Gen. 3:34). Who could make a way? Who could make it possible for anyone to pass by the fiery sword? Just as no one could make a way in the sea except by God's power and by the pillar of fire and the pillar of light that come from God (see Ex. 14:24), just as no one could make a way in the Jordan except Joshua [in Greek, Jesus] (for this Jesus was the type of the real Jesus) (Jos. 3:16), so Samuel could not pass by the fiery sword and Abraham could not pass. That is why Abraham was seen by the rich man who was being punished and, being in torments, the rich man lifted up his eyes and saw Abraham, even if he saw him from far off, and he saw also Lazarus in his bosom (Lk. 16:23). The patriarchs, the prophets, and all men therefore awaited Christ's advent, so that he might open the way. "I am the way" (Jn 14:6). "I am the door" (Jn 10:9). He is the way to the tree of life, so that "If you pass through fire, the flame will not burn you" (Isa. 43:2) will come to pass. Of what fire? "He posted cherubim and a fiery sword turning to and fro to guard the way of the tree of life" (Gen. 3:34). This is why the blessed waited there, accomplishing a plan[12] that prevents them from going where the tree of life is, where the paradise of God is, where God is the farmer, and where the blessed, the elect, and the holy ones of God eventually will be.

10 There is therefore no stumbling block in this passage, but everything is marvelously written and is understood by those to whom God reveals the interpretation (see 1 Cor. 2:10; Mt. 11:25–7). We have something in excess of this, we who have come to the completion of the ages (Heb. 9:26). What is in excess? If we depart from this life after having become fair and good, not bearing the burdens of sin, we ourselves shall pass by the fiery sword and shall not descend to that place where those waited who had fallen asleep before Christ's coming; we shall pass by without being harmed by the fiery sword "for the work of each man, what sort it is, the fire shall prove. If anyone's work is consumed, he will bear the loss, but he himself will be saved as if through fire" (1 Cor. 3:13,15). We therefore pass by [the sword] and we have something more (see Mt. 20:1) than they did, and, if we have lived well, we cannot depart from this life badly. The ancients, neither the patriarchs nor the prophets, could not say what we can say, if we live well: "It would be far better to be dissolved and to be with Christ" (Phil. 1:23). Therefore we have something more and a great gain (see Phil. 1:21) in having come to the completion of the ages, the first to receive the denarius, for listen to the parable in which, beginning, he gave the denarius to those who were last, but the first supposed that they would receive something more (see Mt. 20:8–10). You therefore are the first, who came last, you receive wages from the master of the house, Jesus Christ our Lord, to whom be glory and power for ever and ever. Amen (1 Pet. 4:11).

LETTER TO GREGORY

Introduction

We may presume that the editors of the *Philocalia* preserved this letter because it affirmed the value of the Greek intellectual tradition – and of Greek philosophy in particular – while subordinating it to the Bible and cautioning against its misuse. The striking interpretation of Exodus which Origen used to make this point was to have a great history. Mediated by Augustine in his hermeneutical treatise *On Christian Doctrine*,[1] "despoiling the Egyptians" would provide medieval theologians with a rationale for intellectual openness. The recipient is traditionally identified as Gregory Thaumaturgus, also identified as the author of the *Address to Origen*. If so, the letter must have been written during the 240s. At any rate, the discussion of persons going down to Egypt from Palestine makes it seem likely that it is from Origen's Caesarean period. Origen makes an uncharacteristic error in section 3 (see n. 3).

The translation is from Grégoire le Thaumaturge, *Remerciement á Origène suivi de La Lettre d'Origène à Grégoire*, ed. and tr. by Henri Crouzel = *SC* 148, Paris, Cerf, 1969, pp. 186–94.

Text

When and to whom the learning that comes from philosophy is useful for the interpretation of Holy Scripture, according to Scriptural testimony.

1 Greetings in God, my most estimable and venerable son Gregory, from Origen.

As you know, an innate capacity for understanding can, with disciplined practice, achieve as far as possible what one may call its purpose, the thing for which the exercise is intended. Your natural ability can, therefore, make you an accomplished Roman lawyer or a Greek philosopher of one of the reputable schools. Nonetheless, I have desired that with all the power of your innate ability you would apply yourself, ultimately, to Christianity. I have, for this reason, prayed that you would accept effectively those things from the philosophy of the Greeks that can serve as a general education or introduction for Christianity and those things from geometry and astronomy that are useful for the interpretation of the Holy Scriptures. For just 'as the servants of philosophers say concerning geometry, music, grammar, rhetoric and geometry that they are adjuncts to philosophy, we say this very thing about philosophy itself with regard to Christianity.

2   And indeed Scripture hints[2] at this principle in Exodus, where, with God himself the person speaking, the children of Israel are told to ask their neighbors and cohabitants for vessels of silver and gold and for clothing (Ex. 11:2 and 12:35). Having in this way despoiled the Egyptians, they may find material among the things they have received for the preparation of divine worship. For, from the spoil taken from the Egyptians the children of Israel prepared the appurtenances of the holy of holies, the ark with its covering, the cherubim, the mercy-seat, and the golden vessel in which was stored the manna, the bread of angels. These articles appear to have been made from the finest of the Egyptians' gold. From gold of second quality they made the wide solid gold candelabrum, close to the interior veil; and the golden table, on which was placed the bread of offering; and between them the golden incense altar. They used any gold of third or fourth quality, if available, for the construction of the holy vessels. The silver of the Egyptians became other things. For, while sojourning in Egypt, the children of Israel had an abundant quantity of such precious materials for the worship of God to show for their experience there. From the clothing of the Egyptians it seems that they had such things as they needed for what Scripture describes as embroidered works. Assisted by God's wisdom, tailors stitched the articles of clothing together to serve as veils and tapestries for the interior and exterior.

3   Why did I need to make this time-consuming digression, demonstrating that things taken from the Egyptians were useful to the children of Israel, things which the Egyptians themselves did not use appropriately, but the Hebrews, through the wisdom of God, used for divine worship?

Scripture recognizes, nonetheless, that there was a bad outcome for some who descended from the land of the children of Israel into

Egypt, hinting that there will be a bad outcome for some who dwell among the Egyptians, that is, among the learned disciplines of the world, after being nurtured in God's law and Israelite worship of him. Thus Hadad the Idumaean did not fabricate idols in the land of Israel until, after fleeing the wise Solomon, he descended into Egypt and became a part of Pharaoh's household by marrying his wife's sister, so that he brought forth and reared children among the children of Pharaoh. Therefore, when he went back up into the land of Israel, he did so in such a way as to tear asunder the people of God and have them say to the golden calf, "These are your gods, O Israel, which led you up out of the land of Egypt" (Ex. 32:4 and 8; 1 Kings 12:28).[3] I could speak from knowledge gained by experience that few are those who have taken anything useful from Egypt and have come out from there and have prepared objects for the worship of God, but many have followed the example of Hadad the Idumaean. These are those who have used some Greek ingenuity to beget heretical ideas and have, so to speak, prepared golden calves in Bethel, which means "house of God." It seems to me that through these things the Word hints that they have set up their own idol beside the Scriptures, where the Word of God dwells, so that they are symbolically referred to as Bethel. The Word says that another idol was set up in Dan. Dan is in the frontier district, close to the regions of the gentiles, as is evident from the book of Joshua the son of Nun (Jos. 19:47). Thus certain idols are close to gentile districts, the very ones which the brothers of Hadad constructed, as we have explained.

4   You, then, my lord and son, apply yourself to the reading of the divine Scriptures, but do apply yourself. We need great application when we are reading divine things, so that we may not be precipitous[4] in saying or understanding anything concerning them. Also, applying yourself to divine reading with the intention to believe and to please God, knock at what is closed in it, and it will be opened to you by the doorkeeper, concerning whom Jesus said, "To him the doorkeeper opens" (Jn 10:3). As you apply yourself to divine reading, seek correctly and with unshakable faith in God the sense of the divine Scriptures hidden from the many. Do not be content with knocking and seeking, for prayer is most necessary for understanding divine matters. It was to exhort us to this very thing that the Savior did not only say, "Knock, and it shall be opened to you" and "Seek, and you shall find," but also, "Ask, and it shall be given to you" (Mt. 7:7; Lk. 11:9). I have dared to say these things out of my fatherly love for you. If my boldness was good or not,

God alone would know, and his Christ, and he who participates in the Spirit of God and in the Spirit of Christ. May you be such a participant, and may you always grow in such participation, so that you may not only say, "We have become participants with Christ" (Heb. 3:14), but, "We have become participants with God."

COMMENTARY ON JOHN, BOOK 32.1–140

Introduction

In this, a late work,[1] Origen elaborates on the symbolic meaning of feet, walking and the way, that he set out decades earlier in the *Commentary on Lamentations* and Book 1 of the *Commentary on John*. Here Jesus' footwashing represents the divine pedagogy by which, as the incarnate Logos, he transforms rational beings so as to make them like himself. This is a ministry in which human teachers, women as well as men, participate. As in Book 1.44–5, where Origen speaks of the need for the New Testament to be transformed into the spiritual gospel, and in Book 13.27–35, where he discusses things above Scripture to which Scripture provides only a meager introduction, so here Jesus' taking off his clothes before he washes the disciples' feet symbolizes his laying aside Scripture's "fabric of passages joined with passages and sounds joined with sounds" (45).

The translation is from Origène, *Commentaire sur S. Jean*, vol. 5, ed. Cécile Blanc = *SC* 385, Paris, Cerf, 1992, pp. 188–248.

Text

I 1   Helped on the way by God through Jesus Christ, let us proceed on the way of the gospel, which for us is great and living, as long as it is known and traveled by us through to the end. 2   Now of course, we shall try to make the thirty-second encampment, as it were, in our discussions, and may the column of glowing cloud, Jesus, accompany us, leading us where we need to go, and stopping us where we need to halt (see Ex. 14:19–20),[2] until, Ambrosius, holy brother and man of God (see 1 Tim. 6:11), by the dictation of those things in the gospel, we traverse the whole gospel, neither quailing at the length of the journey nor being discouraged by our own weakness, but forcing ourselves to proceed in the steps of the column of truth (see 1 Tim. 3:15). **3** Whether or not God wishes our interpretation to complete through dictations the journey through the whole Gospel according to John, God knows. **4** Only – both remaining present in the body and leaving it and being present with the Lord (see 2 Cor. 5:6, 8) – let us not proceed beyond the gospel, so that we may also enjoy the deeds (see Jn 13:17) and words affording blessedness in God's paradise of delights (see Gen. 3:23–4).

During the dinner, the Devil having already pierced the heart of Judas Iscariot with the intention to betray him, knowing that the Father had given all things into his hands, and that he had come from God and was returning to God, he arose from supper and put aside his garments and taking a towel he girded himself. Then he poured water into a basin and began to wash the disciples' feet and to wipe them off with a towel with which he was girded (Jn 13:1–5).

II **5** In the *Homilies on Luke*,[3] we have compared the parables, and have sought what "breakfast" signifies in Scripture and what "supper" means. **6** Suffice it to say that "breakfast" is the first meal, appropriate for beginners, before the completion in this life of the spiritual day, but that "supper" is the final meal offered with reason to those who have already made considerable progress. **7** One might also say that "breakfast" is the sense of the ancient Scriptures, but "supper" is the mysteries hidden in the new covenant.

8 This is said to preface our discussion of how, during the supper, Jesus arose and, pouring water into a basin, began to wash the disciples' feet. **9** I suppose that those who sup with Jesus and, in the last day of his life, participate in a meal with him, need some sort of cleansing, not indeed a cleansing of one of the foremost parts of the soul's body,[4] so to speak, but, if I may say so, they require washing for their furthermost and last parts, those necessarily in communication with the earth. **10** The first cleansing can be done only by Jesus and him alone, but the second can also be done by his disciples, to whom he says: "And you ought to wash one another's feet, for I have given you an example, that as I have done to you, you ought to do to one another" (Jn 13:14–15).

11 It seems to me that here the evangelist, directing our mind to the intelligible reality of these things, has abandoned the order of events in which a bodily washing would occur, because it is before the supper and before reclining to eat that those who need their feet washed have that done. Neglecting that moment in his account, it is, on the contrary, when Jesus had already reclined for the supper that he has him arise from the supper so that he, their teacher and lord, might begin to wash the feet of the disciples who were already eating. 12 In fact, they had already bathed before the supper, and they had become entirely clean according to the words: "Wash yourselves, become clean, lift evil-doing from off your souls and from before your eyes," and so on (Isa. 1:16 LXX), but after this bath they needed a second for their feet only, that is, for the lowest part of the body. 13 For I suppose that it is impossible for the soul, in its furthermost and lowest parts, not to be soiled, even in the case of someone who would appear to be perfect among men. 14 Therefore the majority are covered with the dust of sins, even after washing, from the head, or a little below it, all the way down, but those who are genuinely Jesus' disciples, who can even sup with him, need to have only their feet washed by the Word. 15 Considering the differences between sins, and recognizing what are sins in the accurate and strong sense of the word, which the many do not even consider to be sins, you will see what those things are from which the feet require Jesus' cleaning. 16 And if such is indeed the case with smudges on the feet, what are those to do who have never been able to sup with Jesus, who do not have only their feet soiled? For Jesus had said to Peter, who did not know, but who would understand later (see Jn 13:7) the mystery of the washing of feet cleansed by Jesus, "If I do not wash you, you have no part with me" (Jn 13:8). 17 You seek what this reveals, whether it means: "unless I wash you who are supping with me, but have not been washed by me, you have absolutely no good part" or "not with me, your teacher and lord, but with those lesser than me, those who, after having been bathed, have neither supped at my supper nor had their feet washed by me."

18 Because of "See, I stand at the door and knock; if anyone opens the door to me, I shall enter in to him and sup with him and he with me" (Rev. 3:30) I ask if Jesus never has breakfast with anyone – for such a person does not need an introduction or first teachings – nor does anyone breakfast with him, but anyone who eats with him must sup, "Indeed," he says "a greater than Solomon is here" (Mt. 12:42), concerning whom it is written: "And this was Solomon's breakfast" (1 Kings 2:46 LXX), as recounted in Third Kingdoms.[5]

19 As a consequence of "If I do not wash you, you have no part with me" (Jn 13:8), I would dare say that he did not wash Judas's feet, because the Devil had already pierced his heart with the intention to betray his teacher and lord, finding him not girded with the whole armor of God and not having the shield of faith, with which one can quench all the fiery darts of the evil one (see Eph. 6:13–16). **20** For our passage, "The Devil having already pierced," I hear teaching about this in the same way as the passage in Psalm 7, namely that the Devil is an archer, working his will with fiery darts on those who do not guard their hearts with all diligence (see Prov. 4:23). **21** Here is the text of the Psalm: "If you do not turn around, he will flash his sword, he has strung his bow and prepared it, in it he has prepared his implements of death, and he has fabricated his darts for those who burn. See, he has groaned at injustice, he has conceived travail, he has given birth to lawlessness" (Ps. 7:13–15 [7:12–14]). **22** Everyone recognizes that "See, he has groaned at injustice, he has conceived travail, he has given birth to lawlessness" can be referred to the Devil, but it is absurd to suppose that they are not spoken in the same sense as "If you do not turn around, he will flash his sword, he has strung his bow and prepared it, in it he has prepared his implements of death, and he has fabricated his darts for those who burn." No one else has prepared implements of death on the bow which he has strung except the one through whose envy death entered the world (see Wis. 2:24). **23** From these arrows, then, which he had fabricated for those who burn, the Devil pierced the heart of Judas Iscariot, who was already pierced at the supper, with the result that it displeased him. This was because the food and wine in this supper could not enter the heart of someone pierced by an arrow of the Devil intended to betray the one who was perhaps offering the meal – in this passage it is not actually clear who it was who was responsible for the meal, as it was in the preceding passage, "They prepared a supper there, and Martha served, but Lazarus was one of those reclining with him" (Jn 12:2). **24** Concerning Judas it is written: "the Devil having already pierced the heart of Judas Iscariot with the intention to betray him." Following this one could say of each of those wounded in the heart by the Devil that the Devil had already pierced his heart – in one, so as to fornicate; in one, so as to steal; in one, so as to accept, out of insane vainglory, the idolatry of those who seem to be advanced in dignity;[6] and in the same manner with regard to the rest of the sins with which the Devil pierces the heart not protected by the shield of faith – by the shield of faith one can quench, not just one or two, but all the darts of the evil one (see Eph. 6:16).

III 25   As the plan[7] of the passion was approaching – in view of which Judas Iscariot, wounded by the Devil, was going to betray him – after the supper has already started, "knowing that the Father had given all things into his hands, and that he had come from God and was returning to God, he arose from supper." 26   What, therefore, had not previously been in Jesus' hands was given by the Father into his hands, not some things but not others, but all things, the event concerning which David, seeing in the Spirit, said: "The Lord said to my lord, 'Sit at my right hand, until I make your enemies the footstool of your feet'" (Ps. 109:1 [110:1]). 27   Indeed, even Jesus' enemies were part of the "all things" concerning which Jesus knew, in so far as he depended on fore-knowledge, that they had been given to him by the Father. But so that we may contemplate more clearly what is meant by "the Father had given all things into his hands" let us pay attention to "Just as in Adam all died, so also all shall be made alive" in the Lord (1 Cor. 15:22).

28   But if the Father had given all things into his hands, and in Christ all shall be made alive, neither God's justice nor his saving plan[8] for each person according to merit is invalidated, as is apparent from the words following "so all shall be made alive in Christ," however, "each one in his own order" (1 Cor. 15:23). 29   Again concerning the different orders of those who are to be made alive in Christ when "The Father has given him all things in his hands" is fulfilled, you will understand it by discerning the meaning of "Christ is the first-fruits, then those who belong to Christ at his advent, then the end" (1 Cor. 15:23–4). The "end" is established with Christ at his advent, when "He will hand over the kingdom to his God and Father" having first "brought to naught every dominion, authority and power" (1 Cor. 15:24). 30   It is these beings, I think, with whom there is contention (see Eph. 6:12). He does this so there may be no more dominion, authority, and power against which to have a contention, and therefore no contention will exist, since all dominion, authority, and power will be brought to naught. 31   What moves me to believe that the contention is against every dominion, authority, and power that is being brought to naught is what is added by Paul, namely, "He must reign until he has put all enemies under his feet" (1 Cor. 15:25). Then "the last enemy is death" (1 Cor. 15:26). 32   This agrees with "the Father had given all things into his hands," which

the Apostle expounds more clearly, saying: "When it is said that everything will be subjected to him, it is evident that this does not include the one who has subjected all things to him" (1 Cor. 15:27). 33   But if all things are subjected to him, it is equally evident that "this does not include the one who has subjected all things to him" and that he concerning whom it is written "Before the Lord Almighty he has bent the neck" (Job 15:25 LXX) is among those who are subjected to him, having been vanquished so as to yield to the Word and to be subjected to God's image (see Col. 1:15) and to become the footstool of his feet. 34   Seeing then that the plan[9] was already advancing toward its beneficial conclusion because the Devil had already pierced the heart of Judas Simon Iscariot with the intention to betray him, he knew that the Father had given all things and had given them into his hands which hold everything, so that all things might be subject to him – or that "the Father had given all things into his hands," that is, into his deeds and redemptive acts – indeed he said: "My Father works up to now, and I work" (Jn 5:17).

35   He departed from God for the sake of those who had departed from God – and he who would not initially depart from the Father came to be apart from God – so that what had departed might come with method and order[10] into the hands of Jesus, and so that their return to God, following him, might be planned, so that, by following him, they might be with God (see Jn 1:1). 36   For it was once said to Peter "Where I go, you cannot follow me now, but you can follow me later" (Jn 13:36), because Peter still had something that prevented him from following the Word at that time. 37   It is to be understood that the same thing may be said, according to a fair analogy, concerning each one of the "all things" which the Father has given into the hands of the Son, for to each one of the "all" it could be said "You shall follow me later". 38   But if they do not all follow together, the "later" in "You shall follow me later" does not refer to the same time in the case of each of those who will follow. 39   And it means this to me also concerning all those who are being set at naught, when he shall set at naught every dominion, every authority, and every power (see 1 Cor. 15:24), that is, "until he puts all his enemies under his feet, and the last enemy to be set at naught is death" (1 Cor. 15:25–6). 40   Jesus therefore "knowing that the Father had given all things into his hands, and that he had come from God and was returning to God" and knowing how much and by what things we are moved, as we have explained in presenting our statement on the passage from "He had

219

come from God" to "He was returning to God,"[11] "he arose from supper," which we shall explain after this, in what follows. 41 See if you can say with regard to these matters that he was enjoying a carefree supper with his disciples, but that with care and under duress he arose from the table because of his disciples and interrupted the supper for a moment, until he cleansed the disciples' feet, because they could have no part with him unless he washed them.

IV 42 Let us consider what is said after "He arose from supper." He "put aside his garments," it says, "and taking a towel he girded himself." 43 To those who do not wish to go beyond statements and to understand intellectually the nourishment offered to the soul in this passage, we would say: "What prevented him from washing the disciples' feet while fully clothed?" 44 But if somehow we see in a manner worthy of Jesus the clothing that he wore as he was supping and enjoying himself with his disciples, shall we not consider with what sort of adornment the Word made flesh was clothed (see Jn 1:14)? 45 This adornment – consisting of a fabric of passages joined with passages and sounds joined with sounds – he lays aside, and became more bare, with a servile posture, which is evident in the words "taking a towel he girded himself." He does this so as not to be entirely bare and so that, after the washing, he may dry his disciples' feet with a more appropriate fabric. 46 Consider in these things how the great and glorious Word diminishes himself in becoming flesh, so that he may wash the disciples' feet, for it says: "he poured water into a basin." 47 Thus when Abraham, "lifting up his eyes, looked and, see, there were three men before him, and seeing them he ran ahead to greet them from the door of his tent and prostrated himself on the ground and said 'Lord, if I have found grace before you, do not pass by your servant'" (Gen. 18:2–3), he did not himself take water or promise to wash their feet as guests coming to him, but said: "Take water, and wash their feet" (Gen. 18:4). 48 Neither did Joseph take water and wash the feet of his eleven brothers, but it was the man in charge of Joseph's household "who brought Simeon to them and brought them water to wash their feet" (Gen. 43:23–4). 49 But he who said: "I come not as one sitting at table but as one who serves" (Lk. 22:27), who justly said: "Learn from me, because I am meek and humble of heart" (Mt. 11:29), himself poured water in the basin, for he knew that no one else could so wash the disciples' feet so that, through this washing, they might have part with him. 50 But as far as the water is concerned, it was, according to me, a

220

word of such a sort as to wash the disciples' feet as they came before the basin which Jesus had offered to them.
51   I shall now seek why it is not written that he "washed the disciples' feet, but he "began to wash the disciples' feet." 52   Is such an expression a Scriptural usage, when it seems irrational, according to ordinary usage, to add he "began"?[12] Or did Jesus at that time begin to wash his disciples' feet but not finish washing their feet? 53   Indeed he washed and later finished the washing, since they were soiled according to "You will all stumble because of me this night" (Mt. 26:31) and what he said to Peter: "The cock shall not have crowed before you deny me three times" (Jn 13:38). 54   Once these sins had occurred, the soiled feet of the disciples, which he began to wash when he arose from the table, required washing again, and he finished washing them by cleansing them so that they would not again become soiled. 55   In the same way he began at that time to dry the disciples' feet, but he finished drying them, when he had finished washing.

He therefore went to Simon Peter, who said: "Lord, do you wash my feet?" Jesus answered and said to him: "What I am doing you are not aware of now, but later on you will know." Peter said to him: "You shall never wash my feet." Jesus replied to him: "If I do not wash you, you have no part with me." Simon Peter said to him: "Not only my feet, but also my hands and my head." Jesus said to him: "He who has taken a bath need only wash his feet, but he is entirely clean, and you are clean, but not all of you." For he knew who was to betray him, therefore he said: "You are not all clean" (Jn 13:6–11).
V 56   We shall use the words spoken by Peter as a timely example, if needed, that someone can, with the best intentions, ignorantly say something utterly to his own disadvantage. 57   If indeed having one's feet washed by him had the advantage of giving him a part in Jesus, Peter, nonetheless, ignorant of this advantage, initially said, as if he were trying to discourage Jesus, "Lord, do you wash my feet?" and then "You shall never wash my feet," words which would have prevented an action which would have enabled him have part with the Savior. Clearly, then, even if he said this with a healthy, reverent attitude toward his teacher, he spoke in a manner injurious to himself. 58   This kind of mistake fills the life of believers who ignorantly say or even do things that frustrate their excellent intentions. 59   Such, for example, are those who say, about each thing that is perishable and destined for human use, "do

not take, do not taste, do not touch" (Col. 2:21–22), according to a teaching much inferior to "you shall die as a man" (Ps. 81:7 [82:7]).[13] 60   What is there to say concerning those who are tossed about and carried away by every wind according to human trickery (see Eph. 4:14), calling destructive things salvific and holding false opinions about Jesus as if they revered him?

61   Often Scripture has indicated this about Peter: that he was too ardent to prefer what seemed best to him, as when he impetuously contradicted Jesus' prophecy concerning the disciples: "You will all stumble because of me tonight" because: "Indeed it is written, 'I shall strike the shepherd, and the sheep of the flock shall be scattered'" (Mt. 26:31; see Zech. 13:7). Concerning this he impetuously said, contradicting Jesus' assertion, "Even if all should stumble because of you, I shall not stumble" (Mt. 26:33). 62   And this impetuousness[14] in his soul became, I think, the reason why he stumbled more seriously than the others, when he denied Jesus three times before cock crow (see Jn 18:25–7). 63   Therefore, since he was aware of how impulsive he had been earlier, he derived the greatest benefit, becoming the most steadfast and patient.[15] This character manifested itself when Paul said to him, before all, "If you, a Jew, exist as a gentile and do not live as a Jew, why do you compel the gentiles to act like Jews?" (Gal. 2:14), and so on. He remained steadfastly silent and with great forbearance restrained himself from asserting his reasonable position on the matter (These things will be discussed more opportunely in a work on the Epistle to the Galatians.)[16] 64   In the Acts of the Apostles (see Acts 15:7–11) also his resoluteness – "having been transformed into his image" (2 Cor. 3:18) – will appear to all who examine and observe each detail.[17]

VI 65   Here, then, Jesus got up from supper, having put aside his clothing he was girded by a towel that he had taken up. Pouring water in a basin, he was beginning to wash the feet of the disciples and to wipe them off with the towel with which he was girded. The disciples were all presenting their feet to him, perceiving, according to their opinion of Jesus, that one so great would not wash their feet irrationally[18] out of the desire to embarrass them, as ordinary people would say, but rather – reflecting that he must be acting symbolically – that he would accomplish something useful to them that would be apparent to them later. Only Peter – not looking beyond the immediate situation and applying to it no further consideration – out of reverence for Jesus did not present his feet to be washed, but first tried to discourage him by saying "Lord, do you wash my feet?" Even after he should have been persuaded by "What I am doing you are not aware of now, but later on you will know," he said: "You shall never wash my feet." 66 Even though the other disciples placed their confidence in Jesus and avoided contradicting him, Peter, in spite of apparently good intentions, implicitly censured Jesus for acting irrationally in starting to wash his disciples' feet and also implicitly censured his fellow-disciples. 67 For if he, in trying to stop Jesus, was actually acting in the proper way, and they had not realized this, he was censuring them for having behaved impertinently in presenting their feet to Jesus. If it had occurred to him that one must not oppose what is reasonable and if he had considered reasonable Jesus' action in washing his disciples' feet, he would not have opposed what was taking place. 68 Apparently, then, he uncritically considered unreasonable Jesus' desire to wash his disciples' feet.

Nonetheless, if we ought to be examining even details in Scripture that might be considered trivial, this is a topic for investigation: how it is that, even though Peter came first in the list of disciples (doubtless because of his preeminent worthiness, since Judas, ultimately rejected on account of his bad character, came last), nonetheless, when Jesus started to wash the feet of the disciples and wipe them off with the towel with which he was girded, he did not start with Peter. 69 It should be said in response to this that, just as a physician, serving with his skill a great number of invalids, begins his treatment with those whose case is most urgent and who are most grievously ill, so Jesus, washing the soiled feet of his disciples, began with the more soiled ones, and perhaps came to Peter last, because his feet least needed washing. 70 Perhaps an awareness that his feet were almost clean motivated Peter to contradict Jesus.

VII 71 A consideration of Jesus' words "He who has taken a bath need only wash his feet, but he is entirely clean, and you are clean, but not all of you" suggests, perhaps, that the disciples had already washed their feet. As a result of this bath, they no longer had any need to be washed by Jesus, and perhaps Peter was already clean, even before Jesus washed his feet. 72 If someone should seek in this regard why Jesus who had said: "He who has taken a bath need only wash his feet, but he is entirely clean" went ahead and washed his disciples' feet, even though they did not need it, the response is: "To him who has will be given and more will be added" (see Mt. 25:29).[19] 73 Since they were already clean, Jesus added to their cleanness by washing their feet. He would not even have washed them if they had not already taken a bath and become entirely clean, clean enough to say that they were so, for if one is perfect among the sons of men, but lacks the perfection that comes, so to speak, from Jesus, he will not be considered clean.

74 I shall take up these ideas later, because they are presented to me after having dictated what precedes. But let us keep to the order in which things have come to our attention. In as much as we have already seen that the disciples' soiled feet needed Jesus' washing, we now see that he washed their feet because they were clean enough for men, but not for God. Apart from Jesus, no one is clean before God, even if he might otherwise be thought to have worked hard enough to make himself clean. 75 But when they are bathed with the baptism of Jesus and their feet are washed by him, the Holy Spirit is able to dwell in those who have already become clean by human standards, and power from above covers them like a garment (see Lk. 1:35).

76 But Peter, not understanding Jesus' intention when he began to wash the feet of the disciples and to wipe them off with the towel with which he was girded, said to him "Lord, do you wash my feet?" He said this out of confusion and embarrassment, but Jesus answered and said to him, teaching that this was a mystery, "What I am doing you are not aware of now, but later on you will know."

77 What did Jesus do when he washed the disciples' feet? Did he not, by washing their feet and wiping them off with the towel with which he was girded, make them beautiful, so that they might be ready to preach the good news? 78 Indeed I think that, when Jesus washed the disciples' feet, the prophecy was fulfilled that had been spoken concerning the apostles: "How beautiful are the feet of those who proclaim good news of good things" (Rom. 10:15; Isa. 52:7). 79 If, by washing the disciples' feet, he made them beautiful, what shall we say about the genuine beauty that comes to those who are entirely immersed[20] in the Holy Spirit and in fire (see Mt. 3:11)? 80 But the feet of those who preach good news of good things have become beautiful, so that, once they have been washed, cleansed, and wiped off by Jesus' hands, they can proceed on the holy way and walk on the one who said "I am the way" (Jn 14:6). 81 For all those who have had their feet washed by Jesus, and they only, walk to the Father on that living way, a way that is no place for feet which are still soiled because they have not yet been cleansed. 82 For this reason Moses had to remove the sandals from his feet, for the place where he was standing was holy ground (see Ex. 3:5). This was also the case with Joshua[21] the son of Nun (see

Jos. 5:15). **83**   But the disciples of Jesus, in order to make their way on the living and animated way, must not only not have sandals for the way – this was commanded by Jesus to the apostles (see Mt. 10:10) – but they must also, in order to walk on this way, have their feet washed by the Jesus who put aside his garments, perhaps in order to make their clean feet still more clean, perhaps also to take the stain on the disciples' feet onto his own body through the towel, by which alone he was girded. Indeed, he bears our infirmities (see Isa. 53:4; Mt. 8:17).

VIII **84**   Consider then that it is recounted that Jesus was about to wash the disciples' feet at the precise moment when the Devil had already pierced the heart of Judas Iscariot with the intention to betray him, and the plan[22] for humanity was about to come about. **85**   Beforehand it was not an appropriate time for the disciples' feet to be washed by Jesus – for who would then wash off the soil that had accumulated in the interval before the passion? – and at the passion it would not have been possible either, since there was no other Jesus[23] available to wash their feet. **86**   Nor would it have been appropriate after the plan[24] was accomplished, for that was the time for the dwelling of the Holy Spirit with the disciples once they were clean and their feet had been washed, and they already had their feet ready and beautiful for preaching in the Spirit good news of good things. **87**   The meaning of "What I am doing you are not aware of now, but later on you will know" is "Having your feet washed by me is a symbol of the cleansing of the foundations[25] of your souls, so that they may become beautiful, because you are about to preach good news of good things and walk upon the souls of men with clean feet. **88**   This is the mystery which you are not aware of now; since you are not yet capable of understanding it, it will be a better time to understand it when I have washed your feet, after that you will know when you understand it, having been enlightened by a knowledge of a reality that is neither contemptible nor insignificant.

89   When Jesus had said these things to Peter, the disciple made an unintelligent response, one giving the appearance, specious in the event, of honoring and revering Jesus. **90**   Therefore, because Peter's response was not appropriate for him, Jesus does not allow it to come true, since, in keeping with his benevolence, he prevents things from coming true in a way that would injure the speaker. **91**   For Peter says: "You shall never wash my feet," meaning that, even though Jesus had decided to wash his feet, they would not be washed by him and would not be washed for all eternity. But he, seeing that it would be more advantageous for Peter to be speaking falsely in this matter than for him to be saying the truth, indicates the advantage to him of not saying the truth in this matter, saying: "If I do not wash you, you have no part with me." 92   If, therefore, Peter was about to say plainly: "You shall never wash my feet," and saying the truth in this would entail his having no part in Jesus – but he would have a part by not saying the truth in what he had come to say impetuously – what should he do but not say the truth? 93   Thus saying the truth in this matter would not deprive him of a part in Jesus, who would make him a liar by washing his feet. 94   In any event, it is written: "Every man is a liar" (Ps. 115:2 [116:11]). We shall make appropriate use of this verse in the case of persons who say impetuously and uncritically that they are going to do something which will not be advantageous to them if they persist in their bad judgment. 95   By indicating to them that they would not have part in Jesus, if they kept their impetuous promise, but that they might have hope for a good outcome by repudiating their previous statements, we encourage them to refrain from persisting in their bad judgments, even if, in their great impetuousness, they accompanied them with oaths. 96 And we shall say: "Just as Peter, who said 'You shall never wash my feet,' was prevented from acting according to his words so as to deprive himself of a part in Jesus, so you who have been mistaken in some way out of impetuousness and have promised uncritically to do something will do better by abandoning your bad judgment and doing something more reasonable."

97   By giving heed to "What I am doing you are not aware of now, but later on you will know" and "If I do not wash you, you have no part with me," let those who object to a figurative interpretation of this and similar passages be reconciled to such an interpretation of the gospels. If not, let them show how it is reasonable for a disciple who, by their own account, spoke out of reverence in saying to Jesus, "You shall never wash my feet," to hear from his teacher that he would have no part in the Son of God, because it was a great mistake not to have his feet washed by him. 98   The statement that, if you commit this transgression "you have no part with me" would seem appropriate if they were said in reference to an obviously sinful act, but "If I do not wash you, you have no part with me" has no reasonable basis for someone who contends that Peter had not wanted him to wash his bodily feet. 99   In his foot-washing, the teacher seems to have responded with extreme cruelty

(something we must not say) to a disciple who was honoring him (which is most absurd).

IX 100   Therefore let us offer our feet to Jesus, who even now is arising from the supper table, laying aside his garments, taking a towel, girding himself, pouring water into a basin, and starting to wash our feet, as in the case of the disciples, and wiping them off with a towel with which he is girded, having become like one who serves (see Lk. 22:27) in our midst. 101   If we do not do this, in fact, we shall have no part with him, nor shall our feet become beautiful. Let us do it chiefly because, being zealous for the higher gifts (1 Cor. 12:31), we wish to be counted among those who preach good news of good things.

102   Nonetheless, because he acted impetuously, Peter – when he heard "If I do not wash you, you have no part with me" requesting him to offer his feet to Jesus – wished to exceed the request, and to offer for Jesus' cleansing not just his feet, but also his hands, which Jesus no longer required to be washed, when they ate bread, despising those who said: "Your disciples do not wash their hands when they eat bread" (Mt. 15:2) and, after his hands, his head, which Jesus no longer even required to be covered, for the image of the glory of God was already upon it (see 1 Cor. 11:7). 103   Let it suffice for us, if we come into the same situation as Jesus' disciples, to offer only the feet for him to wash and dry, for "he who has taken a bath need only wash his feet, but he is entirely clean," but if someone is not entirely clean, it is because he has not taken a bath.

104   If it is true that someone "who has taken a bath need only wash his feet, but he is entirely clean" and the disciples of Jesus were clean, because they had bathed, someone may seek how it is that Jesus poured water into a basin and began to wash the disciples' feet. 105   We have already partially anticipated this investigation in our response, to which we now add what follows. 105   "We have need" refers to things that are necessary, without which we cannot continue living. Regarding bodily existence, we have relatively few necessities, only those about which Paul says: "If we have food and clothing, that will suffice for us" (1 Tim. 6:8). On the other hand, things pertaining to wealth and luxury, arising from the excess of those who live softly, are not indispensable necessities but superfluities. The same principle applies to more divine matters: we have need for those that introduce us to life and make us exist in him who said "I am the life" (Jn 11:25), but things exceeding these, those concerning which he said: "Take delight in the Lord, and he will give you your heart's desire" (Ps. 36:4 [37:4])

and those comprehended in "the paradise of luxury" (Gen. 3:23) and the wealth and glory in wisdom's left hand according to "Length of life and years of life are in her right hand, in her left hand are wealth and glory" (Prov. 3:16 LXX) are beyond necessity. **107** Does not the privilege of having one's feet washed by such a teacher and savior after one has bathed belong to this category? For the gracious gift of God exceeds necessity, just as does the privilege of being in the glory of the sun or the moon or the stars in the holy resurrection of the dead (see 1 Cor. 15:41–2). **108** Therefore the one who is clean and has bathed has no necessity for being washed, but he is washed, according to our preceding explanation, because to him who has more will be added (see Mt. 25:29), as John said: "Let him who is clean still make himself clean and let him who is holy still make himself holy" (Rev. 22:11).

109 "[Y]ou are clean" applies to the eleven, to which "but not all of you" is added because of Iscariot. He knew that he was going to betray him, since he was already unclean, first, because he did not take care of the poor, but, being a thief, he appropriated what had been put in the chest, and, second, because, when "[d]uring the dinner, the Devil having already pierced the heart of Judas Iscariot with the intention to betray" Jesus, he did not repel the suggestion. **110** Therefore the eleven, who had bathed and had become clean, now became cleaner by having their feet washed by Jesus, but Judas was already not clean, for "he who is soiled" it says "let him still be soiled" (Rev. 22:11) when, after the morsel, Satan entered into him.

When he had washed their feet, taken up his clothes, and reclined again, he said to them: "[Do you] Know what I have done.[?]²⁶ You call me teacher and lord, and you do well to say so, for I am. If therefore I, your teacher and lord, have washed your feet, you also ought to wash each other's feet, for I have given you an example that, as I have done to you, so you should do" (Jn 13:12–15).

X **111** Perhaps those who perceive the magnitude of Jesus' power and understand what he had done in washing the disciples' feet – cleansing what came last and was ordinary in them, by cleaning those things in contact with the ground (the parts of the body functioning symbolically) – would not presume, out of their admiration for what this washing accomplished, to do something like it themselves. If Jesus, on resuming his place to give them this teaching while they dined, had not exhorted them in the words just cited, they would consider themselves too unimportant to wash the feet of "the inner man in secret" (Rom. 7:2, 2:29) of those who have received the same teachings from God. 112   For in a manner that was very disconcerting, intended to exhort them to a comprehension of what had just happened, he said: "[Do you] Know what I have done.[?]" 113   This can be understood as a question, to reinforce the importance of what had occurred, or as a command, to arouse their minds to pay attention to this action so as to understand it. 114   It is in a highly pedagogical manner, even if disconcerting, that he says: "You call me teacher and lord and you do well to say so, for I am. If therefore I, your teacher and lord, have washed your feet, you also ought to wash each other's feet." 115   Jesus washes his disciples' feet as their teacher and his servants' feet as their lord[27]. 116   It is by teaching that the dust that comes from the earth and from worldly affairs– which had touched nothing but the furthermost and lowest parts of the disciples – is wiped off; it is by the lordship of the sovereign who has authority over those who, because they still have the spirit of servitude (see Rom. 8:15), receive whatever pollution may befall them, that he sweeps off what soils their feet. 117   No one with good sense would say that it is as the door, or as the shepherd, or as the physician that Jesus washes the feet of disciples and servants. But I think that the feet of the disciples need to be washed by the teacher, because they have not yet received everything that they need, but still lack what is implied in "Let it be enough for the disciple to become as his teacher is" (Mt. 10:25). 118   And this is the purpose of the teacher – in his capacity as teacher – in relation to his disciple, to make the disciple like himself, so that he may no longer require his teacher in that capacity, even if he still needs him in some other capacity. 119 Indeed just as the purpose of a physician – who is needed by those who are ill even though those who are well do not need a physician – is to relieve those ill of their illness so that they may no longer need him, so the purpose of the teacher is to endow the disciple with the "enough" in "Let it be enough for the disciple to become as his teacher is." 120   In the Savior, in so far as he is lord, one sees a characteristic other lords do not have, for they do not wish for their servants to become lords like them. 121   The Son of the goodness and love of the Father is such that, even as lord, he activates in his servants the ability to become like their lord, so that they no longer have "the spirit of servitude that leads to fear, but have received the spirit of sonship, in which they cry 'Abba, Father'" (Rom. 8:15). 122   Before becoming like the teacher and like the lord, they must have their feet washed. This is because they lack certain teachings, so that they still have the spirit of servitude that leads to fear. But when one of them – according to "Let it be enough for the disciple to become as his teacher is and the servant to become as his lord is" – becomes like his teacher and lord, then he can imitate him who washed the feet of the disciples, and wash the feet of disciples in his capacity as teacher, an office which God established in the church after apostles, who have obtained the first place, and after prophets, who have obtained the next place (see 1 Cor. 12:28).

XI 123   If "You shall serve your brother" (Gen. 27:40) refers to those who are inferior and "Become lord of your brother" (Gen. 27:29) refers to those who, like Jacob, are superior, it is evident that the servant, becoming like his lord, washes the feet of those who serve by the teaching received from him, since "You call me teacher and lord, and you do well to say so, for I am" deserves a sense deeper than that perceived by ordinary people, for not to everyone who says "Lord, lord" is told by Jesus: "You call me teacher and lord, and you do well to say so." 124   For they who will say on that day: "Lord, lord, have we not eaten in your name and drunk in your name and in your name cast out demons and performed miracles" (Mt. 7:22, Lk. 13:26) will not "do well to say so." 125   But Jesus will say to them: "Depart from me, I have never known you, you workers of injustice" (Mt. 7:23, Lk. 13:27). But if they do say "Lord, lord" well, he will not tell them: "Depart from me". 126   But also "Not all who say to me 'Lord, lord' will enter the kingdom of heaven" (Mt. 7:21) demonstrates that, unlike the apostles, to whom he is speaking here, not everyone who says "Lord, lord" has his testimony "you do well to say so, for I am." 127   For truly vices no longer exercised sovereignty over them, but the Word, in effect, their Lord, is complete, animated, and living virtue.

128   But if indeed "No one can say 'Jesus is Lord' except by the Holy Spirit" (1 Cor. 12:13) – and we understand what it means to say "Jesus is Lord" – he who says "Jesus is Lord" in the Holy Spirit does well to say so. 129 But you will seek to determine if he who "does well to say so" must speak in the Holy Spirit, by comparing "you do well to say so" to "For the Spirit was not yet, for Jesus had not yet been glorified" (Jn 7:39). 130   It is the task of one who is genuinely serving the Word to do well saying "Jesus is Lord," and to the disciple who is like him to do well calling the Savior "teacher." It is to such a person that he would say "for I am," but this would not be said by the Word to someone who is a servant of sin or a disciple of lies.

XII 131   Nonetheless, someone who is holy may need to receive the washing of the feet, since the widow inscribed as such in ecclesiastical honor is examined concerning, among other good qualities, whether "she has washed the feet of the saints" (1 Tim. 5:10). For I think it would be absurd to stick to the letter and to say, for example, that a holy widow who possesses all the other qualifications but this one should not be enrolled in the ecclesiastical honor, even though, in a time when she lived comfortably and had all her needs met, she had often through household servants looked after the needs of strangers and anyone else with a claim to her bounty. 132   But do not be shocked it you need to seek a higher meaning for "if she has washed the feet of the saints" where, along with the male elders, female elders are commanded to be good teachers (see Titus 2:3).[28] 133   See if it is not also vexatious that all without distinction who are disciples of Christ, wishing to fulfill the prescription "you also ought to wash each other's feet," should consider themselves bound to wash the bodily and sensible feet of their brothers, as if believers who happened to be in any station of life whatsoever were to do this, even bishops and presbyters who are apparently[29] in a prominent ecclesiastical position and those who have honorable secular rank. Following this reasoning a master would be required to wash the feet of a slave who was a believer and parents those of their child, something which has never been customary or, if so, rarely and among simple rustics. 134   In this regard, what we said about "If I do not wash you, you have no part with me" should be recalled along with what was said about "Know what I have done for you." 135   It was appropriate for Jesus to have provided as an example for us a footwashing similar to what is said figuratively by the bridegroom in the Song of Songs: "I have washed my feet, how shall I sully them?" (Song 5:3).

136   Pay attention to "as I have done to you, so you should do," comparing it to "If I do not wash you, you have no part with me". 137   What if someone should say about this that, even if it is an allegory, the footwashing took place, so that what is actually said must be accepted along with the figurative sense of the text that says "If therefore I, your teacher and lord, have washed your feet, you also ought to wash each other's feet, for I have given you an example that, as I have done to you, so you should do"? The answer is: "If indeed, when Peter said: 'You shall never wash my feet' the reply was 'If I do not wash you, you have no part with me,' shall we actually speak and dare to say to those who, out of consideration, do not present their feet for us to wash, 'If I do not wash you, you have

no part with me'?" **138**   If, at this point, what I say does not disconcert you, what must you say to the question: "Must we observe the text meticulously?"?

139   That it may sometimes be appropriate to wash the feet of one or another disciple of Jesus, and for that person to offer his feet to be washed – the one performing it and the other receiving it out of love and hospitality – I would admit. **140** But if you say that everyone who is not conscious of having done this (that is, of having thus washed the feet of the saints) is under a strict obligation to obey "You ought to wash each other's feet," understand that just about everyone fails to honor this commandment.

COMMENTARY ON JOHN,
BOOK 32.318–67

Introduction

In dealing with one of many enigmatic passages in John, Origen develops a subtle understanding of glory.[1] Here he recognizes that the Bible uses the Greek word for glory, *doxa*, in a distinctive way. This means that a piece of his mental furniture, the Platonic differentiation between *doxa*, understood as "opinion," and *epistêmê*, understood as rationally founded "science," is not helpful for interpretation. By tracing the word's usage in the Septuagint, he retrieves the notion of glory implied in the Hebrew word, *kabod*. This glory is the actual presence of God. In such glory we, like Moses, participate by the personal transformation that occurs through the contemplation of God. This process demonstrates how, far from applying philosophical categories foreign to the text, Origen lets the text speak to him so as to modify the assumptions he brings to it. In addition, in his discussion of divinization and his recognition of the inadequacy of human language, Origen addresses topics that were elaborated in the following century by the Cappadocians and remain central to the Greek theological tradition.

The translation is from Origène, *Commentaire sur S. Jean*, vol. 5, ed. Cécile Blanc = *SC* 385, Paris, Cerf, 1992, pp. 324–44.

Text

Therefore after [Judas's] departure, Jesus said, "Now the Son of Man has been glorified, and God has been glorified in him. If God has been glorified in him, God will also glorify him in himself and will immediately glorify him" (Jn 13:31–2).

XXV 318   After the glories due to signs and wonders and the glory of the transfiguration, the beginning of the Son of Man's

233

glorification was Judas's departure, once Satan had entered into him, from the place where Jesus was. **319** That is why the Lord said: "Now the Son of Man has been glorified." In addition, the Savior said: "If I be lifted up from the earth, I shall draw all to me" (Jn 12:32), to signify "by what sort of death he was to glorify God" (Jn 21:19); indeed, even in dying, he glorified God. **320** Therefore, at the beginning of the plan[2] that would culminate in Jesus' death, namely when Judas, after the morsel of bread, had departed to plot against Jesus, he said: "Now the Son of Man has been glorified." **321** In addition, since the Messiah could not be glorified without the Father's being glorified in him, "and God had been glorified in him" is linked to "now the Son of Man has been glorified."

322 Nonetheless, the glory of the death on behalf of humankind does not belong to the only-begotten Word, Wisdom, and Truth which, by nature, cannot die, or to any of the other diviner aspects of Jesus. It belongs rather to the man who was the Son of Man, born of the seed of David according to the flesh (see Rom. 1:3). **323** For the same reason that, earlier, he said: "Now you seek to kill me, a man who has spoken the truth to you" (Jn 8:40), he says, in the passage we are now examining, "Now the Son of Man has been glorified." **324** This is the one who, I suppose, God also highly exalted, the one who "became obedient to death, even death on a cross" (Phil. 2:8–9). The Word who was in the beginning with God, the Word who was God (Jn 1:1), could not be further exalted. **325** The exaltation of the Son of Man, which occurred when he glorified God in his own death, is this: he was no longer anything but the Word, that is, utterly identical with it. **326** If indeed "he who joins himself to the Lord is one spirit" (1 Cor. 6:17), so that it is no longer possible to say with regard to him and the Spirit "They are two," how much more reason do we have to say that the humanity of Jesus has become one with the Word – so that he has been exalted who "did not consider equality with God a thing to be grasped" (Phil. 2:6)[3] – while the Word has remained in its own exalted place or has been restored to it, when God the Word, being a man, is back "with God" (see Jn 1:1)? **327** In the death of Jesus, glorifying God, have been accomplished the words "Having despoiled the principalities and powers, he has made them a public spectacle, having triumphed over them on the tree" (Col. 2:15) and "Having reconciled through the blood of his cross what is on earth and what is in heaven" (Col. 1:20) * * * In all this, in fact, the Son of Man was glorified, and God was glorified in him.

XXVI 328   Since the one who has been glorified has been glorified by someone, in the words "Now the Son of Man has been
glorified" you search for the one by whom he was glorified, and the
same goes for "and God has been glorified in him." 329   For the
sake of terminological clarity, let us first attend carefully to the
words "Now the Son of Man has been glorified"; second to "and
God has been glorified in him"; third to the statement linked to
them, "If God has been glorified in him, God will also glorify him
in himself"; and fourth to "and will immediately glorify
him."330   Unless one should say that this last phrase should be
considered as part of the conclusion of the conditional proposition,
so that the conditional proposition would begin with "God has been
glorified in him" and conclude with "God will also glorify him in
himself and will immediately glorify him."

We must necessarily attend to the word "glory," which is not
used neutrally here as among some Greeks, who define "glory" as
praise accorded by the many. The word clearly has a different
meaning in this passage in Exodus: 331   "And the glory of the
Lord filled the tent. And Moses could not enter the tent of witness,
because the cloud had overshadowed it and the tent was filled with
the glory of the Lord" (Ex. 40:34–5). 332   In Third Kingdoms
[= 1Kings] also we have the following description: "And it happened
as the priest left the sanctuary, that the cloud filled the house of the
Lord, 333   and the priests could not stand at their service before the
cloud, because the glory of the Lord filled the house" (1 Kings
8:10–11). 334   Also, in relation to Moses' glory it says in Exodus:

> As Moses came down from the mountain and the two
> tablets of the covenant were in Moses's hands, as he was
> coming down from the mountain Moses did not know that
> the appearance of the skin of his face had been glorified as
> he was speaking with him. And Aaron and all the children
> of Israel saw Moses, and the appearance of the skin of his
> face was glorified, and they were afraid to come near him.
>
> (Ex. 34:29–30)

XXVII 335   This meaning of "glory" is clear in the Gospel
according to Luke when it says:

> And it came to pass while he was praying the appearance of
> his face was altered, and his clothing was changed to
> dazzling white. And, see, two men were conversing with

him, who were Moses and Elijah. Appearing in glory, they
spoke of the departure he was about to accomplish in
Jerusalem.

(Lk. 9:29–31)

336 See also how Paul employs "glory," when he says, for
instance:

If the ministry of death, graven in letters on stones, took
place in glory, so that the children of Israel could not bear
to fix their attention on Moses's face because of the
exceeding glory of his face, even though that glory was
temporary, how shall the ministry of the Spirit not be in
glory? If indeed there was glory in the ministry of condemnation, how much more will the ministry of justification
exceed in glory? Indeed what was glorified then was not
glorified as far as regards the exceeding glory; if indeed
what is temporary was manifested by glory, how much
more will that which is permanent be manifested by glory?

(2 Cor. 3:7–11)

and where he says:

All of us, with unveiled face reflect the glory of the Lord;
we are transformed into the same image from glory to
glory, as by the Spirit of the Lord.

(2 Cor. 3:18)

337 Shortly thereafter he says :

If our gospel is hidden, it is hidden from those who are
being destroyed, in whom the god of this world has
blinded the intelligence of unbelievers, so that the enlightenment of the gospel of Christ, who is the image of God,
may not radiate to them.

(2 Cor. 4:3–4)

338 Again, a little farther down, he says:

Because it is the God who said "Let light shine out of darkness," who has shone in our hearts for the illumination of

the knowledge of the glory of God in the face of Jesus
Christ.

(2 Cor. 4:6)

The interpretation of the gospel text before us does not now
require a precise interpretation of each of these passages. Suffice it
to say that to the extent that, following a bodily interpretation, a
more divine manifestation occurred in the tent and in the temple
when they were completed and in the face of Moses when he was
conversing with the divine nature, to that same extent, following an
elevated interpretation, one might refer to things that are known
accurately concerning God, things that are contemplated by a mind
rendered capable by extreme purity, as "a vision of the glory of
God." The mind that has been purified and has surpassed all material things, so as to be certain of the contemplation of God, is
divinized by those things that it contemplates. 339   It must be
said that this is what it means for the face to be glorified of one who
contemplates God, converses with him, and passes time with him in
such contemplation, so that when it is said figuratively that Moses's
face was glorified, it means that his mind was divinized.
340   Accordingly, also, the Apostle said: "All of us, with unveiled
face reflect the glory of the Lord; we are transformed into the same
image." 341   Just as the brightness of the nocturnal luminary is
dimmed at the rising of the sun, so is the glory on Moses by that in
Christ. 342   Indeed the superiority in Christ, who, knowing the
Father, was glorified by him, bore no comparison with the things
known by Moses that glorified the face of his soul. 343   Therefore
it is said that the glory of Moses is temporary in comparison to the
exceeding glory of Christ.
XXVIII 344   After dealing with the passages cited as briefly as
possible, let us proceed to "Now the Son of Man has been glorified,
and God has been glorified in him." 345   Knowing the Father,
then, he is glorified by that very knowledge, which is the greatest
good and one that he brings to a perfect knowledge, that by which
the Son knows the Father. 346   I suppose that, because he knows
himself, something not far from knowing the Father, he is glorified
by this knowledge of himself. 347   Whether the knowledge of the
universe completes the magnitude of his glory, since he knows
hidden things as well as things that are openly seen, you may investigate if this is what it means for him to be wisdom-in-itself or if, in
the case of the so-called Son-in-himself of Man, glorification comes
from being united to wisdom. Nonetheless all this glory, by which

the Son of Man has been glorified, is a glorification bestowed by the Father as a gift. **348**   There are many things that contribute to the whole glory of the man, but the one *par excellence* is God, who is not simply glorified by being known by the Son, but is glorified in the Son.

349   Concerning this matter, even if it is daring and beyond our abilities for us to scrutinize such a saying, we must nonetheless dare to suggest a potential topic for investigation. **350**   I seek to know if it is possible for God to be glorified in some way besides being glorified, as I have explained, in the Son. Is God glorified to a greater extent in himself, because, in gazing on himself, he is pleased with an unspeakable satisfaction, contentment, and joy at his knowledge of himself and contemplation of himself – greater than contemplation in the Son, as one must understand and say such things about God – as he takes pleasure and rejoices in himself? **351**   I employ these terms not as if they could properly be applied to God, but for lack of what might be termed unspeakable words (see 2 Cor. 12:4), which he alone can, along with his only-begotten Son, speak or think about himself in the proper sense.

352   Since we have come to the topic of God's glorification in Christ, we should investigate as a corollary how he would be glorified in the Holy Spirit and in all those beings in whom the glory of the Lord has appeared or will appear. **353**   In this regard I suppose that the Son is the radiance of the whole glory of God, according to what Paul said: "Being the radiance of his glory" (Heb. 1:3), but that partial radiances in anticipation of this radiance of the whole glory come to the rest of the rational creation, but I do not think than any being can contain the entire radiance of God's glory except his Son.

354   Now therefore, since the plan[4] involving the passion of the Son of Man on behalf of all did not take place apart from God (see Heb. 2:9), "therefore God has highly exalted him" (Phil. 2:9). It says not only that "the Son of Man has been glorified," but "indeed God has been glorified in him" and thus one could explain this passage.

355   It is written: "No one has known the Son, except the Father" (Mt. 11:27) and it is said: "Blessed are you, Simon bar Jonah, for flesh and blood have not revealed this to you, but my Father who is in heaven" (Mt. 16:17). **356**   Therefore, in so far as the Son is not known by the world – "He was in the world, and the world was made by him, but the world did not know him" (Jn 1:10) – he has not yet been glorified in the world, and his not being glorified in the world does not discredit the one who has not been glorified, but it discredits the world that does not glorify him. 357   When the heavenly Father revealed the knowledge of Jesus to those from the world to whom he did reveal it, the Son of Man was glorified in those who knew him (see Jn 17:10) and by the glory by which he was glorified in those who knew him, he procured glory for those who knew him, those indeed who with unveiled face reflect the glory of the Lord, and are transformed into the same image (see 2 Cor. 3:18).

XXIX 358   See "from" what "glory" and "to" what "glory" (2 Cor. 3:18), from the glory of the one who was glorified to the glory of those glorifying. 359   This is why, when Jesus came to the plan[5] at the conclusion of which he was going to rise upon the world[6] and, once known, to be glorified in the glory of those who were glorifying him, he said: "Now the Son of Man has been glorified," and since "No one knows the Father except the Son, and him to whom the Son reveals him" (Mt. 11:27), and since the Son was coming by plan to reveal the Father, therefore, "and God has been glorified in him". Compare "and God has been glorified in him" to "He who has seen me has seen the Father who sent me" (Jn 14:9, 12:49). The Father who begot him is contemplated in the Word, who is God (Jn 1:1) and the image of the invisible God (see Col. 1:15), since he who beholds the image of the invisible God is immediately able to behold the prototype of the image of God.

360   Still one may thus comprehend more clearly what is expressed in this place: just as, through certain persons, God's name is blasphemed among the gentiles (see Rom. 2:24; Isa. 52:5; and Ez. 36:20), so, through the saints, among whom men see the most brilliant good works, the name of the Father who is in heaven (see Mt. 5:16) is glorified. 361   In whom, then, has this name been so glorified as in Jesus, since he did not commit sin nor was guile found in his mouth (see 1 Pet. 2:22), nor did he know sin (1 Cor. 5:21)? 362   Therefore, being such, the Son has been glorified, and the Father has been glorified in him. 363   But if God has been glorified in him, the Father will give him in return something greater than what the Son of Man has achieved, greater indeed for the one who has glorified God – for the lesser glorifying the one far greater, as in "The Father who sent me is greater than me" (Jn 14:28) – namely the glorification of the Son of Man in God, the lesser in the greater. 364   For the glory that is in the Son when the Father glorifies him far exceeds that in the Father when the Father is glorified in the Son. 365   And it was fitting that the greater,

responding to the glory with which the Son had glorified him, should graciously allow the Son to glorify him in himself, so that the Son might be glorified in God. And since such a great thing should not keep waiting – I speak of the Son's being glorified in God – he added "and will immediately glorify him."

366   We are not ignorant that these observations are far inferior to the implications of the subject being examined – when God reveals himself and his word is present to manifest the glory of God – and the Father who bestows the knowledge of the whole glory of God on him on whom he can bestow it. 367   Thus, as briefly as possible, and in a manner far beneath the value of the words, we still confess our thanks to God, even for these expositions, which are far better than we deserve.

NOTES

A NOTE ON TRANSLATIONS

1 Nautin, pp. 223–60.
2 Caroline P. Hammond Bammel, ed., *Der Römerbriefkommentar des Origenes: Kritische Ausgabe der Übersetzung Rufins*, Buch 1–3, Freiburg, Herder, 1990.

1 THE MAKING OF A SCHOLAR AND THEOLOGIAN

1 See Patricia Cox [Miller], *Biography in Late Antiquity: A Quest for the Holy Man*, Berkeley, University of California Press, 1983.
2 Nautin.
3 Notably Timothy D. Barnes in *Constantine and Eusebius*, Cambridge, Mass., Harvard University Press, 1981, and Henri Crouzel in *Origen: The Life and Thought of the First Great Theologian*, tr. by A. S. Worrall, San Francisco, Harper & Row, 1989.
4 *EH* 6.2.10–11.
5 See Christopher Haas, *Alexandria in Late Antiquity: Topography and Social Conflict*, Baltimore, Johns Hopkins University Press, 1997.
6 See Walter Bauer, *Orthodoxy and Heresy in Earliest Christianity*, ed. and tr. by Robert Kraft, Gerhard Krodel *et al.*, Philadelphia, Fortress Press, 1971, pp. 44–60.
7 See C. H. Roberts, *Manuscript, Society and Belief in Early Christian Egypt*, Oxford, Oxford University Press, 1979, and A. Rousseau and L. Doutreleau, eds, Irénée de Lyon, *Contre les hérésies*, Bk 3, vol. 1 (= *SC* 210), Paris, Cerf, 1974, pp. 126–31.
8 See *Str.* 6.15.124.5–131.1, where he uses both terms and ascribes this tradition to the apostles, and commends it as a rule for the interpretation of Scripture. See also 6.18.165.1, 7.7.41.3 and 7,15.105.5 on the rule of the church and 7.17.108.1 on the united testimony of the apostles to the church's tradition.
9 See Richard P. C. Hanson, *Tradition in the Early Church*, London, SCM Press, 1962, pp. 75–129.
10 Hal Koch, *Pronoia und Paideusis: Studien über Origenes und sein Verhältnis zum Platonismus*, Berlin, De Gruyter, 1932, p. 309.

11 *HJer* 4.3.
12 Justin Martyr, *First Apology* 29.
13 *HEzek* 4.8.
14 Nautin, p. 414.
15 See Bernhardt Neuschäfer, *Origenes als Philologe* = *Schweizerische Beiträge zur Altertumswissenschaft* 18, 2 vols, Basel, Friedrich Reinhardt, 1987.
16 I largely follow the description of these stages in Henri-Irénée Marrou, *A history of Education in Antiquity*, tr. by George Lamb, New York, Sheed and Ward, 1956, pp. 229–34.
17 Marie-Joseph Rondeau, *Les Commentaires patristiques du Psautier (IIIe–Ve siècles)*, vols 1 and 2 = *Orientalia Christiana Analecta* 219 and 220, Rome, Pont. Institutum Studiorum Orientalium, 1982 and 1985, esp. vol. 2, pp. 21–135.
18 In the discussion of *technikon* and *metrikon*, I follow Neuschäfer, *Origenes als Philologe*, pp. 202–46.
19 See Ibid., p. 397, n. 236.
20 Ibid., pp. 276–85.
21 *Address* 8.111.
22 Origen's knowledge and use of medicinal lore has not yet received the detailed attention it deserves. An excellent essay on a particular case, Origen's reliance on medicine in his discussion of God's therapeutic hardening of Pharaoh's heart, is found in Amneris Rosselli, "'Ο τεχνίτης θεός: la pratica terapeutica come paradigma dell'operare di Dio in Phil. 27 e PA III 1," in Lorenzo Perrone, ed., *Il cuore indurito del Faraone: Origene e il problema del libero arbitrio*, Bologna, Marietti, 1992, pp. 65–83.
23 *EH* 6.2.13–14.
24 See Robert M. Grant, *Heresy and Criticism: the Search for Authenticity in Early Christian Literature*, Louisville, Westminster/John Knox Press, 1993.
25 Holger Strutwolf, *Gnosis als System: Zur Rezeption der valentinianischen Gnosis bei Origenes* = *Forschungen zur Kirchen- und Dogmengeschichte* 56, Göttingen, Vandenhoeck und Ruprecht, 1993, p. 23. Other authors who have dealt with Origen's relationship to Gnosticism are Hans Jonas, in *Gnosis und spätantiker Geist,*vol. 2, *Von der Mythologie zur mystischen Philosophie*, ed. by Kurt Rudolph, reprint, Göttingen, Vandenhoeck und Ruprecht, 1993, and Allain le Boulluec in "Y-a-t-il des traces de la polémique antignostique d'Irénée dans le *Péri Archôn* d'Origène?" in *Gnosis and Gnosticism: Papers read at the Seventh International Conference on Patristic Studies (Oxford, September 8th–13th, 1975)*, ed. Martin Krause, Leiden, Brill, 1977, pp. 138–47 and in *La notion d'hérésie dans la littérature grecque IIe–IIIe siècles*, vol. 2, Paris, Études Augustiniennes, 1985.
26 See Salvatore R. C. Lilla, *Clement of Alexandria: A Study in Christian Platonism and Gnosticism*, Oxford, Oxford University Press, 1971.
27 Marguerite Harl speaks of "almost constant employment of a vocabulary borrowed simultaneously from the Bible and from Greek culture" (Clément d'Alexandrie, *Le Pédagogue*, Livre I, Paris, Cerf, 1960 = *SC* 70, p. 102).

28 See *Str.* 1.5.28.3.
29 See Guy G. Stroumsa. *Hidden Wisdom: Esoteric Traditions and the Roots of Christian Mysticism*, Leiden, Brill, 1996.
30 On this subject, see Gunnar af Hällström, *Fides Simpliciorum according to Origen of Alexandria*, Helsinki, Societas Scientiarum Fennica, 1984,
31 See *Str.* 4.2.4.1.
32 See Joseph W. Trigg, "Receiving the Alpha: Negative Theology in Clement of Alexandria and its Possible Implications," in SP 31 (1997), 540–45.
33 See Nautin, pp. 293–302.
34 Brian E. Daley, "Origen's 'De Principiis': A Guide to the 'Principles' of Christian Scriptural Interpretation," in John F. Petruccione, ed., *Nova et Vetera: Patristic Studies in Honor of Thomas Patrick Halton*, Washington, DC, CUA Press (forthcoming). The comment is on *Str.* 4.1.3.1–3.
35 See Annewies van den Hoek, *Clement of Alexandria and his Use of Philo in the Stromateis: An Early Christian Reshaping of a Jewish Model*, Leiden, Brill, 1988.
36 David T. Runia, *Philo in Early Christian Literature: A Survey*, Assen, Van Gorcum and Minneapolis, Fortress, 1993, p. 156.
37 See Christoph Riedweg, *Mysterienterminologie bei Platon, Philon und Klemens von Alexandrien*, Berlin, De Gruyter, 1987.
38 *HJer* 20.2.
39 Nautin, pp. 132–3, 417.
40 See Nicholas R. M. de Lange, *Origen and the Jews: Studies in Jewish–Christian Relations in Third-Century Palestine*, Cambridge, Cambridge University Press, 1976.
41 *EH* 6.19.6.
42 Porphyry, *Life of Plotinus* 3, 14 and 20.
43 For a summary of the reasons for postulating two men named Origen, see Joseph W. Trigg, *Origen: The Bible and Philosophy in the Third-Century Church*, Atlanta, John Knox Press, 1983, pp. 259–60.
44 Plato, *Theaetetus* 176b. This passage is cited as Plato's definition of the purpose (*telos*) of human existence in Alkinoos, *Didaskalos* 28. The *Didaskalos*, written as a handbook of Platonic doctrine during the early Imperial period, provides our best witness to the Platonism of Origen's time.
45 Henri Crouzel, *Origène et Plotin: Comparaisons doctrinales*, Paris, Pierre Téqui, 1991.
46 *Address* 7.106
47 See Pierre Hadot, *Philosophy as a Way of Life*, tr. by Michael Chase, Oxford, Basil Blackwell, 1995, esp. pp. 264–76.
48 *EH* 6.3, 6–7. See Plato *Republic* 3.400d.
49 Justin, *Dialogue with Trypho*, 8.
50 See, among numerous examples, *Str.* 1,13.57.6, 1.16.77.4, 2.2.5.1, 5.14.96.5, and 8.1.1.2.
51 See *Address* 13–14.

52 *CSong*, Prologue 3 where Proverbs = ethics, Ecclesiastes = physics, and the Song of Songs = enoptics (the mystical knowledge of God bestowed on the initiated).
53 *EH* 6.3.1–7.
54 See *CMt* fr. DV–DVI and *HJer* 20.3.
55 *EH* 6.3.8.
56 Ibid. 6.3.8–12.
57 *Phil.* 7.
58 See *EH* 6.8.1–2 and *CMt* 15.1–5.

2 THE MATURE YEARS AT ALEXANDRIA

1 See Joseph W. Trigg, "The Charismatic Intellectual: Origen's Understanding of Religious Leadership," in *Church History*, 50 (1981), 5–19, reprinted in *Studies in Early Christianity*, vol. 9, ed. Everett Ferguson, New York, Garland, 1992, pp. 107–21 and "Origen, Man of the Church," in *Origeniana Quinta*, pp. 51–6. See also Gunnar af Hällström, *Charismatic Succession: A Study on Origen's Concept of Prophecy*, Helsinki, Finnish Exegetical Society, 1985.
2 *EH* 6.14.10.
3 Ibid. 6.23,1–2.
4 Ibid. 6.19.15.
5 Ibid. 6.21.3.
6 Ibid. 6.8.5. See Nautin, p. 103.
7 *CJn* 6.2. See Nautin, pp. 366–8.
8 A good introduction to current studies on the *Hexapla* are three articles by Olivier Munnich ("Les Hexaples d'Origène à la lumière de la tradition manuscrite del la *Bible* grec"), G. J. Norton ("The Fragments of the *Hexapla* of the Psalter and the Preparation of a Critical Edition of the Hebrew Psalter"), and Pierre Jay ("Jérôme et la Septante origénienne") in *Origeniana Sexta*, pp. 167–214. See also the discussion of Origen's intentions in Adam Kamesar, *Jerome, Greek Scholarship and the Hebrew Bible: A Study of the Quaestiones Hebraicae in Genesim*, Oxford, Oxford University Press, 1993, pp. 4–28 and Nautin, pp. 303–61.
9 Origen also employs it in *HJos* 6.3.
10 In *HJer* 20.1, Origen, in a discussion of the potential ambiguity of Scriptural language, quotes the definition of this term in Aristotle, *Categories* 1.1: " 'Homonyms' are things that have only the word that refers to them in common, the definition corresponding to that word being different."
11 See José Antonio Alcain, *Cautiverio y redención del hombre en Orígenes*, Bilbao, Mensajero, 1973, pp. 67–86.
12 See Ives-Marie Duval, "Vers le Commentaire sur Aggée d'Origène," in *Origeniana Quarta*, pp. 7–15.
13 Origen, *On First Principles*, tr. by G. W. Butterworth, London, SPCK, 1936, most recently reprinted in 1973, Gloucester, Mass., Peter Smith, 1973. Butterworth faithfully follows Paul Koetschau's 1913 *GCS* edition. He does not, of course, reflect significant new under-

standings of Origen's work that have emerged since its publication. Modern editions that do reflect them are Origenes,*Vier Bücher von den Prinzipien*, ed. and tr. by Herwig Görgemanns and Heinrich Karpp, 3rd edition, Darmstadt, Wissenschaftliche Buchgesellschaft, 1992, and Origène, *Traité des Principes*, ed. and tr. by Henri Crouzel and Manlio Simonetti = *SC* vols 252–3, 268–9 and 312, Paris, 1978, 1980 and 1984. See also the translation of Rufinus's text by Marguerite Harl, Gilles Dorival, and Alain le Boulluec: Origène, *Traité des Principes (Peri Archôn)*, Paris, Études Augustiniennes, 1976, particularly valuable for its documentation of subsequent controversies surrounding the work on pp. 253–300.

14 See Nautin, pp. 368–71. See Lothar Lies, *Origenes' "Peri Archon": Eine undogmatische Dogmatik*, Darmstadt, Wissenschaftliche Buchgesellschaft, 1992.

15 We find the Greek in Eusebius, *Contra Marcellum* 1.4.25.

16 See Nicola Pace, *Ricerche sulla tradizione di Rufino del "De principiis" di Origene*, Florence, La Nuova Italia Editrice, 1990.

17 *PA*, Preface, 2.

18 In setting forth his belief in creation *ex nihilo*, Origen alludes to the *Shepherd of Hermas*, Mandates 1.1: "First of all, believe that God is one, who created and ordered all things and made all things to be out of what is not." Like Irenaeus and Clement, Origen considered the *Shepherd* a work close, at least, to Scripture in authority.

19 *PA*, Preface, 4.

20 "Generated" assuming the original Greek word was *egenêthê*, which Rufinus evidently sought to conform to fourth-century standards of Trinitarian orthodoxy by translating it as *natus* ("born"). Jerome translated it is as *factus* ("made") in *Letter to Avitus* 2 in order to make Origen appear heretical by those same standards. It is doubtful that Origen saw any theological difference between *egenêthê* and *egennêthê* ("begotten"); both would have implied to him that the Father was the source of the Son's existence, the Son being clearly distinguished from creatures, properly speaking, by his sharing, along with the Holy Spirit, in God's eternal existence, not having come into being in time.

21 The "common death" is physical death, which Origen contrasts with death to sin, on the one hand, and to death to God, on the other. Origen also makes this distinction in *CJn* 13.140.

22 *PA*, Preface, 4.

23 Ibid.

24 Ibid., Preface, 5.

25 Ibid., Preface, 6.

26 Ibid., Preface, 7.

27 Ibid., Preface, 8.

28 Ibid.,Preface, 10.

29 Ibid., Preface 3.

30 Ibid., Preface, 4–10.

31 I here follow the translation in Herwig Görgemanns and Heinrich Karpp, *zusammenhängendes und organisches Ganzes*, on p. 99 of their

NOTES

edition and translation. They justify this translation on the basis of
early Christian usage, where the Greek *sôma* ("body," Rufinus's *corpus*)
implies an organic and systematic unity. Origen himself appears to
use the term with such an implication in *CJn* 13.302–3 where, in
commenting on Jn 4:36b, "so that the sower and the reaper may
rejoice together," he speaks of "one body (*sôma*) of truth":

> I suppose that for every art and science that involves many
> propositions, the sower finds the principles, which others take
> and elaborate, who themselves transmit the things they have
> discovered to others. Thanks to their discoveries, these become
> to their successors (who cannot discover the first principles
> [*archas*], join together their consequences, and bring to perfec-
> tion their arts and sciences) that which enables them to
> collect, as in a harvest, the fruit of these arts and sciences
> which have been brought to perfection.
>
> If this is true with arts and certain sciences, it remains to
> be seen how much more is it true of the art of arts and science
> of sciences. For after elaborating those things discovered by
> the very first, their successors have, with those things discov-
> ered, transmitted to those who follow them, so that they may
> examine them attentively, raw materials for gathering
> together with wisdom one body of truth.

32 *PA*, Preface 10.
33 Basilius Steidle, "Neue Untersuchungen zu Origenes 'Peri Archon,'"
    in ZNW 40 (1942 for 1941), 236–43.
34 See Gilles Dorival, "Remarques sur la forme du Peri Archon" and
    Marguerite Harl, "Structure et cohérence du Peri Archon," in
    Origeniana, pp. 11–45 and, more recently, Gilles Dorival, "Nouvelles
    remarques sur la forme du *Traité des Principes* d'Origène," in *Recherches
    Augustiniennes* 22 (1987), 67–108.
35 Brian E. Daley, "Origen's 'De Principiis': A Guide to the 'Principles'
    of Christian Scriptural Interpretation," in John F. Petruccione, ed.,
    Nova et Vetera: Patristic Studies in Honor of Thomas Patrick Halton,
    Washington, DC, CUA Press (forthcoming).
36 See Pierre Hadot, *Philosophy as a Way of Life*, tr. by Michael Chase,
    Oxford, Basil Blackwell, 1995.
37 *PA* 4.2.7–8.
38 Henri Crouzel argued that Origen never intended to produce a
    system in the article "Origène est-il un systématique?" in his *Origène
    et la philosophie*, Paris, Aubier, 1962, pp. 179–215. Franz Heinrich
    Kettler makes a powerful case to the contrary in *Der ursprüngliche Sinn
    der Dogmatik des Origenes* = ZNW Beiheft 31 (1966).
39 *PA* 1.3.4. On the Jewish sources of this tradition, see Gedaliahu Guy
    Stroumsa, *Savoir et salut*, Paris, Cerf, 1992, pp. 23–123.
40 See *CC* 6.18 and *H1Sam* 1.2 & 4.1 and Joseph W. Trigg, "The Angel
    of Great Counsel: Christ and the Angelic Hierarchy in Origen's
    Theology," in *Journal of Theological Studies* n.s. 42 (1991), 35–51.

41 For a penetrating discussion of this issue, see Norbert Brox, "Spiritualität und Orthodoxie: Zum Konflikt des Origenes mit der Geschichte des Dogmas," in Ernst Dassmann and K. Suso Frank, eds, *Pietas: Festschrift für Bernhard Kötting = Jahrbuch für Antike und Christentum*, Ergänzungsband 8 (1980), pp. 140–54.

42 See Rowan Williams, *Arius: Heresy and Tradition*, London, Darton, Longman and Todd, 1987.

43 See *PA* 1.2.2–4.

44 See ibid. 2.9.2.

45 Athanasius, *On the Decrees of the Synod of Nicaea* 27.1–2

46 See, among other passages, *PA* 1.3.3 and 2.1.5

47 For a summary of Arius's position as best we can arrive at it, see Richard P. C. Hanson, *The Search for the Christian Doctrine of God*, Edinburgh, T. & T. Clark, 1988, pp. 3–27.

48 *PA* 1.2.1. The best work on Origen's Christology remains Marguerite Harl, *Origène et la fonction révélatrice du Verbe incarné*, Paris, Seuil, 1958.

49 On the New Testament background, see J. Reumann, "OIKONOMIA-terms in Paul in Comparison with Lucan *Heilsgeschichte*," in *New Testament Studies* 13 (1966–7), 147–67. On Irenaeus, see Robert M. Grant, *Irenaeus of Lyons*, London, Routledge, 1996, pp. 49–50.

50 *PA* 2.6.2.

51 Ibid. 2.6.3.

52 Ibid. 2.6.5.

53 Ibid. 1.2.4.

54 Ibid. 2.8.3.

55 Ibid. 4.4.10.

56 Ibid. 2.1.1.

57 See Hal Koch, *Pronoia und Paideusis: Studien über Origenes und sein Verhältnis zum Platonismus*, Berlin, De Gruyter, 1932

58 PA 2.1.2.

59 Ibid. 3.6.1.

60 Ibid.1.5.5.

61 Hendrik S. Benjamins, *Eingeordnete Freiheit: Freiheit und Vorsehung bei Origenes*, Leiden, Brill, 1994.

62 *PA* 3.1.21–2.

63 Ibid. 3.1.19.

64 Brian E. Daley, *The Hope of the Early Church: A Handbook of Patristic Eschatology*, Cambridge, Cambridge University Press, 1991, p. 47.

65 Ibid., p. 48.

66 *PA* 3.6.6.

67 Ibid. 2.11.4.

68 Ibid. 2.11.6.

69 Ibid. 2.11.5–7.

70 Ibid. 2.11.6.

71 Ibid. 2.7.4.

72 Ibid. 1.6.2. See also ibid. 3.6. 3.

73 See also *CLk* on Lk. 14:19–20.

74 *PA* 2.3.1.

75 *PA* 2.10.4

76 See Georg Anrich, "Clemens und Origenes als Begründer der Lehre von Fegfeuer," in W. Nowak, ed., *Theologische Abhandlungen: Eine Festgabe zum 17. Mai 1902 für Heinrich Julius Holtzmann*, Tübingen, J. C. B. Mohr (Paul Siebeck), 1902, pp. 97–120

77 See *HJer* 20. On the possibility that eternal punishment is a medicinal lie, see Joseph W. Trigg, "Divine Deception and the Truthfulness of Scripture," in *Origen: His World and His Legacy*, ed. Charles Kannengiesser, Notre Dame, Indiana, University of Notre Dame Press, 1988, pp. 147–64 and David Satran "Pedagogy and Deceit in the Alexandrian Theological Tradition," in *Origeniana Quinta*, pp. 119–24.

78 *PA* 2.3.1.

79 Ibid. 2.3.4.

80 Ibid. 1.6.3.

81 Ibid. 2.11.2.

82 Ibid. 2.3.2.

83 Ibid. 3.6.2.

84 See Daley, *The Hope of the Early Church*, pp. 48–9.

85 See Henri Crouzel, *Les fins dernières selon Origène*, Aldershot, Variorum, 1990 and Charles E. Hill, *Regnum Caelorum: Patterns of Future Hope in Early Christianity*, Oxford, Oxford University Press, 1992, see esp. pp. 127–41.

86 The classic discussion of Origen's biblical interpretation is Henri de Lubac, *Histoire et Esprit: L'intelligence d'Écriture d'après Origène*, Paris, Aubier, 1950. Richard P. C. Hanson provides an important corrective in *Allegory and Event*, Richmond, John Knox Press, 1959. Marguerite Harl's discussion of Origen's hermeneutic in her introduction to the *Sources chrétiennes* edition of *Philocalia 1–21* (*SC* 302, Paris, Cerf, 1983, pp. 42–157) provides a clear and balanced account.

87 *PA* 4.1.1.

88 Ibid. 4.1.4–6.

89 Ibid. 4.1.6–7.

90 Ibid. 4.2.1.

91 Ibid. 4.2.4. See Karen Jo Torjesen, *Hermeneutical Procedure and Theological Method in Origen's Exegesis*, Berlin and New York, Walter de Gruyter, 1986.

92 *PA* 4.2.5.

93 Ibid. 4.2.9. See Jean Pépin, "L'absurdité, signe d'allégorie," in *La tradition d'allégorie: de Philon d'Alexandrie à Dante*, Paris, Études Augustiniennes, 1987, pp. 167–86. The word "planned" is *ôikonomêse*, the verb corresponding to the noun *oikonomia*. See Hendrik S. Benjamins, " Οἰκονομία bei Origenes: Schrift und Heilsplan," in *Origeniana Sexta*, pp. 327–31.

94 *PA* 4.2.6.

95 Ibid. 4.2.8

96 Ibid. 4.3.4

97 Ibid. 4.3.3.

98 See *The Great Code: The Bible and Literature*, New York, Harcourt Brace Jovanovich, 1982, pp. 60, 60–2 and *Words with Power Being a Second Study of the Bible and Literature*, San Diego, Harcourt Brace Jovanovich, 1990, pp. 5–6

99 *PA* 4.3.5 and 4.3.11.

100 Ibid. 4.2.3.

101 Manlio Simonetti, *Lettera e/o allegoria: Un contributo alla storia dell'esegesi patristica*, Rome, Institutum Patristicum "Augustinianum", 1985, pp. 79–80.

102 See Theresia Heither, *Translatio Religionis: Die Paulusdeutung des Origenes*, Cologne and Vienna, Böhlau Verlag, 1990.

3 MAN OF THE CHURCH AT CAESAREA

1 See John Anthony McGuckin, "Caesarea Maritima as Origen Knew It," in *Origeniana Quinta*, pp. 3–25.

2 See Robert L. Wilken, *The Land Called Holy: Palestine in Christian History and Thought*, New Haven, Yale University Press, 1992.

3 See David J. Halperin, *The Faces of the Chariot: Early Jewish Responses to Ezekiel's Vision*, Tübingen, Mohr, 1988, pp. 337–8 and Origen, "Homily 1 on Ezekiel," intr. and tr. by Joseph W. Trigg in Vincent L. Wimbush, ed., *Ascetic Behavior in Greco-Roman Antiquity: A Sourcebook*, Minneapolis, Fortress, 1990, pp. 45–65.

4 See David T. Runia, *Philo in Early Christian Literature: A Survey*, Assen, Van Gorcum and Minneapolis, Fortress, 1993, pp. 24–5.

5 Grégoire le Thaumaturge, *Remerciement à Origène suivi de la Lettre d'Origène à Grégoire*, ed. Henri Crouzel, Paris, Cerf, 1959 = *SC* 148. Crouzel proposes the earlier date on p. 22. Pierre Nautin proposes the later date in Nautin, p. 382.

6 Nautin, in Nautin, pp. 83–6 and 182–97, has challenged the traditional attribution to Gregory Thaumaturgus while accepting the authenticity of the *Address* as a testimony by a student of Origen. Crouzel effectively defends the traditional attribution in 'Faut-il voir trois personnages en Grégoire le Thaumaturge?" *Gregorianum* 60 (1979), 287–320. The question of attribution, like that of dating, remains open.

7 *Address*, 2.13 and 5.55.

8 Ibid., 4.45 and 5.48–72.

9 Ibid., 5.72.

10 Robert L. Wilken, "Alexandria: A School for Training in Virtue," in Patrick Henry, ed., *Schools of Thought in the Christian Tradition*, Philadelphia, Fortress Press, 1984, pp. 15–30.

11 *Address*, 15, 175, and 179.

12 Ibid., 4.42. See Joseph W. Trigg, "The Angel of Great Counsel: Christ and the Angelic Hierarchy in Origen's Theology," in *Journal of Theological Studies* n.s. 42 (1991), 35–51.

13 *Address*, 15.174.

14 Ibid., 8.109.

15 Ibid., 8.111.

16 Ibid., 9.123.
17 Ibid., 5.59
18 Ibid., 7.97.
19 Ibid., 7.107–08.
20 Ibid., 14.171.
21 Ibid., 14.163–7
22 Ibid., 7.103–4.
23 See Nautin, pp. 389–409.
24 An additional seventy-five homilies in Jerome's *Tractate or Homilies on the Psalms* are, in effect, reworked homilies by Origen. See Vittorio Peri, *Omelie origeniane sui Salmi*, Vatican City, Biblioteca apostolica, 1980.
25 See Daniel Sheerin, "The Role of Prayer in Origen's Homilies," in *Origen of Alexandria: His World and His Legacy*, ed. Charles Kannengiesser and William L. Peterson, Notre Dame, Ind., Notre Dame University Press, 1988, pp. 200–14.
26 On Origen's preaching style, see Pierre Nautin, "Origène prédicateur," in *SC* 232, pp. 100–9 and Adele Monaci Castagno, *Origene predicatore e il suo pubblico*, Turin, FrancoAngeli, 1987.
27 *HJudg* 8.4.
28 *HLev* 4.6.
29 *HPs* 36.2.
30 *HEx* 13.3.
31 See *HGen* 10.1 and *HJer* 20.6.
32 See Origène, *Sur la Pâque*, ed. and tr. by Octave Guérand and Pierre Nautin, Paris, Beauchesne, 1979.
33 *EH* 6.2.20.2 (on Beryllus as a celebrated author) and 6.33.1–3.
34 *DH* 5.
35 Gregory of Nazianzus, *Letters* 101.32.
36 *DH* 7.
37 Ibid. 16.
38 Namely in John Ernest Leonard Oulton and Henry Chadwick, eds and tr., *Alexandrian Christianity*, Philadelphia, Westminster, 1954; in John J. O'Meara, tr. Origen, *On Prayer and Exhortation to Martyrdom = Ancient Christian Writers* 19, New York, Paulist, 1954; and in Rowan Greer, *An Exhortation to Martyrdom, Prayer and Selected Works*, New York, Paulist, 1979. Oulton's translation has the fullest notes. All of these volumes also include the *Exhortation to Martyrdom*.
39 *OP* 1.
40 Ibid. 5–8.1.
41 Ibid. 8.2.
42 Ibid. 9.2.
43 Ibid. 13.2–3.
44 Ibid. 12.2.
45 Ibid. 32.
46 *EM* 12.
47 Ibid. 4.
48 Ibid. 5.

49 Ibid. 46. See John M. Rist, "The Magical Power of Names in Origen and Later Platonism," in *Origeniana Tertia*, pp. 203–16.

50 *EM* 4.

51 Ibid. 13.

52 Ibid. 3.

53 Nautin, pp. 411–36.

54 *CSong*, Prologue 1.1.

55 On exegesis of the Song of Songs before Origen, see Roland E. Murphy, *The Song of Songs*, Minneapolis, Fortress Press, 1990, pp. 12–16. Murphy stresses the paucity of evidence concerning early Jewish interpretation.

56 Henri Crouzel, *Origène et Plotin: Comparaisons doctrinales*, Paris, Pierre Téqui, 1991, p. 220.

57 *CSong*, Prologue, 1.4.

58 Ibid., Prologue, 1.6.

59 Ibid., Prologue, 1.7.

60 Ibid., Prologue, 2.43.

61 Ibid., Prologue, 2.4–19.

62 Ibid., Prologue, 2.2.20–27.

63 See Anders Nygren, *Agape and Eros*, tr. by Philip A. Watson, Philadelphia, Westminster Press, 1953, pp. 387–92. For more recent treatments of Origen on love, see John M. Rist, *Eros and Psyche: Studies in Plato, Plotinus, and Origen*, Toronto, University of Toronto Press, 1964; Henryk Pietras, *L'amore in Origene*, Rome, Institutum Patristicum "Augustinianum," 1988; Catherine Osborne, *Eros Unveiled: Plato and the God of Love*, Oxford, Oxford University Press, 1994. Osborne makes a strong case that Origen not only understood the Bible better than does Nygren, but he also had a better understanding of Plato.

64 *CSong* 3.1.4.

65 Ibid. 1.5.3.

66 On the meaning of *nous* in this context, see Henri Crouzel, *Origène et la "connaissance mystique,"* Bruges, Desclée de Brouwer, 1961, pp. 41–2.

67 *CSong* 1.5.4.

68 *PA* 4.9–11 and 2.11.5.

69 *CSong* 2.1.

70 Ibid. 3.6.9.

71 Ibid. 1.1.11.

72 See Patricia Cox Miller, "Pleasure of the Text, Text of Pleasure: Eros and Language in Origen's Commentary on the Song of Songs," in *Journal of the American Academy of Religion* 54 (1986), 241–53.

73 Charles Bigg, *The Christian Platonists of Alexandria: The 1886 Bampton Lectures*, Oxford, Oxford University Press, 1913, p. 173.

74 Caroline P. Hammond Bammel, ed., *Der Römerbriefkommentar des Origenes: Kritische Ausgabe der Übersetzung Rufins, Buch 1–3*, Freiburg, Herder, 1990.

75 Peter Gorday, *Principles of Patristic Exegesis*, New York and Toronto, Edwin Mellen: 1983 and Lorenzo Perrone, ed., *Il cuore indurito del*

Faraone: Origene e il problema del libero arbitrio, Bologna, Marietti, 1992.

76 Theresia Heither, *Translatio Religionis: Die Paulusdeutung des Origenes*, Cologne and Vienna, Böhlau Verlag, 1990, p. 2.

77 The fragments of these homilies were collected by Claude Jenkins in "Origen on 1 Corinthians," in *Journal of Theological Studies* 9 (1908), 231–47, 353–72, 500–14 and 10 (1909), 29–51.

78 Francesca Cocchini, *Il Paolo di Origene: Contributo all storia della recezione delle epistole paoline nel III secolo*, Rome, Edizione Studium, 1992

79 Gedaliahu Guy Stroumsa, in *Hidden Wisdom: Esoteric Traditions and the Roots of Christian Mysticism*, Leiden, Brill, 1996, pp. 11–26, shows how Platonists used *ainigma* and the related verb *ainittomai* to speak of the true, philosophical meaning of myths.

80 Robert M. Grant, *Miracle and Natural Law in Graeco-Roman and Early Christian Thought*, Amsterdam, North Holland, 1952, p. 258.

81 *CJn* 20.7. See also fr. II on 1 Corinthians in Jenkins, "Origen on 1 Corinthians," p. 232.

82 See Nautin, pp. 375–6.

83 See James Francis, *Subversive Virtue: Asceticism and Authority in the Second-Century Pagan World*, University Park, Pennsylvania, Pennsylvania State University Press, 1995, pp. 133–5.

84 See Karl Pichler, *Streit um das Christentum: Der Angriff des Kelsos und die Antwort des Origenes*, Frankfurt, Peter D. Lang, 1980, pp. 43–50.

85 *EH* 6.38.1.

86 *CC*, Preface, 3.

87 Ibid. 1.28.

88 Ibid. 4.54.

89 Ibid. 8.12.

90 Ibid. 8.66.

91 Ibid. 5,27.

92 Robert L. Wilken, *The Christians as the Romans Saw Them*, New Haven, Yale University Press, 1984, p. 124. See also Michel Fédou, *Christianisme et religions païennes dans le Contre Celse d'Origène*, Paris, Beauchesne, 1988.

93 *CC* 4.88.

94 Ibid. 1.9.

95 Ibid. 1.41 and 2.55.

96 Ibid. 4.54.

97 Ibid. 4.14.

98 Ibid. 2.75.

99 Ibid. 5.25.

100 Ibid. 3.5.

101 See Grant, *Miracle and Natural Law*, pp. 182–208.

102 *CC* 2.30.

103 Ibid. 5.14–16.

104 Ibid. 5.18–19.

105 Ibid. 5.23.

106 Ibid. 1.28 See Marie-Joseph Rondeau, *Les Commentaires patristiques du Psautier (IIIe–Ve siècles)*, vols 1 and 2 = *Orientalia Christiana Analecta* 219 and 220, Rome, Pont. Institutum Studiorum Orientalium, 1982 and 1985, vol. 2, pp. 51–8.

107 *CC* 7.42. See John Whittaker, " Ἄρρητος καὶ ἀκατανόμαστος" in *Platonismus und Christentum, Festschrift für Heinrich Dörrie*, ed. H. D. Blume and F. Mann = *Jahrbuch für Christentum*, Ergänzungsband 10, Münster, Aschendorffsche Buchhandlung, 1983, pp. 303–306, repr. in John Whittaker, *Studies in Platonic and Patristic Theology*, London, Variorum Reprints, 1984.

108 Plato, *Republic* 330a. Seriphos is one of the smallest Aegean islands.

109 *CC* 1.29–30.

110 Ibid. 7.48 and 3.68.

111 *CMt* 15.15.

112 *CC* 7.44.

113 Ibid. 7.31.

114 Adolf Harnack, *History of Dogma*, tr. by Neil Buchanan, London, Williams & Norgate, 1900, vol. 2, pp. 330–80.

115 *CC* 4.79.

116 Ibid. 4.3.

117 Ibid. 4.5.

118 Ibid. 4,71,

119 Ibid. 7.42.

120 Ibid. 6.68

121 *EH* 6.39.5. See Nautin, p. 441.

4 A CONTROVERSIAL LEGACY

1 Henri de Lubac, *Exégèse Médiévale: Les Quartre sens de l'Écriture*, 4 vols, Paris, Aubier, 1959–64. He quotes Richard Simon, *Histoire critique du Vieux Testament*, 1.3.1 (1685 edn, p. 403) in vol. 1, p. 212.

2 Manlio Simonetti, *Lettera e/o allegoria: Un contributo alla storia dell'esegesi patristica*, Rome, Institutum Patristicum "Augustinianum", 1985, pp. 73–4.

3 See Manlio Simonetti, *Lettera e/o allegoria: Un contributo alla storia dell' esegesi patristica*, Rome, Institutum Patristicum "Augustinianum", 1985 and Bernhardt Neuschäfer, *Origenes als Philologe* = *Schweizerische Beiträge zur Altertumswissenschaft* 18, 2 vols, Basel, Friedrich Reinhardt, 1987. See also Jean-Noël Guinot, "La fortune des *Hexaples* d'Origène aux IVe et Ve siècles en milieu antiochien," in *Origeniana Sexta*, pp. 215–25.

4 See Andrew Louth, *The Origins of the Christian Mystical Tradition: From Plato to Denys*, Oxford, Oxford University Press, 1981.

5 Brian E. Daley, *The Hope of the Early Church: A Handbook of Patristic Eschatology*, Cambridge, Cambridge University Press, 1991, p. 50.

6 Samuel Rubenson, *The Letters of St. Antony: Monasticism and the Making of a Saint*, Philadelphia: Fortress Press, 1995.

7 See Rebecca Hardin Weaver, *Divine Grace and Human Agency: A Study of the Semi-Pelagian Controversy*, Macon, Ga, Mercer University Press, 1996.

8 André Godin, *Érasme lecteur d'Origène*, Geneva, Droz, 1982, pp. 449–89.

9 Henri Crouzel, *Origen: The Life and Thought of the First Great Theologian*, tr. by A. S. Worrall, San Francisco, Harper & Row, 1989, p. xi.

10 Manlio Simonetti, "La controversia origeniana," *Augustinianum* 25 (1986), 7–31.

11 Ulrich Berner, *Origenes*, Darmstatt, Wissenschaftliche Buchgesellschaft, 1981.

12 On Methodius, see A. Vitores, *Identitad entre el cuerpo muerto y resusitado en Orígenes según el "De Resurrectione" de Metodio de Olimpo*, Jerusalem, Fransciscan, 1981 and Lloyd G. Patterson, "Methodius, Origen and the Arian Dispute," *SP* 17.2 (1982), 912–23 and *Methodius of Olympus: Divine Sovereignty, Human Freedom, and Life in Christ*, Washington, CUA Press, 1997.

13 On Eustathius, see Joseph W. Trigg, "Eustathius of Antioch's Attack on Origen: What is at Issue in an Ancient Controversy?" in *Journal of Religion* 75 (1995), 219–38.

14 On Pamphilus and Eusebius see Nautin, pp. 99–153.

15 See Joseph W. Trigg, *Biblical Interpretation* = *The Message of the Fathers* 9, Wilmington, Del., Michael Glazier, 1988 and Simonetti, *Lettera e/o allegoria*, pp. 140–230.

16 See Elizabeth A. Clark. *The Origenist Controversy: The Cultural Construction of an Early Christian Debate*, Princeton, Princeton University Press, 1992.

17 Berthold Altaner, "Augustinus und Origenes," in *Kleine Patristische Studien* = *Texte und Untersuchungen* 83 (1967), 224–52. Henry Chadwick, "Christian Platonism in Origen and Augustine," in *Origeniana Tertia*, pp. 217–30.

18 See Aloys Grillmeier with Theresia Hainthaler, *Christ in the Christian Tradition, Volume 2: From the Council of Chalcedon (451) to Gregory the Great (590–604), Part Two: The Church of Constantinople in the Sixth Century*, tr. by Pauline Allen and John Cawte, Louisville, Westminster John Knox Press, 1995. pp. 385–410.

19 See Giulia Sfameni Gasparro, "Il problema delle citazioni del Peri Archon nella Lettera a Mena di Giustiniano," in *Origeniana Quarta*, pp. 54–76.

20 See Antoine Guillaumont, *Les "Képhalaia Gnostika" d'Évagre le Pontique et l'Histoire de l'Origénisme chez les Grecs et chez les Syriens*, Paris, Seuil, 1962 and Francis X. Murphy, "Evagrius Ponticus and Origenism," in *Origeniana Tertia*, pp. 254–69. But see J. G. Bunge, "Origenismus – Gnostizismus: zum geistesgeschichtlichen Standort des Evagrius Pontikos," *Vigiliae Christianae* 40 (1986), 24–54.

21 Antoine Guillaumont, "Le Gnostique chez Clément d'Alexandrie et chez Évagre le Pontique," in *ΑΛΕΞΑΝΔΡΙΝΑ: Hellenisme judaique et christianisme à Alexandrie, Mélanges offerts au P. Claude Mondésert*, Paris, Cerf, 1987, pp. 195–201.

22 Irena Backus, ed., *The Reception of the Church Fathers in the West*, 2 vols, Leiden, Brill, 1997. See also Max Schär, *Das Nachleben des Origenes im Zeitalter des Humanismus*, Basel, Helbing & Lichtenhahn, 1979 and André Godin, *Érasme lecteur d'Origène*, Geneva, Droz, 1982.

COMMENTARY ON PSALMS 1–25, FRAGMENT FROM PREFACE

1 Charles Bigg, *The Christian Platonists of Alexandria: The 1886 Bampton Lectures*, Oxford, Oxford University Press, 1913, p. 173.
2 Origen's unnamed Jewish teacher at Alexandria. See chapter 2, pp. 11–12.
3 Initially the analogy is the one the Psalmist makes between pure, refined silver and the Holy Scriptures. Origen generalizes this into an analogy between Scripture and the created world.
4 "Artisan" here is Greek *technitês*, "one who exercises skill or art (*technê*)."
5 "Rational principle" is Greek *logos*.

COMMENTARY ON LAMENTATIONS, SELECTED FRAGMENTS

1 Nautin, pp. 368–71.
2 See chapter 1, p. 6.
3 Origen relies on a traditional interpretation of "Jerusalem" as "vision of peace," making it an appropriate image of the soul's contemplative nature. See Philo, *On Drunkenness* 1.369 and *On Sleep* 3.692,
4 From the context, we must assume that the "fourfold" character of the Old Testament refers to the four translations into Greek, mentioned below, which Origen arranged together in his *Tetrapla* or "fourfold" text.
5 The Greek word for the four elements (*stoicheiai*) is also the word for letters of the alphabet.
6 "Confusion" is the supposed etymology of "Babylon." See Gen. 11:9.
7 The contrast is between *agapê* and *philia*.
8 Greek *tôn eschatôn*, which Origen takes to refer to the punishments that sinners will suffer after death.
9 Origen's interpretation of this passage in John in *CJn* 32.77–82 below, one of his last works, is entirely consistent with his treatment here, in one of his first. In both cases he connects the footwashing passage in John with the Old Testament examples of Moses and Joshua and in both he interprets the passage spiritually as referring to the soul. See also *HJos* 6.3.
10 Greek *logos*.
11 Greek *logos*.
12 Greek *philanthrôpia*. This is a term Origen often uses for disinterested love, especially God's love of humanity. See Catherine Osborne, *Eros Unveiled: Plato and the God of Love*, Oxford, Oxford University Press, 1994, pp. 164–84.
13 Greek *logos*.

14 Greek *logos*. See *CJn* 1.11.

15 Greek *hēgemonikon*, originally a Stoic term. The "governing faculty" is the part of the soul responsible for decisions, whether of intellect, affection or will.

16 That is, God's punishments either purify the sinner or deter others from following his example. For a discussion of such deterrence, see *HJer* 12.4 below.

17 Here Origen follows the text of Symmachus instead of the LXX, which reads "he spurned."

18 This is one of the earliest references to Palestine as the "holy land". See chapter 3.

19 That is, a state of confusion.

20 Origen employs a similar image for heretics in our selections below from *CJn* 13.

21 See Josephus, *Jewish War* 6.5.3.

22 For a discussion of how Origen draws on an earlier Christian use of this verse as a testimony to Christ, see Jean Daniélou, *Études d'exégèse judéo-chrétienne (Les Testimonia)*, Paris, Beauchesne, 1966, pp. 76–95.

23 This passage is obscure, probably because the fragment drastically condenses Origen's argument. This leaves it unclear whether Origen accepts or rejects the identification of Josiah as a type of Christ. The statement in 2 Chr. 35:25 that Jeremiah, the supposed author of Lamentations, made a lament for Josiah had apparently suggested to earlier interpreters the identification of Josiah as the subject of the lament. Although the origin of this interpretation was probably Jewish, the interpreters Origen refers to were Christians who identified Josiah as a "type" of Christ. In their interpretation, Josiah was a type of Christ because he was a righteous king who died because of the lawless behavior of the Jewish people. The reference to Neco's unwillingness to fight, which appears to be Origen's own, suggests that Origen accepted this interpretation. Given Origen's consistent identification of Pharaohs as types of Satan, "the prince of this world" (see especially *HEx* 2.1), he may have seen in Neco's unwillingness to fight against Josiah a reflection of 1 Cor. 2:7–8. There the princes of this world "would not have crucified the Lord of Glory" had they not been ignorant of the hidden "wisdom of God in a mystery"; by implication they, like Neco, would not have fought against him willingly.

24 The implication is that, in this oracle, Christ must be speaking through the prophet Jeremiah (and, by implication, through all the prophets) since he is privy to a knowledge otherwise withheld from the Jewish people. To clinch this identification, Origen turns to Isaiah 52, where, according to ancient Christian tradition, the prophet, assuming the *prosōpon* of the coming Messiah, predicts his passion. It is thus the incarnate Christ who, in Isaiah, says "I am present, the very one who is speaking" just as he says to the Samaritan woman, "I am he, the one who is speaking to you." On Christ's effective incarnation in Scripture, see *CJn* 1.33–4 below.

25 That is, those who took away the Old Testament prophets, including Jeremiah, were, in effect, taking away Christ. Origen possibly found

this idea in a work written *c.* AD 165, Melito's *On the Passover* (57): "But first the Lord had planned in advance [*proôikonomêsen*] his own sufferings in the patriarchs and prophets and in the whole people, so that he was confirmed by the seal of the law and the prophets."

26 Thus the prophets belong, before the fact, to the Christian church, where their ministry continues in the church's teachers, whom Origen endows with the prophetic role. See Gunnar af Hällström, *Charismatic Succession: A Study on Origen's Concept of Prophecy,* Helsinki, the Finnish Exegetical Society, 1984, pp. 39–60.

27 Justin Martyr wrote in his *First Apology* 36.2 (*c.* 152), of the prophets speaking, at times, in the "person" (*prosôpon*) of God or of Christ. Greek drama established the identification of the "person" or character speaking in a play with that character's mask or "face".

28 Greek *prosôpon*.

29 Greek *prosôpon*.

30 Greek *prosôpa*, the plural of *prosôpon*.

COMMENTARY ON GENESIS, FRAGMENT FROM BOOK 3

1 Nautin, pp. 370–1.

2 For detailed commentary, see the Éric Junod's introduction to the *SC* edition (pp. 24–65) and Hendrik S. Benjamins, *Eingeordnete Freiheit: Freiheit und Vorsehung bei Origenes,* Leiden, Brill, 1994, pp. 70–86.

3 See Lorenzo Perrone, "Perspectives sur Origène et la littérature patristique des 'quaestiones et responsiones,'" in *Origeniana Sexta,* pp. 150–64.

4 Plotinus, *Enneads* 3.1.6.

5 Marcionites made a point of distinguishing between a good God of the New Testament and a merely just God of the Old Testament, whom they, like the Valentinians, designate with the Platonic term Artisan (Greek *dêmiourgos*, the term Origen uses consistently in this passage).

6 "Powers" (Greek *dunameis*) is the normal term for angelic beings.

7 Junod (*SC* 226.152, n. 1) argues that these "Greeks" (i.e. pagans) are Academic philosophers from the Hellenistic period opposed to the early Stoics and that Origen may have known them only vaguely through handbooks. On the other hand, Benjamins (*Eingeordnete Freiheit,* p. 82, n. 63) argues that they were contemporary Platonists who affirmed providence as a general direction of the universe but denied that providence entails comprehensive divine foreknowledge of individual human actions.

8 That is, God knows what will happen in the future, but he knows contingent events as contingent.

9 "Common notions" is a Stoic term; see Cicero, *De fin.* 3, 6, 21 and 10.33 and Epictetus, *Diss.* 1.22.9ff. and 2.11.3.

10 *Oikonomôn,* referring to God's *oikonomia*.

11 Origen takes the opportunity, having demonstrated that God has good reason to blind us to the future, to clarify this difficult passage in Exodus, which could be used by Gnostics as evidence that the God of

the Old Testament is cruel and arbitrary, deliberately and for no good reason making some people blind and others sighted.

12 This work is known only from this citation and a longer one in *CJn* 2.188–90 (not in this volume). The notion of heavenly tablets played an important role in other Jewish apocalyptic literature, notably the Book of Jubilees, as well as I Enoch, and the Testaments of Levi and Asher. Origen also mentions this idea twice in *CJn* 1.68 and 221 below.

13 Plotinus makes the same argument in *Ennead* 3.1.5.

14 This theory developed by Hipparchus, an astronomer of the second century BC, is known as the precession of the equinoxes. Using data from earlier astronomers, Hipparchus demonstrated, to the embarrassment of astrologers, that so-called "fixed" stars are not, from our perspective, really fixed.

15 Origen discussed a distinction made by astrologers between the theoretical concept (*to noêton*) of a sign of the zodiac (i.e. a twelfth part of the ecliptic) and the actual form of the constellation. Astrologers may claim that the theoretical concept, rather than the constellation itself, determines the future, but the precession of the equinoxes means that the theoretical concept cannot be determined accurately from the actual position of the stars, which are gradually slipping eastwards so as to occupy a different place on the ecliptic.

16 Origen explains this curious citation in *CJn* 2.188–90, where he states that, according to *The Prayer of Joseph*, which he describes as a Jewish apocryphal writing, Jacob was actually the highest archangel. When the Archangel Uriel meets him in Syrian Mesopotamia, Jacob fights with him for pretending to be his superior when Uriel is, in fact, eight ranks below him. This appears to be a midrash on Genesis 32, where Jacob struggles with an angel and receives the name Israel. Origen's point is that the book that speaks of Jacob's reading future events in the stars also ascribes to him a superhuman dignity, so that, even if he could read the stars, that does not mean that we can.

17 This is one of Origen's strongest statements of the absolute transcendence of God. God is uniquely an "ingenerate mind" (*nous agenêtos*), that is, a mind that has no origin outside itself.

18 Greek *tais ta anthrôpina oikonomousais*, a reference to the angels as the administrators of the divine *oikonomia*.

19 Here Origen probably has in mind the demonic resistance to Christ predicted by the prophets.

COMMENTARY ON JOHN, BOOK 1

1 See Ronald E. Heine, "The Introduction to Origen's *Commentary on John* Compared with the Introductions to the Ancient Philosophical Commentaries on Aristotle," in *Origeniana Sexta*, pp. 3–12.

2 In 1 Peter 3 Christian women are exhorted to adorn themselves inwardly rather than outwardly and to be subject to their husbands, following the example of women in the old covenant and of Sarah in particular. The implication is that, since the same principles of

behavior apply under both covenants, it may be presumed that the peoples of the old and new covenants are also similar in their organization. Origen often cites biblical texts this way, quoting a few words on the assumption that intelligent readers will fill in the rest of the text in such a way as to advance his argument. He may have learned the technique from Clement, who employed such fleeting allusions deliberately to hide his message from those unworthy of it.

3 Note that Origen does not question either the canonical status or the Johannine authorship of the Revelation to John.

4 That is, when they present their own tithes and first-fruits, these offerings are taken from tithes and first-fruits previously offered to them, since, by depending on offerings from the people, they have nothing to offer that is not already consecrated.

5 Genuine priests are evidently so constituted, not by episcopal ordination, but by their total dedication to studying Scripture. Pierre Nautin (Nautin, p. 467) finds here an implicit rebuke of Demetrius for not ordaining him as a presbyter.

6 Nautin (ibid., pp. 366–7) argues that this return to Alexandria was in 231 after a lengthy sojourn in Palestine, where Origen sought refuge after Demetrius condemned his recently published *Commentary on Genesis* and *Peri Archon*. The rapprochement was temporary and he left Alexandria permanently a year later.

7 The original text here is corrupt. Origen seems to be pointing out that, while Paul assumes considerable authority, he avoids speaking as an oracle, as if he were simply a mouthpiece for the Holy Spirit.

8 Four, since they correspond to the four elements: earth, air, fire, and water.

9 That is, the Gospel of John deals with Christ in his human and divine natures: it speaks of the man Jesus, given a genealogy by Matthew and Luke, but it begins its account with the Logos, who, like Melchizedek in Hebrews, has no genealogy.

10 Here again the text is corrupt, but there seems to be little doubt about the point Origen is making.

11 Literally "obtain the intelligence" (*ton noun labein*). The use of the word *nous*, also translatable as "mind," "sense," or "meaning," recalls 1 Cor. 2:16b, "But we have the mind (*nous*) of Christ" cited in 24 below. The implication is that we can know the meaning (*nous*) of the Gospel according to John only if we have the mind (*nous*) of Christ.

12 Here and elsewhere Origen affirms the perpetual virginity of Mary. On Origen's Mariology, see Henri Crouzel, "La théologie mariale d'Origène," in *SC* 87, pp. 11–64. Jean Leclerq, in *The Love of Learning and the Desire for God: A Study of Monastic Culture* (tr. by Catharine Misrahi, New York, Fordham University Press, 1961), p. 121, recounts a testimony of a nun, Elizabeth of Schönau, disturbed by allegations that Origen was a heretic. When the Blessed Virgin appears to her in a vision, she asks: "My Lady, I beg of you, kindly reveal to me something concerning the great doctor of the church, Origen, who in so many places in his works has sung your praises so magnificently. Is he saved or not?" She receives the reply:

Know only that Origen's error did not come from bad will; it came from excess of fervor with which he plunged into the depths of the Holy Scripture he loved, and the divine mysteries which he was wont to scrutinize to an excessive degree. For this reason the punishment he is undergoing is not severe. And because of the glory his writings have given to me, he is illuminated by a very special light on each feast commemorating me. As for what will happen to him on the last day, that must not be revealed to you, but must remain hidden among the divine secrets.

13 Origen frequently cites these verses together in this way. See note 11 above.

14 Greek *epidêmia*, in contrast to *parousia*, "advent." The term *epidêmia*, from *epi* "to" and *dêmos* "humanity," is sometimes translated "incarnation" and, more clearly than *parousia*, implies Christ's assumption of humanity to be present with humanity.

15 There is a lacuna here, but the sense is evidently that, just as a little leaven leavens the whole loaf, so the gospel testimony transforms the whole Old Testament into a gospel by providing a key to its previously hidden meaning.

16 This is the same point made above in *CLam* fr. CXVI.

17 Greek *oikonomous*, i.e. those who exercise God's *oikonomia* on their behalf. As we shall see, these are normally angels, although spiritually advanced human beings may also exercise this ministry.

18 Discourses (*logoi*, plural) prepare the way for the Word (*logos*, singular) of God.

19 Origen refines the distinction between the two Testaments by arguing that, in both dispensations, Christ is present to some more immediately than he is to others. Just as Christ was present in a way prefiguring his incarnation to certain preeminent figures under the old covenant, so, under the new covenant, he is not fully present, as God the Word, to immature souls.

20 Greek *oikonomia*. The "plan" may be God's plan of salvation encompassing both Jews and gentiles. More likely Origen has in mind the exercise of *oikonomia* by the apostles themselves, who accommodate themselves to the Jews at Jerusalem. Origen goes on to argue that they acted the same way with simple Christians. In doing so they may exercise deliberate deception. See John Reumann, " Οἰκονομία as 'Ethical Accommodation' in the Fathers, and its Pagan Backgrounds," in *SP* 3 (1961), pp. 370–9.

21 A statement of Origen's Christian esoterism. Just as Paul acted as though he accepted the law's continuing validity in order to reach Jews, so, by implication, the person seeking to improve simple Christians should act as though there are no higher, secret teachings.

22 Origen cites this verse, testifying to the power of Scripture in the human heart, at least twenty-three times in his extant works.

23 Origen consistently argued that the power of the gospel to change lives distinguishes Christian teaching from Greek rhetoric and philosophy. See chapter 3, pp. 58–60. The distinction between *logos* ("discourse" or

"word") and *dunamis* ("power"), taken from Paul, echoes the contrast between *logos* and *ergon* ("word" and "deed") that is a commonplace in Classical Greek literature.

24 Note how Origen, many years later, elaborated on this theme in *CJn* 32.78–83 below.

25 Greek *kat'epinoian*. For a discussion of *epinoiai*, see J. Wolinski, "Le recours aux ἐπίνοιαι du Christ dans le *Commentaire de Jean* d'Origène," in *Origeniana Sexta*, pp. 465–92. John A. McGuckin makes the fascinating suggestion that the fourteen *epinoiai* from John listed in 9 and 21 determined the scope of his entire commentary . See "Structural Design and Apologetic Intent in Origen's *Commentary on John*," in *Origeniana Sexta*, pp. 441–57.

26 See *CGen* 15, n. 12.

27 This appears to be an allusion to the cosmology of *Peri Archon*. How is the "joy which shall be to all people" also a "glory" "when those who have been humbled to the ground return to their rest"? Most likely Origen had in mind the glory that occurs in souls that are divinized as a result of their contemplation of God; see *CJn* 32.138–40, translated below. Such souls "return" to the original unity with God that they lost in a pre-cosmic fall.

28 Neither Greek nor Hebrew distinguishes between the words meaning "messenger" and "angel".

29 This is the characteristic position of the Gnostics, including Heracleon. See chapter 1, p. 8.

30 Precisely because of this wide range of meaning, the Greek word *archê* cannot be translated by a single English word. In the paragraphs below it is translated either as "beginning" or "principle". It also means "rule" in the sense of "control". Cécile Blanc (*SC* 120 bis, p. 114, n. 1) points out that, in the course of these few paragraphs, Origen examines *archê* in terms of the four causes recognized by Aristotle: efficient, the "by which" of 110–11; material, the "from which" of 103; formal, the "in accordance with which" of 104–5; and final, the "end" here.

31 This distinction, and the priorities implied, is fundamental to Origen's understanding of the Christian life.

32 Greek *apokatastasis*. Here Origen does employ this term often associated with him.

33 Origen believed that the sun, along with other heavenly bodies, was animated. In *On First Principles* 1.7.5 he applies Romans 8:20–22 and Philippians 1:24, cited here, to the heavenly bodies. See Alan Scott, *Origen and the Life of the Stars: A History of an Idea*, Oxford, Oxford University Press, 1991.

34 Greek *dêmiourgos*. This term, meaning "artisan" (literally "one who works for the people"), was applied by Plato (*Timaeus* 40c) to the Creator of the world. Gnostics used it to refer to an inferior Creator-God, identified with the God of the Old Testament and distinct from the God of the New Testament who is the Father of Jesus Christ. Here Origen appropriates the term to designate the Son as the one "through whom all things were made."

35 That is, Aristotelians and most contemporary Platonists.

36 Here Origen alludes to the philosophical use of *archê* in the sense of a first principle of existence, a sense in which it may have been used by Anaximander in the sixth century BC. Origen clearly distinguishes himself as a Christian from the general consensus of the Greek philosophical tradition that the world came into being out of preexisting matter. He finds this position put forward in two works that were certainly marginal to the Bible as he understood it but to which he ascribed a certain authority. He correctly appeals to them, rather than to Genesis 1:1, for an unambiguous statement of creation *ex nihilo*.

37 That is, "the Logos was in the image (*eikôn*) of God." Origen assimilates the biblical "image" (*eikôn*) to the Platonic "form" (*eidos*) by which a thing is what it is. This is already attested in Philo, *Legum Allegoriae* 1.53, in Irenaeus, *Demonstratio* 22 and in Clement, *Protrepticus* 10.98.4.

38 Origen's concise Greek is open to several interpretations, depending on the translation of the key words *sustasis* (which I have translated "structure" but can also mean "substance") and *theôria* (which I have translated "theoretical consideration"). My interpretation of the Greek *noêmata* as "the designs by which it [the universe] is constituted" follows Origen's description of Wisdom in *PA*, a roughly contemporary work. There he wrote that "In Wisdom, subsisting by itself, are found every power and form of the future creation, both those that first came into existence and those that happened as a result of them, formed and disposed in advance by the power of foreknowledge" (*PA* 1.2.2). As Cécile Blanc points out (*SC* 120 bis, p. 118, n. 1), this is Origen's first effort to define – and, one might add, to distinguish between – "Word" and "Wisdom" as *epinoiai* of the Son. Thus, as Blanc points out, "The same reality is called 'Wisdom' according to its essence, which is to be united to God, and 'Word' in so far as it inclines toward creatures." Origen makes the same distinction in the passage from *PA* already referred to, writing that "Wisdom' is called "Word" in so far as it reveals to the whole creation "the meaning of the mysteries and secrets contained in the wisdom of God" (*PA* 1.2.3). Origen understands Proverbs 8 as providing essentially the same picture of Creation as Plato's *Timaeus*. The Son as Word, acting in the capacity of Plato's Artisan (*dêmiourgos*), creates the universe after an unchangeable pattern contained in the Son as Wisdom.

39 Greek *kata tên sophian kai tous tupous tou sustêmatos tôn en autôi {tôi logôi} noêmatôn*. The "system of designs" theoretically considered in Wisdom provides the "patterns" of the creative activity of the Word.

40 Greek *logous* (the acc. plural of *logos*).

41 Greek *hin' houtôs eipô*. That is, "created" of Prov. 8:22 is not intended in the precise sense of the term. The interpretation of this verse became a major issue in the Arian controversy.

42 That is, "life" cannot be a first principle, because being "in" the Word, "Word" is logically prior to it and therefore its first principle.

43 Greek *philanthrôpia*. See *CLam* fr. XXV, n. 12 above.

44 Greek *prosôpon*.

45 The words for "distinct existence" and "essence" are *hupostasis* and *ousia*.

46 Peter Widdicombe states, in relation to this passage:

> Origen is aware that the very words he uses to describe the
> Son, such as Wisdom, Word, and Light, which emphasize the
> Son's closeness to the Father, are taken by some as grounds for
> denying the Son a distinct existence. But the Word is not to
> be thought of as existing only in the mind of God or as a mere
> utterance of the Father, existing as syllables. Such a concep-
> tion fails to grant him a distinct ὑπόστασις.
>
> (*The Fatherhood of God from Origen to Athanasius*,
> Oxford, Oxford University Press, 1994, p. 86)

47 Here Origen assumes the Platonic distinction between being,
approached through the intellect, and becoming, approached through
the senses. As we have seen in chapter 3 (pp. 59–60), he believes that
Moses and the prophets originated this distinction.

48 On the notion of analogy, see the selection above from the Alexandrian
Commentary on the Psalms.

49 A reference to the rational beings embodied in the stars. See n. 33
above. Origen interpreted Job 25:5 to mean that the stars sin. See 257
below and *PA* 1.7.2.

50 That is, the dignity of being greater than the heavenly beings. See
172–3 above.

51 Greek *logos*.

52 It is hard to see how the reference to "the ways of a serpent upon a
rock" supports Origen's argument. Perhaps Origen had in mind Isa.
35, especially verse 9, where lions and other "wicked wild beasts" are
excluded from the way of the redeemed, but, uncharacteristically, he
did not precisely recall it.

53 Greek *logos*.

54 Cécile Blanc accepts Pierre Nautin's emendation of the text to add the
word "not" as the only way to make sense of this phrase. Note that in
HLk 19.1 below Origen ascribes a similar argument, appealing to
God's glory, to those who would deny the divinity of the Savior.

55 We do not know if Origen had anyone in particular in mind in raising
this hypothetical point. Presumably he himself would have felt a need
to reconcile the Platonic philosophy so vital to his thought, in which
the first divine hypostasis is not an object of knowledge, even to itself,
with the Christian belief that the Son knows and reveals the Father. See
Henri Crouzel's comparison of Origen with Plotinus on this point in
Origène et Plotin: Comparaisons doctrinales, Paris, Pierre Téqui, 1991, pp.
159–68. Origen appears to reject the possibility of the Son's partial
ignorance because truth cannot be lacking in knowledge. Here
Origen's faithfulness to the biblical witness pushes him toward the
eventual Nicene position that accords the Son equality with the Father.

56 Greek *philanthrôpos*.

57 This is a characteristic reference to Christ's human soul, which is vital
to Origen's Christology, one of the most significant ways in which he
foreshadows later Christological developments.

58 We find this same distinction below in *CJn* 13.39.

59 Greek *logos*.

60 The "aspects" (Greek *epinoiai*) of the Logos are vital to Origen's Christology because they allow the Logos to have multiple effects while remaining the same essentially.

61 See the fuller treatment of this theme in *CJn* 32.111–22.

62 Because God belongs to the realm of being rather than of becoming, he is not subject to time, so that, from God's perspective, "today" is eternity. This enables Origen to avoid the implication that "today" is a point in time, implying that the Son's generation is not eternal. See *PA* 1.2.9.

63 See Cécile Blanc, "L'angélologie d'Origène," in *SP* 14 (1976), 79–109.

64 Origen knows the meaning of the phrase but seems not to recognize a Hebrew plural or to understand the construct state, an indication of very limited knowledge of Hebrew when he wrote this work.

65 This appears to be a mistranslation of a Hebrew phrase meaning, literally, "wonder of a counselor". See Joseph W. Trigg, "The Angel of Great Counsel: Christ and the Angelic Hierarchy in Origen's Theology," in *Journal of Theological Studies* n.s. 42 (1991), 35–51.

66 Here Origen leaves open the possibility of the salvation of the demons.

67 See also **68** above and *CGen* 15, n. 12.

68 In Phil. 12 (= *HJos* 20.2) Origen compares Scripture to a "drug" against serpents, understood allegorically as vices in the soul.

69 A reference to the preexistent soul of Christ, already united with the Logos long before its union with human body in the Incarnation. See chapter 2, p. 25.

70 See *H1Sam* 5.7 below.

71 See nn. 33 and 49 and above. Although the modern reader may take it for granted that the expression in Job is a figure of speech, we cannot be sure that it was so intended.

72 Greek *oikonomôn*, another reference to Christ's administration of the divine *oikonomia*.

73 Evidently David's taking the kingdom from Saul prefigures Christ's supplanting Satan's kingship.

74 *Teleios* and related words mean both "mature" and "perfect".

75 "By means of reason" could just as easily be "by means of the Word". For, Origen, human reason is, in fact, a participation in the divine Logos: see *PA* 1.3.6. Interestingly, Origen does not use *logos* for "word" in its fundamental English sense, an individual unit of speech; for "word" in this sense he employs *prosêgoria* ("title"), *onoma* ("name" or "term") and *phônê* ("sound").

76 Origen argues that Jn 15:22 refers to Christ's coming as reason to all people, not to his coming in the Incarnation. There is no sin in those who have not yet reached the age of reason, when they can be responsible for their actions. See *PA* 1.3.6.

77 Origen anticipates modern developmental psychology in seeing early childhood as a period of magical thinking.

78 Or, possibly, "the perfection of the Word."

79 That is, the Word becomes flesh for those who participate in the Word merely as reason, but the Word is God for those who have become perfect, a common distinction in Origen. See 43 above.

80 Marguerite Harl (*Origène et la fonction révélatrice du Verbe incarné*, Paris, Seuil, 1958, p. 126, n. 24) provides a helpful explanation of this enigmatic text:

> We think that Origen seeks progressive stages in the growth of human reason and there is in this text an expression of Origen's anthropology. See Plotinus, for whom man is triple, because there is, intermediate between man αἰσθητικός [sensible] and man ἐν νῷ [in intellect], rational man. There is an effort to situate the soul between body and mind.

81 "Angel" here and "messenger" in the previous paragraph are the same word in Greek, from which is derived the word translated "announce".

82 Among those before Origen who had applied this verse to the generation of the Son are Justin Martyr (*Dialogue* 38.6–7), Theophilus of Antioch (*To Autolycus* 2.10.6) and Tertullian (*Against Praxeas* 7). Although, as we have seen, Origen provides an interpretation of this verse in case it is attributed to the Father, he rejects it on philological grounds, arguing that the ensuing words attributed to the same *prosôpon* are not consistent with such an identification. On the concept of "person" or *prosôpon*, see chapter 1, p. 6.

83 That is, "Lord of Hosts."

COMMENTARY ON JOHN, BOOK 13.3–192

1 Jean-Michel Poffet, *La méthode exégétique d'Héracléon et d'Origène commenteurs de Jn 4: Jésus, la Samaritaine et les Samaritaines*, Fribourg, Éditions Universitaires, 1985.

2 Origen, in *CJn* 6.92, characterizes this, the earliest interpretative work on a book of the New Testament, with the vague term *hupomnêmata* ("notes" or "treatises"). We do not know its title. It may not have been a full-fledged commentary like his, but a set of relatively brief comments. It survives only in fragments preserved here and in other books of Origen's *CJn* and works by Clement of Alexandria. We must recognize that Heracleon would almost certainly appear to better advantage if we had his work in its entirety. Alain le Boulluec (*La notion d'hérésie dans la littérature grecque II*e*–III*e* siècles*, vol. 2, Paris, Études Augustiniennes, 1985, pp. 514–19) shows how Origen, by juxtaposing brief citations with his own carefully argued interpretations, sought to make Heracleon appear arbitrary and inane

3 Presumably in the (now lost) Book 12, to which he refers more than once.

4 Greek *logos*.

5 See *CJn* 1.64 above.

6 This seems to be a reference to the two stages of Origen's eschatology. See chapter 2, p. 32.

7 Greek *ôpheleia*.

8 Origen seems to suggest that the "unspeakable words" Paul heard were
not, strictly speaking, beyond all human language. In his *Homilies on
Joshua* (22.4), which he may have preached at Caesarea at about the
same time as he was composing this book of the *Commentary on John*,
Origen used 2 Cor. 6:12 to argue that, even if the reasons for the division of cities in Joshua are not explicitly given, they can be understood
by someone who, like Paul, has had those reasons revealed to him by
the Spirit:

> It is certain that these mysteries were understood and entirely
> apprehended by that person who was "taken up as far as the
> third heaven" (2 Cor. 2:2) and while in heaven, saw heavenly
> things. He saw Jerusalem, the true city of God, and he saw
> Bethelelem, Hebron, and all these cities concerning which
> the division by lot is now described. And he did not simply
> see them, but he understood in the Spirit the reasons for them,
> since he testifies that he heard words and reasons. What
> words? "Unspeakable words," he says, "which it is not
> permitted to utter." You see, therefore, that Paul knew and
> understood all things in the Spirit, but he was not permitted
> to divulge them to men. To what men? Those, doubtless, to
> whom he said repoachfully, "Are you not men and walking
> according to man?" (1 Cor. 3:3). But he probably told them to
> those persons who no longer walk according to man. He told
> them to Timothy, to Luke, and to other disciples whom he
> knew to be capable of receiving unspeakable mysteries. Only
> he did make a mysterious allusion to them when he exhorted
> Timothy saying: "Remember the words which you have heard
> from me, which are to be conveyed to trustworthy men who
> are able to instruct others" (2 Tim. 2:2).

Thus what is humanly impossible is not impossible for those who, by
becoming spiritual, have passed beyond the human condition (see
34–6 below). Thus, as Peter Widdicombe points out in *The Fatherhood
of God from Origen to Athanasius*, Oxford, Oxford University Press,
1994, p. 57: "The capacity to understand the 'ineffable mysteries'
depends on our moral condition."
9 See *CLam* fr. III above.
10 "Becoming similar," that is, by a process of spiritual transformation.
11 Greek *logos*.
12 The Samaritan woman thus represents a person who, out of dissatisfac-
tion with a "simpler" Christianity, is seduced by the pretensions of
Gnostic groups. Earlier in the commentary, Origen had addressed his
patron, Ambrosius, as someone in the same position:

> You yourself, through lack of persons espousing better things,
> and because your love for Jesus did not permit you to put up
> with an irrational and ignorant faith, once gave yourself over
> to doctrines [*logois*] which you later rejected when, having

accepted the intelligence that was offered to you, you properly
judged them to be false.

(*CJn* 5.8)

13 Greek *logos*.
14 Greek *plêrôma*. In Valentinian theology the "Fullness" is the spiritual
    realm from which spiritual natures in this world have been alienated.
    See Jn 1:16; Col. 2:9; Eph. 3:19.
15 Greek *suzugos*, from Phil. 4:3. Gnostics, as attested in Irenaeus, *Against
    Heresies* 1.21.3 and Clement of Alexandria, *Excerpta* 63.2, seem to have
    considered the "comrade" a spiritual prototype in the Fullness with
    whom those who are spiritual enter into a spiritual marriage.
16 Evidently the Valentinian Gnostics whom Heracleon represents.
17 The Greek word *kyrios*, translated "Lord" and used as a name of God,
    can also be translated here as the polite form of address, "Sir."
18 Origen speaks of the woman as "considering herself in a state of
    contemplation" (*en theôria ... gegonenai*) because she uses the verb
    theôrô ("behold" or "contemplate"). The terminology harks back to the
    pagan mysteries and was taken over by philosophy to refer to the
    achievement of deeper insight.
19 On the concept of "Artisan" (*dêmiourgos*) as creator of the world,, see
    CJn 1, n. 34 above.
20 Greek, *kanôn*. On this concept, see chapter 1, especially p. 4.
21 Here Origen seems to allude to Galatians 4:6, in which of our adop-
    tion as sons of God enables us to cry "Abba, Father." He appears to
    identify this ability to cry "Abba, Father" with the concept (expressed
    in such passages as Eph. 3:2, Heb. 4:16 and 10:19, and 1 Jn 2:28 and
    3:21) that Christians can approach God with bold confidence (*parrêsia*).
    Parrêsia is the ability to speak openly and frankly, especially in the
    presence of a person of superior rank.
22 Here Origen's use of the term "Artisan" for the God whom the Jews
    worship in order to emphasize that, unlike the Gnostics, those who
    follow the rule of the church can, by means of a spiritual interpretation
    of the Old Testament (the "Jewish discourses"), identify the Creator of
    the world as the same God as the Father of Jesus Christ.
23 This is an apocryphal work known to Clement of Alexandria. Whether
    it is the same work referred to as the *Teaching of Peter* in the Preface to
    Peri Archon is debatable.
24 That is, to Jewish rituals.
25 Greek *oikonomia*.
26 Plato noted that a mirror image is reversed in *Theaetetus* 193a, and
    Aristotle discussed further defects of such images (*Meteor* 374b 16).
    Ancient mirrors were, in any event, inferior to ours.
27 Origen, of course, sought to do precisely this himself. See, in partic-
    ular, his homilies on Exodus and Leviticus.
28 That is, the spiritual natures have been lost in the material world
    created by the Artisan.
29 The meaning of the last phrase is obscure, perhaps because of a corrupt
    text. In *PA* 1.1.1–4, Origen argues at greater length that this verse

does not imply that God is corporeal, as would be implied in a materialistic Stoic concept of spirit.

30 A reference to Aristotle's doctrine of a fifth nature, not constituted by the four elements, earth, air, fire, and water. See Alan Scott, *Origen and the Life of the Stars: A History of an Idea*, Oxford, Oxford University Press, 1991, pp. 24–38.

31 The original text is defective here. I follow Cécile Blanc's reconstruction of its sense.

32 In Paul's image in 1 Cor. 3:12, one to which Origen often recurs, the combustible wood, hay, and stubble are building materials tested by fire.

33 In the LXX 1 and 2 Sam. and 1 and 2 Kings are designated 1–4 Kingdoms, so that Third Kingdoms is our 1 Kings.

34 Greek *pneuma* = spirit.

35 Greek *homoousious*, the same word to be used of the Father's relation to the Son in the Nicene Creed. The succeeding argument seems to indicate that Origen would not have wanted to apply the term to the relationship between the Son (or the Holy Spirit) and the Father.

36 Greek *christos* v. *êlimmenos*. This appears to be a distinction without a difference. See Cécile Blanc, *SC* 222, pp. 295–6.

37 Dositheus is an obscure figure, often listed as the originator of a heresy. Origen's belief that he was a Samaritan Messianic pretender, also expressed in *CC* 1.57 and 6.11, may be the most reliable information about him. According to the latter, only about thirty Dositheans remained in Origen's time.

38 That is, the Samaritan woman who symbolizes heterodox thought.

39 Greek *logos*.

40 Greek *logos*.

41 Greek *logos*.

42 Greek *Oikonomia tês ôpheleias*.

HOMILY 12 ON JEREMIAH

1 This is the Septuagint version of the Authorized Version's "my cup runneth over."

2 It is daring to speak of God as having hands, since it suggests that God has a body.

3 This seems to indicate that, for instruction at the eucharist, the church at Caesarea regularly read through the entire Bible, from beginning to end, in the course of some fixed period of time. Pierre Nautin argues (Nautin, pp. 389–401) that this occurred in the course of a three-year cycle.

4 Greek *dioikonomoumenon*, that is, administering *oikonomia*.

5 Greek *oikonomei*.

6 Greek *oikonomei*.

7 A reference to esoteric doctrines hidden in Scripture, which are only accessible to more advanced Christians. See Guy G. Stroumsa, *Hidden Wisdom: Esoteric Traditions and the Roots of Christian Mysticism*, Leiden, Brill, 1996, pp. 109–31.

8 "Be sound moneychangers" is an unwritten saying ascribed to Jesus
which Origen often quotes. It is also found in *Pistis Sophia* 134 and in
Str. 1.28.177.2.

9 Through, that is, the Roman *cursus honorum*. Augustine, in *Confessions*
6.11, 19, confesses to having sought to become a governor (*praeses*), a
position that conferred authority to administer a capital punishment.

10 In *On the Passover* 2.16 Origen notes that in Rom. 13:12 ("The night is
advanced, the day is at hand"), "night' signifies this world and "day"
the world to come.

11 Notice that Origen, while citing temperance, justice, and courage,
three of the cardinal virtues of Greek philosophy, adds the specifically
Christian virtues of endurance and holiness. He probably omitted
mentioning here the fourth cardinal virtue, normally referred to as
"prudence" (*pronoia*), because he intended to use the same term a little
further on in the sense of "providence." This expansion of the pagan
ethical tradition is characteristic also of Origen's teaching as witnessed
in *Address* 12.149, where Gregory speaks of His adding "endurance" to
the four cardinal virtues. While appreciating and making use of the
pagan ethical tradition, Origen evidently believed that Christian tradition takes precedence over it.

12 Origen here has Gnostics in mind.

13 Origen distinguishes "petty demons" (*daimonia*) from their chief, "the
Devil" (*diabolos*).

14 In Origen's terminology the flesh of the Word is Holy Scripture. See
On the Passover 2.10.12, where he refers to "the fleshes of Christ, that is,
I say, the Holy Scriptures." See also *CJn* 32.45 below. Here Origen
hints at a doctrine for the more sophisticated, who do know "what sort
of thing the flesh of the Word is" in a way calculated not to disturb
those whom he considers more simple.

15 The "bodily unleavened bread" that some members of Origen's congregation celebrate at the time of the Passover is probably a reference to
participation in the Jewish Passover. As we see, Origen also speaks of
members of his congregation who observe the Sabbath and participate
in the celebration of the Day of Atonement. On the well-attested
phenomenon of Christians observing Jewish feasts, see Marcel Simon,
Verus Israel, Paris, Boccard, 1964, pp. 356–93.

HOMILIES 19 AND 20 ON LUKE

1 See Nautin, pp. 406–9 and Hermann-Josef Sieben, ed. and tr.
Origenes, *In Lucam Homiliae* vol. 1 = *Fontes Christiani* 4/1, Freiburg,
Herder, 1991, pp. 28–31.

2 See Gerald Bostock, "Origen's Exegesis of the Kenosis Hymn," in
Origeniana Sexta, pp. 531–47.

3 These are apparently persons who hold views like those of Beryllus of
Bostra, denying that Christ pre-existed His Incarnation, but holding
that he was a human being adopted at some point as God's Son and
Messiah. Origen characteristically warns His hearers against various
purveyors of false teaching in His homilies.

NOTES

4 For Origen the defining characteristic of one whole set of heretics, those we know as Gnostics, is their denial that the God of the Old Testament is the God and Father of Jesus Christ. The followers of Marcion, whom Origen includes in this group, accepted only the Gospel of Luke.

HOMILY 5 ON 1 SAMUEL

1 See Pierre Nautin's introduction to His edition, *SC* 328, pp. 57–60.
2 See K. A. D. Smelik, "The Witch of Endor: 1 Samuel 28 in Rabbinic and Christian Exegesis till 800 A.D.," in *Vigiliae Christianae* 33 (1977), 160–79. See also Patricia Cox Miller, "Origen on the Witch of Endor: Toward an Iconoclastic Typology," in *Anglican Theological Review* 66 (1984), 137–47.
3 This text, along with Origen's homily and a shorter treatise by Gregory of Nyssa, are included in *La maga di Endor*, ed. and tr. by Manlio Simonetti = *Biblioteca Patristica* 15, Florence, Nardini, 1989. See Joseph W. Trigg, "Eustathius of Antioch's Attack on Origen: What is at Issue in an Ancient Controversy?" in *Journal of Religion* 75 (1995), 219–38.
4 Greek *prosôpon*. The identification of the persona speaking was an important technique of classical grammar, see chapter 1, especially p. 6.
5 A demon could not have known that the Lord had already designated David king or that Saul would die the next day, clearing the way for him to ascend the throne and establish His Messianic dynasty. Following Paul and Ignatius, Origen believed that such matters belonged to the divine plan of salvation, the *oikonomia*, which was a mystery deliberately hidden from the demons. Nautin (*SC* 328, pp. 84–6) traces the doctrine that a demon could not prophesy concerning the divine plan of salvation to Ignatius, *Ephesians* 19.1, which Origen cited in *HLk* 6.4. It could just as easily come from 1 Cor. 2:7–9, where Paul says that, had they understood the divine mystery, the (demonic) rulers of this world "would not have crucified the Lord of glory."
6 Origen's remarks do not survive, but the application of Psalm 22, already made, for example, in Mt. 27:35, would appear obvious to any Christian.
7 Origen alludes to the story of the woman with an issue of blood in Mark 5 and parallel passages, which he appears to understand allegorically.
8 Greek *iatrikê philanthrôpia*.
9 The implicit distinction between "Word" and "Savior" is curious. Apparently the former refers to Christ's divine and the latter to His human nature.
10 Origen's point is that since, as Paul testifies, we achieve only partial knowledge in this life, even Isaiah, acknowledged as the greatest of the prophets, only prophesied "in part." Nonetheless, in this particular case, Samuel's words achieve perfection, since His posthumous oracle concerning David was entirely fulfilled. Such perfection is consistent

270

with Paul's promise. On the other hand, if prophets do not continue to exercise the prophetic charism after death, "the perfect" could never come.

11 Greek *hêgemonikon*. See *CL* fr. XXVII, n. 15 above.
12 Greek *oikonomia*.

LETTER TO GREGORY

1 Augustine, *On Christian Doctrine* 2.40.60.
2 Greek *ainissetai*, recalling the words, *en ainigmati* "in a riddle" or "hint" of 1 Corinthians 13:12.
3 Origen has evidently confused Hadad (Ader in Greek) of 1 Kings 11:14–25 with Jereboam of 1 Kings 11:26–12:33.
4 "Impetuousness" (*propetes*) is exactly the wrong way to approach the Scripture. It characterizes the approach of the Gnostics, who assume that they already know what Scripture teaches before seriously considering it. Its opposite is the "attention" (*prosochê*) recommended to Gregory.

COMMENTARY ON JOHN, BOOK 32.1–140

1 Nautin (pp. 378–80) suggests 248 or 249.
2 Origen likens the long process of composing the *Commentary on John* to the Israelite's journey through the wilderness.
3 This passage does not survive.
4 Origen here relies on the principle of homonymy set forth theoretically in the Preface to the *Dialogue with Heraclides* and in the *Commentary on the Song of Songs*. See chapter 3, pp. 41 and 47.
5 The point is that no one receives elementary teachings directly from Jesus, but anyone who has such direct intercourse with the Word is necessarily receiving hidden and mystical teachings not revealed to the many. The account of a sumptuous breakfast occurs in the Septuagint of 1 Kings (called Third Kingdoms in the LXX) alone.
6 Perhaps these are Christians who worship the Emperor out of a desire for worldly advancement.
7 Greek *oikonomia*.
8 Greek *oikonomia*. Origen here argues that the *oikonomia* for all creation in Christ is consistent with God's particular *oikonomia* for each individual rational being.
9 Greek *oikonomia*.
10 See Marguerite Harl, *Origène et la fonction révélatrice du Verbe incarné*, Paris, Seuil, 1958, pp. 224–5:

> God's revelation does not irrupt in the world brusquely, without preparation or plan; this would not be in conformity with the divine pedagogy. God makes himself known "at opportune moments" and "in a certain order." Revelation by Christ is a "moment" of revelation, it constitutes a stage, perhaps privileged and definitive, but still a stage after many others.

NOTES

In the accompanying footnote she cites *CC* 2.66, where Origen describes God as "with a certain judgment distributing to each what is required."

11 This passage also does not survive.

12 This does, in fact, seem to be a Hebraism, taken over from the language of the Septuagint.

13 Concerning this cryptic example, Cécile Blanc writes (*SC* 385, p. 212, n. 1):

> The beginning of this citation – which the reader must have in mind, since it recurs often – said: "You are gods, all of you sons of the Most High." Origen here opposes the grandeur of every man's vocation to a literal and meticulous observance of the Law.

14 Greek *propetes*. See *Letter to Gregory*, n. 4 above.

15 Thus, within the overall context of God's plan for His life, Peter's succumbing to temptation is ultimately profitable to him. This is consistent with Origen's discussion of the temptation in *OP* 29.15–19.

16 Although this work, probably Origen's commentary on the epistle, is lost, we know from Jerome that Origen taught that Paul's rebuke of Peter could not have been sincere, since he himself had made similar compromises, discussed in *CJn* 1.42 above, for the sake of *oikonomia*. See the discussion of this point in Augustine's correspondence with Jerome, especially Jerome, Letter 112 and Augustine, Letters 28, 40 & 82.

17 Origen probably has in mind Peter's defense of Paul in Acts 15, but he may also allude to Peter's ability, in Acts 10, to overcome His initial inclinations and to baptize Cornelius.

18 All but Peter perceive that Jesus, the Incarnate Word (*logos*) would not act irrationally (*alogôs*).

19 Apparently Origen conflated Mt. 25:29 with Mt. 6:33 or with an unwritten saying that he and Clement of Alexandria considered genuine: "Ask for the large things, and the small ones will be added to you". See *Str.* 1.24.158.2 and *CC* 7.44.

20 That is, "baptized".

21 "Jesus" in Greek.

22 Greek *oikonomia*.

23 The implication is that, later, the apostles themselves, and those who are like them, can become "another Jesus." See *CJn* 1.23 above. Origen goes on to argue that human beings can and should fulfill the spiritual ministry symbolized by footwashing.

24 Greek *oikonomia*.

25 The Greek word here, "*basis*," means, literally, "that on which one steps."

26 The Greek may be interpreted either as a command or as a question.

27 Here Origen employs the doctrine of *epinoiai*, "aspects" of the Logos, set forth most fully in Book 1. According to this doctrine, the Logos ministers in distinct ways to different persons according to their spiritual needs at different levels of transformation.

272

28 Widows who "wash the feet of the saints" are women who have the charism to provide the advanced Christian teaching footwashing symbolizes. In *HIsa* 6.3 Origen restricts women's teaching to other women. In the homily, however, Origen presents the footwashing in this passage as a symbol for all Christian teaching, including elementary instruction in morals, not, as here, for advanced teaching only. Whether the discrepancy is to be ascribed to a development in his thought or to reserve in speaking to a congregation about advanced doctrines it is hard to say.

29 Here, as in *HJer* 12.3 above, Origen specifies that ordination only "seems" to indicate eminence in the church.

COMMENTARY ON JOHN BOOK 32.318–67

1 See John A. McGuckin, "Origen on the Glory of God," in *SP* 25, pp. 316–24.

2 Greek *oikonomia*.

3 For Origen the figure described in Philippians 2 is the preexistent human soul of Christ, which becomes one with the Logos, a process described in *PA* 2.6. On Origen's use of Philippians 2, see Gerald Bostock, "Origen's Exegesis of the Kenosis Hymn," in *Origeniana Sexta*, pp. 531–47.

4 Greek *oikonomia*.

5 Greek *oikonomia*.

6 "Rise upon the world" as the "Sun of righteousness" of Mal. 4:2 (3:20 LXX).

BIBLIOGRAPHICAL NOTE

The notes in this volume provide an introduction to major work related to Origen. For further bibliography see Henri Crouzel, *Bibliographie critique d'Origène* and ibid., *Suppléments* 1 and 2, The Hague, Martinus Nijhoff, 1971, 1982, and 1996.

INDEX OF SCRIPTURAL CITATIONS

15:15 135
15:22 146, 264n
15:35–8 57
15:42–9 57
15:49–51 57
17:1 126
17:21 132
18:25–7 222
18:33 126
18:36 126
19:15 117
19:26 109
20:17 177
21:19 234
21:25 115, 154, 155

Acts

2:27 138
2:27–31 204
3:21 30, 120
4:11 129
4:29 207
5:41 43
7:42 165
7:49 168
7:55 206
8:10–20 141
8:32 119
9:4–5 117
13:46 191
15:1–11 222
16:3 113, 166
16:10 187
17:18 113
17:21 120
17:28 85
18:9 187
18:18 166
17:31 143
21:23–6 166
21:24 113
22:22 117

Romans

1:3 234
1:20 135

1:25 163
2:16 110, 118
2:24 239
2:28 112, 190
2:29 104, 112, 144, 164, 190, 229
2:33 189
3:25 26, 124, 127, 141, 191
3:31 165
5:3–5 132
5:12–14 50, 52
6:4 133
6:9–10 157
6:10 115
7:1 156
7:2 156, 229
7:3 157
7:4 157
7:6 112
7:22 41
7:24 45
8 53
8:7 81
8:9 165
8:15 135, 229
8:19–22 27
8:19 131
8:20 121, 132
8:20–2 261n
8:21 131
8:22 121
9–11 49
9:16 29
9:14–18 49
9:17 101
9:20 164
10:4 85
10:6–8 146
10:7 207
10:10 43
10:15 224
10:18 166
11:7 191
11:11 185
11:28 82
11:33 133
12:1 171
13:2 x
13:12 269n
13:14 32

INDEX

Celsus 52–5
Chadwick, H. 254n
Chalcedon 26
chastisement *see* punishment
Christ, humanity and divinity of
    17, 25–6, 41, 122, 134, 234,
    263n
Christological titles 9
Christology 19–20, 23–34; *see also*
    Christ, humanity and divinity of
church 46
Cicero 257n
circumcision 98, 112, 190
Clark, E.A. 254n
Clement of Alexandria 14, 28, 49,
    265n, 267n, 272n; and Origen
    9–10, 31; on image of God
    262n; on philosophy 13, 59; on
    rule of faith 4; style of 11, 66,
    259n
Cocchini 252n
consort – *suzugos* 159
corporeality and incorporeality 30,
    31–2, 44–5
cosmology 18, 20, 21, 28, 64
Creation, doctrine of 54, 60, 71–2,
    262n; *see also* cosmology
Crouzel, H. 64, 193, 210, 245n,
    246n, 251n, 259n, 274; on
    author of *Address* 249n; on
    Origen and Plotinus 13, 46,
    263n; on Origen's eschatology
    32; on Origen's life 241n

Daley, B. 10, 22, 29, 253n
Daniélou, J. 256n
death, Origen's teaching on 45
Demetrius (Bishop of Alexandria)
    14, 15, 259n
descent into hell, Christ's 206–7
Devil, the – devils – demons –
    adverse powers – Satan: act
    freely 102; causing saints to
    stumble 189–90; did not
    summon Samuel 199, 202, 203;
    fought by God 81, 118;
    ignorant of divine *oikonomia*
    207; piercing the heart of Judas
    217–19, 225, 228, 234; in Rule

of the Church 20; serve divine
    oikonomia 27, 187; taking the
    soul captive 74
Didymus the Blind 66
divinization 233, 237; *see also*
    transformation
Dorival, G. 22, 245n
Dositheus 173–4
drunkenness – inebriation
    (symbolism of) 136, 180

education, divine 29–30
elevated interpretation or sense
    (*anagogê*) 73, 75, 78, 106, 113,
    164, 176, 177, 237
embodiment 121, 132; of Christ in
    Scripture 220; *see also*
    corporeality and incorporeality
enthusiasm 136
Epictetus 257n
epinoia (pl. *epinoiai*) – aspect 17, 26,
    103–49, 273n; *see also*
    Christological titles *and references
    to biblical passages such as* Jn
    11:25; Jn 14:6; 1 Cor. 1:24
Epiphanius of Salamis 65–6
epistêmê 22, 233, 246n
Erasmus 64, 66
eschatology: in Clement and
    Origen 9, 18, 20; controversy
    over Origen's 64; Origen's
    29–32, 44, 50, 55–6, 218–19;
    see also paradise; purification;
    resurrection of the dead
esotericism – hidden or secret
    meaning or knowledge: in
    gnosticism 8, 9–10, 84; in
    Jewish tradition 12, 23, 47; in
    Pauline epistles 51–2, 57, 260n;
    in scriptural interpretation
    32–3, 37, 69–70, 104, 186,
    190–1; *see also* mystery(ies)
eternal generation of the Son 24
evil, God's responsibility for 54
eucharist 40
Eusebius: defender of Origen's
    memory 65; on encounter with
    Beryllus of Bostra 40; on

Origen's character 13; on
Origen's life 3
Eustathius of Antioch 85, 199
Evagrius Ponticus 63, 66
evangelism 117

Fédou, M. 252n
Francis, J. 52
free choice of the will: God's respect
  for 60; gnostic doctrine and 8;
  in *PA* 20; influence of Origen's
  doctrine of 63–4; not destroyed
  by astrology 86–102; and
  providence 27–9, 42;
fullness – *plêrôma* 159, 166

Gasparo, G. Sfameni 254n
glory 233–46
glossalalia 207
God: Celsus on 53–4; creator and
  lawgiver same as Father of Jesus
  Christ 72, 88, 118, 143, 165,
  196; doctrine of 19, 23;
  imitation of 28; incorporeality
  of 23, 24, 25, 31, 167–72;
  knowledge of 44, 61, 120;
  likeness to 32, 42; mind of 101;
  see also Trinity – trinitarian
  theology
Godin, A. 254n, 255n
Gnostics and Gnosticism 15, 16,
  20, 257n, 270n; at Alexandria
  4; influence on Origen 7–9;
  Origen's refutation of 22, 27;
  scriptural interpretation of 33
Gorday, P. 49
Görgemann, H. 245n
gospel – good news: Christians
  called to preach 226–7;
  footwashing as preparation to
  preach 224; hidden from
  unbelievers 236; Jesus
  proclaiming about himself 174;
  meaning of 107–19; power of
  114
governing faculty *see hêgemonikon*
grace, Origen's understanding of 29
grammar – grammarian –
  grammateus: Origen's

abandonment of profession in
  14; Origen's training in 5–7;
  Origen's use of techniques of 17,
  25, 32–3, 42, 44, 45–6, 58, 73
Grant, R.M. 51–2, 242n, 247n,
  252n
Gregory of Nyssa 63, 65
Gregory Thaumaturgus *see Address
  to Origen*
Grillmeier, A. 254n
Guillaumont, A. 254n
Guinot, J.-M. 253n

Hadot, P. 13, 22
Hällström, G. af 243n, 244n, 257n
Halperin, D.J. 249n
Hanson, R.P.C. 241n, 247n, 248n
Harl, M. 22, 69, 242n, 245n,
  247n, 265n, 271n
Harnack, A. 60
healing, divine 143, 205, 223
Hebrew (language) 12, 16, 40, 73,
  74, 173, 233, 264n, 272n
Hebrew, the (teacher of Origen)
  11–12, 70
hêgemonikon – governing faculty 73,
  80, 168, 169, 177, 208
Heine, R.E. 258n
Heither, T. 35, 49–50
Heracleon 16, 150–1, 158–60,
  162–3, 164, 166, 167, 171,
  174, 175, 177–8
Heraclides 40–1
Hexapla 16, 63
hermeneutics *see* scriptural
  interpretation
hidden meaning or knowledge *see*
  esotericism
Hill, C.E. 32
Hipparchus 258n
Hippolytus 46
Hoek, A. van den 243n
Holy Land 36, 82
Holy Spirit: gifts of 50; indwelling
  of 225; inspiration of 20, 21, 22,
  42, 71, 224; relation to Father
  and Son 24; as sanctifier 135;
  why known as "Comforter" 30
Homer 7